THE **TRANSITION** OF **ORGANIZATIONS**

MANAGING FOR GROWTH AT EACH STAGE
OF THE ORGANIZATION'S LIFE CYCLE

LUKAS MICHEL & HERB NOLD

ADVANCE PRAISE

"Much has been written and debated about management and organizations. However, the fact remains that we live in a volatile and complex world that is forever changing — even more so after the advent of Covid-19 and its impact on all organizations. The business world is constantly shifting, and growing ever more complex, as technology advances. The ability to remain agile and adaptable to the changing business environment requires an understanding of the organizational life cycle and the strategies necessary to navigate the changing terrain, which will be essential for success in the 21st century. The Transition of Organizations is a must-read for all who are captivated by the management and oversight of the contemporary organization. It is an indispensable guide to the organizational life of any business."

Jose Perez, Ed.D., MBA, Business Professor,
Polk State College, Lakeland, Florida

"A book for every manager who wants to understand which way the company can go, depending on its development phase, what challenges are waiting and how to overcome them. It has the potential to become a foundational work in the organizational development and management literature."

Guido Bosbach, CEO, ZUKUFTHeute.net, Wachtberg, Germany

Published by
LID Publishing
An imprint of LID Business Media Ltd.
LABS House, 15–19 Bloomsbury Way,
London, WC1A 2TH, UK

info@lidpublishing.com
www.lidpublishing.com

A member of:

BPR
businesspublishersroundtable.com

Printed by Severn, Gloucester
ISBN: 978-1-915951-11-3
ISBN: 978-1-915951-12-0 (ebook)

Cover and page design: Caroline Li

THE **TRANSITION** OF **ORGANIZATIONS**

MANAGING FOR GROWTH AT EACH STAGE OF THE ORGANIZATION'S LIFE CYCLE

LUKAS MICHEL & HERB NOLD

MADRID | MEXICO CITY | LONDON
BUENOS AIRES | BOGOTA | SHANGHAI

To our partners and their support

CONTENTS

FOREWORD		2
PREFACE		6
PART I	**LIFE CYCLE PATTERNS**	10
CHAPTER 1	THE DIGITAL ECONOMY	12
CHAPTER 2	THE GROWTH LIFE CYCLE	24
CHAPTER 3	THE MANAGERIAL MODES & ECOSYSTEM	38
PART II	**MASTERY IN MANAGEMENT**	56
CHAPTER 4	PEOPLE-CENTRIC MANAGEMENT	58
CHAPTER 5	AGILE ORGANIZATION	66
CHAPTER 6	THE DYNAMIC OPERATING SYSTEM	100
CHAPTER 7	A COMPETITIVE ADVANTAGE	124
PART III	**FIVE LIFE CYCLE STAGES**	136
CHAPTER 8	CREATIVITY	138
CHAPTER 9	DIRECTION	148
CHAPTER 10	DELEGATION	158
CHAPTER 11	COORDINATION	168
CHAPTER 12	COLLABORATION	178
PART IV	**FOUR TRANSITION STRATEGIES**	188
CHAPTER 13	PEOPLE FIRST	190
CHAPTER 14	PEOPLE-CENTRIC MANAGEMENT	204
CHAPTER 15	DYNAMIC OPERATIONS	236
CHAPTER 16	AGILE ORGANIZATION	260
PART V	**MANAGING TRANSITIONS**	282
CHAPTER 17	WORK ON THE SYSTEM	284
CHAPTER 18	THREE STEPS	296
CHAPTER 19	THE TRANSITION ROADMAP	312
APPENDIX 1	LIFE CYCLE TRANSITIONS	330
BIBLIOGRAPHY		332
LIST OF FIGURES		334
ACKNOWLEDGEMENTS		336
ABOUT THE AUTHORS		337

FOREWORD

It is widely known that the average start-up lasts between two and five years. An estimated 50% survive for just one year, with 69% of new small businesses surviving just two years and only 90% of start-ups lasting five years. While there are many reasons for this low survival rate, poor planning, poor use of resources and lack of supporting infrastructure are among the most significant.

Start-ups are not the only organizations with finite life spans. One study of companies that were founded in 1976 found that only 10% were still in existence in 1986. Other research found that of the companies created in the United States, less than 0.1% make it to their 40th anniversary. Think about that. The average human life expectancy in the US is nearly 80, so chances are good that you will outlive the company you work for... by a long shot.

To reinforce the point that most organizations have a limited life span, McKinsey & Company innovation consultants Richard Foster and Sarah Kaplan charted the performance of 1,008 large companies over a 40-year period. Of the sample of 1,008 companies in 1962, only 160 survived to 1998. Of the companies listed in the Fortune 500 in 1970, one-third did not survive until 1983. The obvious question is, 'Why and how does this happen?' How is it that highly developed organizations, commanding significant positions in their industry, with advanced capabilities in their value-chains, stumble and fall?

All executives — from those founding a start-up to the CEOs of mega-multinationals — are trying to grow their organizations. However, growth means increasing complexity that presents a dizzying array of obstacles, all conspiring to slow or stop growth entirely. As the rate of change in the VUCA (volatile, uncertain, complex and ambiguous) 21st century business environment accelerates, executives must face and resolve continuously emerging crises.

Successful business leaders in this VUCA environment must demonstrate ambidextrous thinking: working to maximize their current operations while simultaneously laying the groundwork to promote and support future growth. This is not an easy task, because the natural response is to focus on today, and the crisis of the moment, which consumes time and energy. Ambidextrous thinking demands extraordinary discipline and focus, to keep from getting bogged down in the daily minutia.

With more than 30 years in leadership positions, in both the public and private sectors, I've long been intrigued by the study of how managers can best understand the underlying dynamics that impact how well an organization can achieve its objectives in an ever-changing global business environment. When I transitioned to higher education after many years as an organization leader, it was my pleasure to be acquainted with Herb Nold, who was an invaluable mentor as I began my academic career. He is not only a colleague, but a friend.

Herb later introduced me to Lukas Michel, whose decades of research on helping organizations improve performance and adapt to a changing environment is inspirational. While there are many books about management and organizations, their unique perspectives — combined with their innovative diagnostic approach to managing organizations — has always been both fascinating and inspiring. So much so, in fact, that I have incorporated many of their concepts into the business courses I teach. Students have found the concepts relevant and timely because the business world is rapidly changing, and the material provides strategies managers can adopt to lead today's organizations.

Over the years, they have worked independently and in partnership to develop and write about novel ideas that fit the business environment in the 21st century. Lukas's many lectures, papers and books include:

- *The Performance Triangle: Diagnostic Mentoring to Manage Organizations and People for Superior Performance in Turbulent Times*
- *Management Design: Managing People and Organizations in Turbulent Times*
- *Diagnostic Mentoring: How to Transform the Way We Manage*

- *Agile by Choice: A Workbook for Leaders*
- *People-Centric Management: How Managers Use Four Levers to Bring Out the Greatness of Others*
- *Better Management: Six Principles for Leaders to Make Management their Competitive Advantage*

Drawing from Herb's research papers and book chapters on organizational culture, as well as his book, *Agile Strategies for the 21st Century: The Need for Speed*, they have now integrated their observations, conclusions and recommendations into one volume that assimilates all of this.

The Transition of Organizations borrows from and builds upon this body of work to provide a practical roadmap for executives looking to improve performance in their current growth stage while simultaneously laying the groundwork for continued growing. They've leveraged strategic change, organization growth and management expert Larry Greiner's Life Cycle Model, published in 1972, which provides a widely recognized model for growth. The 'Greiner Curve' describes five stages (creativity, direction, delegation, coordination and collaboration), along with crises to be overcome to continue growing into the next state. Additionally, after analysing data from more than 400 organizations that have used the Performance Triangle, a diagnostic tool designed by Lukas to help leaders promote organizational agility, the authors were able to identify clear patterns in the data at each stage.

This book provides the reader with a solid understanding of the Performance Triangle model, various operating modes, and levers that drive productivity, innovation and growth. Gaining insight into key levers that drive performance at the current stage of development, and those needed to overcome a crisis and advance to the next stage, helps promote ambidextrous thinking. *The Transition of Organizations* can help executives visualize and act on what is needed today, while laying the groundwork for what will be needed tomorrow.

As you read this book, you will find extremely valuable concepts and strategies that are very much applicable to today's business environment. I found the chapters that explain the essential ingredients to mastering management to be a great foundation.

For example, Chapter 5 delves into the importance of applying people-centric management. This is a key concept, because human capital — and a manager's ability to utilize this important asset, in any organizational setting — is not only key to great management, but to effective leadership.

The book also describes the importance of remaining agile in a VUCA world. This is an absolute requirement, because the global business climate is fluid and ever-changing. The ability to remain nimble and responsive in the face of relentless change is essential if an organization is to sustain itself, succeed and grow well into the future. Finally, the book offers concrete steps that leaders can use to develop a roadmap for managing the transitions an organization will go through across its life cycle.

As a scholar-practitioner of management and leadership, *The Transition of Organizations* struck me as offering a solid foundation of what it will take to effectively manage in a 21st-century global business organization and overcome obstacles that can stunt growth. It offers the tools, backed up by decades of evidence-based research, to support what you will need to be an effective manager and organizational leader. I think you will find this book to be an indispensable guide to the organizational life of any business.

Jose Perez, Ed.D.
MBA, Professor of Business Administration,
Polk State College, Winter Haven/Lakeland, Florida

PREFACE

Over the past 20 years of helping management teams improve performance, stimulate innovation and plot the path to growth, just about every conversation with top executives started with questions on organizational life cycle. Where are we in the life cycle? Given where we are, how are we doing? What should we be aware of when going to the next level? What is coming next? What should we prepare for? Have we done everything to anticipate potential roadblocks and taken actions to remove them to continue growing? Executives are obviously heavily invested in the development of their organizations, so these questions become a starting point for understanding how they manage people and deliver value to customers and clients.

Context matters. Growth from an entrepreneurial start-up with a few highly motivated people into a mature organization with thousands of employees requires different management techniques and methods. The development of management systems, leadership styles and the emergence of a unique culture is natural. In many cases, however, advice from consultants, the application of recommended practices, and the emergence of rigid cultures, leadership and systems can spawn bureaucracy that inhibits continued growth. The causes are embedded in the inherent structures, capabilities and systems adopted in previous life cycle stages. In transitioning from one stage to the next, executives must recognize the need for individualized design and systemic scaling to successfully operate as internal and external conditions change.

Mastery in management is *better management*. Better management has emerged from the need for speed in the digital economy and the opportunity that distributed knowledge offers to spread leadership to everywhere in the organization. The accelerating rate of both internal and external change means that executives must design organizations to sense changes more quickly in the environment, tap into the knowledge base within their companies, speed up the decision-making process and implement responses faster than ever before.

Traditional management techniques developed in the 20th century, like those espoused by renowned Canadian scholar Henry Mintzberg in *Strategy Safari: A Guide through the Wilds of Strategic Management* (1998), may actually act more like a breaking mechanism in the 21st century. Mintzberg called the conventional approach to strategy the 'Hothouse Model of Strategy Formulation.' This was a methodological, rational process: think – plan – implement – review. This logical, step-by-step approach takes too long in many organizations, resulting in missed opportunities or slow reactions to threats. Effective 21st-century leaders must develop ways to greatly expedite this process and the resulting decision-making.

The development of management processes follows the growth life cycle of an organization. Organizations and managerial approaches, like strategies, initially spring up like weeds in a garden. They are not cultivated like tomatoes in a carefully tended patch. Sometimes, the process of creating managerial systems and processes can be over-managed. In certain situations, it may be better to let ideas emerge naturally, to adapt to whatever the current conditions might be.

Power for the growth life cycle can originate in all kinds of strange places, virtually wherever people have the capacity to learn and the resources to convert learning to action. As organizations grow, day-to-day management typically becomes the dominant management approach. Managers spend their days putting out fires and applying bandages to problems when they pop up, instead of looking to resolve root problems. This results in a proliferation of processes, systems and behaviours that are not consciously managed. Hence, effective development and implementation of management processes as the organization advances through different life cycle stages is not to implement preconceived strategies but to recognize the emergence of new challenges and intervene when appropriate.

The Transition of Organizations explores various common patterns of management styles and offers transition strategies to help managers succeed in the digital economy. Pattern recognition is important because it provides a starting point from which to plot a path most likely to help the organization advance to the next stage of life.

Understanding these patterns makes executives aware of potential systemic malfunctioning within their organizations. This book provides descriptions of common life cycle stages to raise the awareness of their historic roots, so managers can consider active intervention and careful nurturing of better management.

The Transition of Organizations follows previous books mentioned in the foreword:

- *The Performance Triangle* (2013) is the foundational work on organizational agility for executives. It offers the organizational model for mastery in management in the digital economy, not agile software development.
- *People-Centric Management* (2021) introduces four essential levers for better management.
- For those executives who need an extra push to get into dynamic capabilities, *Agile by Choice* (2021) offers 14 nudges and 22 self-guided exercises to gain experience.
- *Management Design* (2021, 3rd edition) is a guided tour of the design of better management.
- *Agile Strategies for the 21st Century: The Need for Speed* (2021) converts recent research into language that managers and students can understand. It brings better management to MBA classes, which is badly needed in a time where leaders unfortunately fall back on the traditional 20th century management techniques they learned in the past.
- *Diagnostic Mentoring* (2021) is the guide for managers during their growth cycles. It is about executing growth management like a gardener.
- In *Better Management* (2022), we suggest people-centric, agile and dynamic capabilities that give managers and their organizations a competitive advantage. We have demonstrated that differences between traditional and better management can lead to a 25% increase in performance, accelerated innovation and growth. Mastery in managing across the life cycle transitions pays off quickly.
- On the drawing board, watch for *The New Leadership Scorecard* (2024), where we will expand on a strategic tool that helps manage transitions.

This book is for managers and consultants. Part I introduces the growth life cycle concept. Part II offers clues to mastery in management. For managers, Part III triggers the thinking about your management patterns. For experts, Part IV offers many suggestions on structures, systems and capabilities to succeed with the transitions. To prepare for and make the transitions, Part V offers techniques to work *on* the system.

The Transition of Organizations is grounded in solid management research and 20 years of application in professional settings. We have used a sample of 400 reference companies to identify the patterns of traits of better management for every life cycle stage. The Leadership Scorecard served as the template to describe these patterns. The Maturity Scale serves as the gauge to compare the levels of better management and management modes, with levers to help identify management approaches. Contrasting traditional with people-centric, agile and dynamic capabilities helped us — and can help you — select 21st-century practices that can guide an organization through the next stages of growth.

The Performance Triangle, management modes, the Leadership Scorecard, the Maturity Scale, the frames for purpose, collaboration and relationships, and the six fitness levels of competitive advantage are all part of the Executive Survey diagnostic instrument. The Executive Survey is our proprietary assessment tool for better management. Commercial versions that accompany this book are available from our website (https://management-insights.ch/en/).

If you like what we are saying and hate the headaches associated with large change initiatives, then you have already taken a big step forward. Rather than embarking on yet another unsuccessful disruptive change project, *The Transition of Organizations* helps you develop what we call dynamic capabilities. These result from people-centric, agile and dynamic capabilities that help you guide your organization and management naturally, without the disruptive side-effects of traditional change programmes.

We are confident that this book will provide you the guidance necessary to successfully navigate organizational life cycle transitions.

Let us know how you do with the gardening in your organization. We would love to hear about your expedition through the wilds of management.

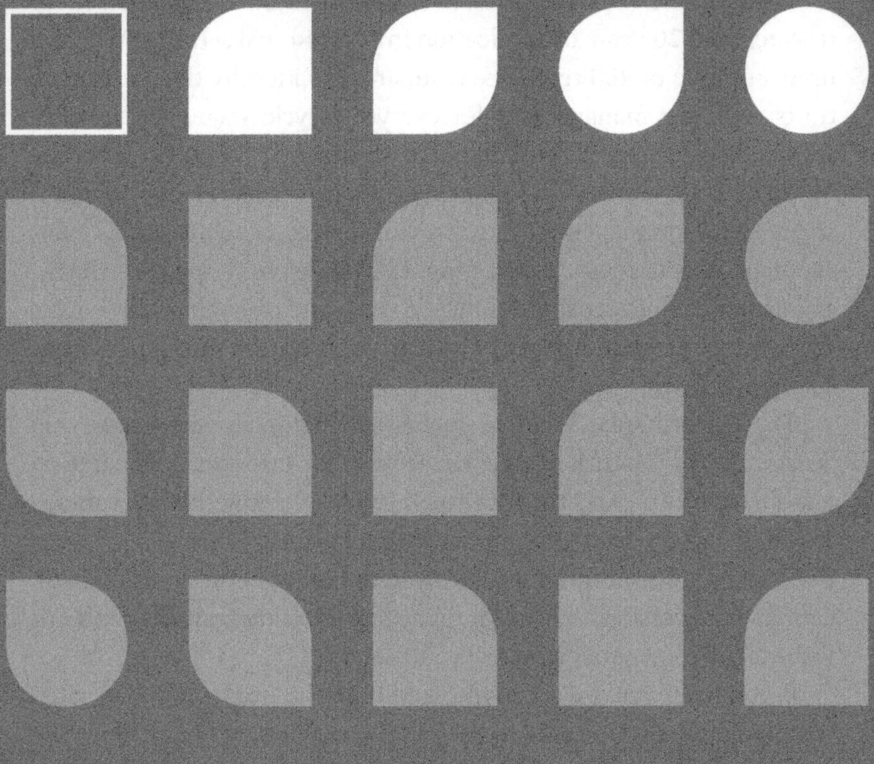

PART I

LIFE CYCLE PATTERNS

The digital economy accelerates the pace of change and organizational development. Organizations advance through growth life cycle stages quicker and experience crisis more often. Using the life cycle framework, managers can identify potential roadblocks with people-centric, agile and dynamic capabilities before crisis hits. With advance warning of impending problems, executives can implement strategies to help navigate the impending storm before it hits. Embedding people-centric dynamic capabilities into the DNA of an organization enables it to absorb the disruptive shock, react quickly and emerge stronger when the crisis passes.

Part 1 outlines *why* managers need to pay attention to life cycle transitions.

CHAPTER 1

THE DIGITAL ECONOMY

Two trends — digitalization and the changing nature of work — fundamentally alter the way we lead people and manage organizations. The disruptive 21st-century business environment and the trend toward remote work for employees and customers accelerate the trends. The digital economy increases the speed of growth, and with this, the need to accelerate the transition from one life cycle stage to another. This is particularly important for younger organizations in a rapid growth stage, but also relevant for more mature companies. Advancing an organization from one stage to the next requires an understanding of the characteristics of each stage and the barriers to advancement. Executives who understand where the organization is and where they want it to go can prepare for potential roadblocks to growth before hitting those barriers.

Chapter 1 outlines the digital environment and why managers need to anticipate and prepare for transitions before bumping up against impediments to growth.

EXPEDITED LIFE CYCLE GROWTH

DIGITALIZATION

Digitalization fundamentally changes the nature of work, how we organize and how we lead people. It lowers information costs and enables new forms of interaction not dreamed of just a few short years ago. Today, information is readily available, large amounts of data can be processed in real time, at near light speed, and communication technologies enable remote work. With instantly accessible information and enhanced analytical tools, organizations can gain new insights into what is happening, identify and capture opportunities early, and promptly mitigate risks from emerging threats. The dramatic reduction in information costs shifts work from being purely material and physical to much more knowledge oriented. Information search and sharing, knowledge creation and learning require engaging the know-how and skills of remotely situated people who are driven by self-determination and self-organization. Such decentralized, collaborative and self-organized management styles are in sharp contrast with traditional approaches dominated by micro-managers focused on command and control and shareholder returns. When work requires the knowledge of employees, teams and communities, people-centric management styles dominate. In such modern, knowledge-driven environments, formal 'control' approaches lose their effectiveness. Today's ease of communication permits management styles rooted in free choice, knowledge sharing, transparency and the absence of rigid command and control structures. The digital economy expedites the development and growth of organizations, which would have been hindered by traditional command and control methodologies.

Old-school management styles dominate in a stable environment where change comes slowly. Leaders refine their decision-making and planning processes in an environment where they methodically analyse, decide, act and control the organization as the situation requires. 'Slow and steady' works just fine if the pace of change is also slow and the business environment is stable.

But in the 21st century, how many industries operate in a slow and stable environment? We suggest that the answer is *not many*, if any at all. With increasing complexity, ambiguity, uncertainty and volatility, agile management approaches that focus on self-responsibility, knowledge sharing, transparency and freedom of choice are necessary to quickly adapt to the new environment.

VUCA

The term VUCA was first used at the US Army War College in Carlisle, Pennsylvania, to describe the military environment after the fall of the former Soviet Union and the end of the Cold War. The concept of a perpetually volatile state of flux has since been expanded to describe other environments, including business, in a rapidly changing world. The VUCA vision of the world emphasizes the unpredictable and rapidly changing nature that affects virtually every aspect of personal and business life. Information, both true and false, is transmitted around the globe at near light speed via social media over the internet, and developments spread worldwide at a previously unimagined pace. The global spread of Covid-19, and the pandemic's far-reaching disruption, is an excellent example. Military doctrine prior to the end of the Cold War was primarily based on the concept of uniformed opponents lining up, and then fighting it out along an identifiable line of combat. The 'good guys' and the 'bad guys' were easily discerned, and followed common, long-accepted rules of engagement. In a VUCA environment, friends and foes may not be easily identified and attack can come from any direction, using unorthodox, totally unexpected new methods. A basic understanding of VUCA helps leaders gain greater insight into how and why systems, people and organizations either fail or succeed in a world that is shaped by rapid technological developments.

Let's take a closer look at the characteristics of the VUCA environment:

- **V = Volatility.** This refers to the nature and dynamics of change, and the nature and speed of forces that drive change, as well as catalysts that accelerate the rate of change.

- **U = Uncertainty.** This denotes the lack of predictability and the probability of unanticipated surprises, and emphasizes the need for a heightened sense of awareness and understanding of issues and events that shape the environment and decisions.
- **C = Complexity.** This encompasses the intertwined interactions of many forces surrounding an organization — the confounding, multiple issues, with no apparent cause-and-effect logic, that confuse and befuddle leaders.
- **A = Ambiguity.** This signifies the haziness of reality, the potential to misinterpret information or events, and the mixed meanings of conditions that lead to confusion about cause and effect.

These elements describe the environment in which organizations must view their current and future state in the 21st century. A clear appreciation of a VUCA environment helps leaders appreciate both the importance and limitations of formal planning and policy making. Acknowledgement and recognition of these elements can help leaders sharpen their ability to look ahead, plan ahead and move ahead by making rapid decisions to adapt to whatever an unsettled world throws at the organization. An appreciation for VUCA sets the stage for managing and leading. In general, the underlying premises of VUCA tend to help shape an organization's ability to:

1. Anticipate the issues that are shaped by internal or external forces.
2. Understand the intended or unintended consequences of issues and actions.
3. Simultaneously appreciate the interdependence of a multitude of variables.
4. Prepare for alternative outcomes and challenges.
5. Interpret and respond quickly and effectively to relevant opportunities or threats.

For virtually all 21st-century organizations — business, the military, education, government and others — VUCA becomes a practical philosophy that promotes awareness, anticipation and readiness along with rapid evolution and action.

Higher volatility is the norm in today's business environment. Globalization, speed, real-time processes, accelerated decision-making, synchronization and immediate responses are required. In a highly dynamic environment, flexibility is essential. Efficiency and scale require rigid command and control routines for consistency and quality that work well in a stable environment.

Too often, when control fails, traditionally trained managers create more of it. They double down with more rules and regulations to force alignment throughout the organization. In a volatile environment, it is hard to maintain focus on what truly matters, such as identifying and exploring new opportunities. Narrow targets that force behaviour intended to improve productivity or quality are always off in the long run. The list of formerly successful companies where executives focused on internal processes and procedures, leading to their decline, is long. It includes Kodak, Sears, Polaroid, Westinghouse and Bethlehem Steel. One-third of the companies in the Fortune 500 in 1970 no longer existed in 1983. They failed to recognize the volatile changes in the business environment they operated in, and turned their focus inward, instead of outward, with disastrous results.

Also, consider the evolution of the mobile phone to smart phones. When Steve Jobs introduced the Apple iPhone in January 2007, Nokia commanded 50% of the market for mobile devices. Nokia, along with RIM, Motorola, Palm and Sony Ericsson, had 75% of the global market. Jobs stated at the iPhone launch that he believed Apple had a five-year head start on the competition. The first Android phone, the G1, was launched less than two years later. Jobs' five-year head start turned out to be less than two years. By the end of 2009, Nokia's market share had shrunk to 39% and all of the other legacy companies except for RIM had exited the business. By the end of 2018, just 11 years after the iPhone disrupted the mobile phone market, none of the companies from 2006 was still operating in the mobile device space.

Uncertainty in the environment challenges strategy. Challenges to corporate strategies include shorter product life cycles, less stable results, higher dependencies on outside resources or forces, increasing need for transparency and greater reputation risks that often appear suddenly, without warning. In an uncertain environment, it is hard for organizations to quickly and effectively act and collaborate — to turn opportunities into benefits. The risks of failure are high, which pushes many executive teams into defensive actions to protect what they have instead of exploring new opportunities that might fail.

When uncertainty rises, people tend to second-guess themselves, mistrust others and limit delegation. Executives issue orders and inhibit the sharing of knowledge by adding layers of hierarchy and rules. In a stable, certain environment, power and authority work well to get things done. Yet, uncertainty cannot be controlled. Therefore, self-responsibility beats command and control in inherently uncertain environments when people do not need to be told what to do. Managers trust them to do the right thing without being told. It is impossible to have a rule or process that covers every conceivable occurrence. Attempting to do so handcuffs people in dealing with clients or customers and slows the response time when they are confronted with unanticipated situations. Self-responsibility gives organizations the dynamic capability to be flexible when uncertain and unanticipated events happen. Digitalization, combined with self-responsible people, helps to decentralize decision-making without losing control. As such, uncertainty demands trust in people at all levels, from the CEO to the line worker, and non-linear approaches to handling people.

Complexity increases with size and scope. In established businesses, the incorporation of sophisticated systems, processes and bureaucratic structures increase complexity. As organizations grow and add complexity, the coordination of activities becomes increasingly important, and significantly more difficult. Self-inflicted complexity is the result of *more of everything*, from the number of employees, operating locations, products on the shelf and segments served, to functions performed and stakeholders with conflicting interests.

In a complex organizational structure, it becomes increasingly hard for executives at the top of the hierarchy to hear weak signals of change, identify opportunities, clearly communicate what is important and help people find purpose in achieving personal and organizational objectives. Typically, when executives lack clarity, they ask for additional detail and data, and then prescribe precise processes to guide implementation of their decisions. The typical executive introduces additional bureaucracy — more rules and coordinating procedures — that would typically work well in a stable environment. Complexity is a natural occurrence and cannot be compacted. However, in the VUCA world, artificially enforced methodologies become another brake to growth by slowing the decision-making process, knowledge sharing, and ultimately innovation. VUCA-aware executives in complex environments must promote self-organization through teams or other forms of people-driven, knowledge-sharing vehicles to overcome the burden of bureaucracy.

Ambiguity refers to the haziness of reality, where it is difficult to differentiate between what is important and all the unimportant information or events. This leads to misinterpretation of what the information means, leading to confusion about cause and effect, which ultimately results in flawed conclusions or actions. In the military context, this would be referred to as the 'fog of war.' Effective response to ambiguity requires choice. Rules of the game change, markets evolve, certainties dissolve, industries merge and change, loyalty vanishes, taboos are broken and boundaries blur in the blink of an eye in the VUCA world. With increasing ambiguity, it becomes necessary to develop strategies and set direction based on unpredictability and a variety of environmental conditions. Flexibility becomes the order of the day, and that requires rapid processing of information and knowledge by people throughout the organization. When the unpredictable happens, managers must adapt quickly to establish new rules and set new limits to the degrees of freedom people have. Managers reestablish stability because they have been taught that this is how to deal with ambiguity.

In ambiguous environments, it becomes hard to select the 'right' response, to take advantage of opportunities or defend against threats, and then move decisively in one direction. Ambiguity cannot be ruled or controlled. In ambiguous environments, delegation is more effective than personal power. People with critical knowledge needed to respond to the unanticipated event may be scattered throughout the organization, so building relationships with those who have special insight and expertise becomes an essential task for modern managers. As such, seeing through the haze of ambiguity and implementing effective responses requires natural, team-based approaches, as opposed to simple, rational, step-by-step management styles that are too slow and cumbersome.

CHANGING NATURE OF WORK

Business is about identifying and exploiting valuable opportunities, and then turning them into client benefits that create value for the organization. This requires information and knowledge, which is the second trigger: the changing nature of work. When knowledge is concentrated at the top of the hierarchy, rigid command and control structures with centralized decision-making dominate. The speed of decisions, and the flexibility for action, depend on the ability of decision-makers to search for information and quickly assimilate relevant knowledge. In a traditionally structured organization, with rigid hierarchy and centralized decision-making, relevant knowledge is slow to get to the decision-makers or never makes it there at all. This slows the decision-making process to a crawl or leads to flawed or ineffective decisions. Organizations miss opportunities or fail to react quickly to emerging threats because it took too long to take affirmative and effective action.

When knowledge is widely distributed throughout a complex organization, managers must engage with people at multiple levels, across various functions, to build relationships that encourage collaboration with a deep sense of purpose. The inhibiting effect of complex organizational structures can be mitigated with various forms of self-organized teams. Whether they are called work groups, project teams, communities of practice or some other term, effective utilization of communication technologies can link people together, even across remote workplaces. This enables and promotes rapid sharing of key pieces of information, allowing executives to sense opportunities early and act on weak market signals. Early detection of changes in the environment is key to being able to form an effective response.

Rapid gathering and assimilation of valuable information and knowledge that is distributed throughout an organization is essential to identifying, selecting, transforming and exploiting opportunities. Sharing knowledge that is buried within the organization, and quickly converting it into action, is the best means to respond to the challenges of a VUCA environment, where knowledge is widely distributed, and changes come with machine-gun ferocity. Leaders and managers at all levels must adapt to a new way of working with people to access the huge base of knowledge in their organization and convert it to action, and to deliver the greatest value to stakeholders.

People who are successful at constantly searching for and uncovering new opportunities that create value are the real stars. They possess unique abilities to sense and see what is happening in the environment with clarity, rapidly assimilate key information and mobilize their energy and that of others to maintain focus on the goal. With the first born-and-bred knowledge worker generation entering managerial jobs, the distinction between managers and employees is becoming increasingly blurred. To quote management guru Peter Drucker, "With the knowledge age, employees become executives. They make decisions." Leaders and managers must develop new methods of working with this new generation of workers to quickly access their collective brainpower and convert emerging, innovative ideas into action. Successful leaders in the VUCA world will find new ways of working effectively with people at all levels.

Organizations grow and must adapt quickly in these times because life cycle stages come faster and expose organizations to more risks if they are not aligned with the needs of the digital economy. Managers must be very aware of the stage their organization is currently in and what is needed to advance to the next stage.

Here are a few questions for you to reflect on regarding the expedited growth of your organization:

- How does the digital economy affect your organization?
- What are the drivers of your growth?
- What are the obstacles that potentially limit further growth?
- Do you have the knowledge resources necessary to make the next transition?
- Do you have the dynamic capabilities to take advantage of the knowledge?

Coming up, Chapter 2 introduces the organizational growth life cycle framework.

THE DIGITAL ECONOMY

Digitalization and the existence of critical knowledge, both internally and externally, accelerate innovation and growth. At the same time, increased complexity, more ambiguity, growing uncertainty and more volatility mask potential opportunities and increase risks that pose obstacles to further growth. Successful leaders in this VUCA environment must understand the factors that stifle or accelerate growth and develop new and innovative ways to collaborate with knowledge workers.

KEY CHAPTER IDEAS

- Digitalization expedites business growth.
- We live in a VUCA world where the need for speed is critically important.
- Complexity increases with size. Ambiguities require choice. Uncertainty challenges strategy. Higher volatility is the norm. In combination, these factors pose limits to growth.
- Knowledge workers challenge traditional command and control operating modes.
- Tapping into the vast knowledge base in an organization requires the attention of top management.

ACTION AGENDA

- Reflect on the factors that expedite or limit growth of the organization you work for, or one that you know well.
- Are there processes or a culture that facilitate knowledge sharing throughout the organization? If yes, how? If no, what could be done to change that?

FURTHER READING

Management perspective on challenges and knowledge:
Michel, L (2020). *People-Centric Management: How Managers Use Four Levers to Bring Out the Greatness of Others*. London: LID Publishing.

Expert perspective on implications of management design:
Michel, L (2021). *Diagnostic Mentoring: How to Transform the Way We Manage*. London: LID Publishing.

The impact of VUCA and how to accelerate knowledge sharing and strategic actions:
Nold, H., (2021). *Agile Strategies for the 21st Century: The Need for Speed*. Newcastle upon Tyne: Cambridge Scholars Publishing Ltd.

Related research on the management context:
Michel, L; Anzengruber, J; Wolfe, M; and Hixson, N (2018). Under What Conditions do Rules-Based and Capabilities-based Management Modes Dominate? *Special Issue Risks in Financial and Real Estate Markets Journal*, 6(32).

THE GROWTH LIFE CYCLE

It is common knowledge that the demands for organizational structures and leadership change as companies advance from start-up to maturity. As noted earlier, only about 10% of start-ups survive beyond five years. Methods for control and leadership in the start-up or early growth stages are wildly different from those needed to successfully manage a complex organization consisting of multiple departments, divisions, product lines or geographic locations. Various models have been proposed over the years to describe the characteristics of each stage of development. These models follow the natural growth of organizations, with each stage exhibiting distinct patterns of structure and behaviours.

Business leaders should be aware of which stage their organization is in, the characteristics of the current stage and the characteristics of the next stage. Successfully and seamlessly navigating an organization from one stage to another is a challenge for even the most talented leaders. To successfully move from one to the next, top executives and entrepreneurs should be aware of what actions must be taken in advance to make a seamless transition. Leaders should proactively prepare for these transitions by laying the foundations or infrastructure needed to prevent a crisis that inhibits further growth. A clear understanding and appreciation of the growth framework helps managers proactively manage the development of their organization.

Chapter 2 introduces the organizational growth life cycle.

FIVE STAGES OF GROWTH

While several life cycle models have been promoted over the years, we have adopted the one proposed by Larry Greiner, the late Professor of Management and Organization at the University of Southern California. Greiner's model follows five stages of development. Current management patterns, methods and behaviours have their roots in the past. The vision, leadership and management structures that were successful earlier became the dominant patterns. However, what worked well in the past may not necessarily work effectively as the organization grows in complexity, in a volatile and uncertain business environment. Failure to recognize and proactively adapt leadership style and management structures to the new internal and external conditions has been widely accepted as the main reason for the short life span of most start-ups and entrepreneurs. Therefore, entrepreneurs, top executives and managers need to pay attention to their current and future life cycle stages. They should be aware of inherent risks in their prevailing structures, leadership and management styles, and systems. The first step is creating awareness, for without that it is impossible to initiate changes *before* encountering a crisis that will prevent further growth.

GREINER'S LIFE CYCLE MODEL

As we've noted, Greiner's widely cited original model, published in 1972 and expanded upon in 1997, suggested that the life cycle of an organization follows five distinct stages (Figure 1). Each has an evolutionary growth phase and a revolutionary crisis phase that must be overcome before the organization can advance and continue to grow.

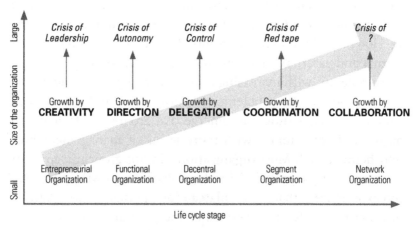

FIGURE 1: GREINER'S FIVE LIFE CYCLE STAGES

According to Greiner, interference with growth potential in organizations is more rooted in decisions made in the past than stemming from present events or market dynamics. In early phases of development, exuberance and excitement by entrepreneurs over their apparent success many times leads them to overlook critical development issues. Consequently, organizations develop patterns of behaviours and methods based on what happened in the past, which proved successful, rather than anticipating and planning for what lies ahead. Flush with early success and growth, managers become absorbed with dealing with the daily array of issues and problems, which consumes them. They simply do not have the time, energy or resources to anticipate and lay the groundwork for future growth because everything goes into dealing with the here and now. Leaders fail to stop and consider that organizations pass through distinct developmental growth phases. Each phase has unique evolutionary characteristics as the organization steadily grows and changes, which inevitably ends with a revolutionary period of considerable organizational challenge or crisis. The actions taken by management to resolve each crisis determine whether the company evolves to the next growth stage.

Over time, control structures and behaviour become accepted as the 'right' way to do business, and part of the DNA of the organization.

These management methods and cultural attributes become rigid, as *this is how we do things here* becomes the common way of thinking. However, these patterns eventually become outdated as both internal and external forces change. As organizations grow in size and complexity, with increasing numbers of employees and greater business volume, the problems of coordination and communication increase. New functions emerge that are needed to maintain control and consistency, with more levels of management hierarchy being added. Most organizations do not grow at a constant pace over multiple periods. They typically have growth spurts, and then experience setbacks or a plateau for a period or two. Plateaus represent relatively quiet periods in the growth phase, inevitably leading up to revolutionary periods of trouble and crisis. Not all organizations survive their crises. They are forced to assess existing management practices that worked in the past, abandon some that got them into trouble and adopt new practices better suited for the next growth spurt.

The critical task for managers is to identify the right time to begin questioning existing practices and implement new ones that work for the next stage of growth. The duration of a phase is closely related to the industry-specific business environment. Innovative or disruptive technology companies are likely to have shorter phases than organizations in established, more stable, industries.

Greiner's five phases of growth framework allows us to identify common patterns of behaviours and management challenges inherent in each phase. Such patterns characterize the dominant managerial and organizational capabilities and systems. Each phase is always the result of actions taken in the previous stage. In each, managers are limited to what they can do to promote growth while in that phase. Leaders cannot go back and reinstall old capabilities, systems or behaviours. They must adopt new practices to position the organization for the subsequent stage.

Creativity characterizes start-ups that develop innovative new products or explore new markets for existing products or services. The founders often are technical experts in a field who engage in informal conversations to get things done. These visionaries see opportunities where others do not and have the will to take risks to pursue the opportunities. Start-ups tend to be nimble, with a rapid decision-making process centred on the founder and minimal bureaucracy. As the company grows, the informal style creates the *crisis of leadership* because one person cannot be everywhere at once and cannot be an expert in all disciplines needed for an efficient and effective organization. A strong manager is needed for the next phase, to provide structure and organization for a business that is growing in complexity. This is the time for rules-based management techniques, which are not typically an area of expertise among founders who are driven by technical knowledge and passion.

Direction is the growth phase when capable managers in key functional areas under directive leadership are brought into the organization. New managers with specialized expertise in areas like human resources, marketing or accounting introduce functional hierarchies that become increasingly segregated. New managers take on roles as functional experts, overseeing departments of other specialists with content-specific training and expertise. Over time, these mangers begin to feel restricted by the centralized directives as they compete for resources to build little fiefdoms. At this point, a *crisis of autonomy* emerges. To overcome this, senior executives and managers must begin to adopt new methods that balance the need for control with flexibility and speed. Processes and actions that promote delegation of responsibility to lower levels in the organization are required in the phase that follows. It is time for engagement-based management.

Delegation refers to the next phase, with decentralized structures and decision-making. Much greater responsibility is given to managers of sub-units, plants and market areas. The delegation process and resulting structural changes separate the roles of top executives at headquarters from overseeing day-to-day activities. That decision-making is entrusted to lower-level managers who are closer to both employees and the customer. Remote managers are granted great autonomy, increasing the speed and quality of decisions that can be made on the spot. Typically, a problem emerges when top management senses that it is losing control. This is the beginning of the *crisis of control*, which requires attention in order to advance into the next stage of growth. This is the time for change-based management techniques to be implemented.

Coordination comes with the introduction of formal systems and processes for greater coordination among the far-flung operations or functional departments. By this point in organizational development, the various entities are led by managers who compete for recognition and resources. Top-level executives residing in the C-suite take responsibility for the management of these systems. Reorganizations become commonplace as decentralized units or functional departments are merged into product segments or other structural units. Incentive programmes designed by top executives emerge, to align behaviours throughout the organization in support of corporate strategic objectives. Over time, with increasing complexity and distance, a lack of confidence builds between headquarters and managers in the field. To maintain the perception of control, headquarter executives add layers of processes, with documentation needed to gain approval for important decisions. At this point, layers of systems and programmes exceed their usefulness. The cost of mountains of bureaucracy in loss of speed and quality of decisions makes the entire process counterproductive. The *crisis of red tape* emerges in an organization that is too complex and cumbersome to take advantage of new opportunities or react to emerging threats. Personal collaboration is needed to overcome this barrier and advance to the next growth stage. Now is the time for capabilities-based management.

Collaboration becomes the next developmental growth stage. The collaboration phase is characterized by spontaneity and skilful confrontation among leaders and managers throughout the organization to overcome differences of opinion or viewpoint. More flexible behavioural controls replace rigid command and control systems or structures with a focus on solving problems in teams. It is here that the unseen factors that make up the culture (shared beliefs, values and assumptions) that have been developing since the creativity stage become a powerful force. In organizations where knowledge is distributed, knowledge sharing throughout the organization — up, down and horizontally — becomes critically important. Collaboration in a large and complex organization connected with intertwined networks creates another crisis to be overcome: one of complexity and identity. New structures and programmes are needed to work across organizational boundaries that promote rapid knowledge sharing. Relevant information must flow freely throughout the organization and into the hands of key decision-makers, so they can move quickly to take advantage of opportunities or respond to emerging threats.

LEVERS OF CONTROL

Top executives and managers at all levels need to know where their organization is in the development cycle. Responses to challenges for one phase are different from those needed to advance to, and deal with problems in, the next phase. Past patterns of behaviour and structure are not helpful in getting through the next growth stage. Existing control structures and unseen rarely discussed elements of the organizational culture act like a breaking mechanism that inhibits further growth. Hence, managers need to identify the current growth phase. They must be aware that patterns that have proved successful in the past may not necessarily support further growth. The life cycle model provides a roadmap to help management be proactive and institute new structures in preparation for the next phase. Additionally, business leaders should be very aware that new solutions to overcome old problems are likely to create a new set of challenges in the next developmental state. Organizational designs cannot be static. They must be constantly evaluated and modified to respond to both internal and external forces of change that can either inhibit an organization's progress or propel it to the next level.

In *Levers of Control* (1994), Harvard Business School professor Robert Simons identified the evolution of management control systems using Greiner's life cycle of an organization model (Figure 2). Additional control systems are introduced and integrated into the organization to solve control challenges as size and complexity increases.

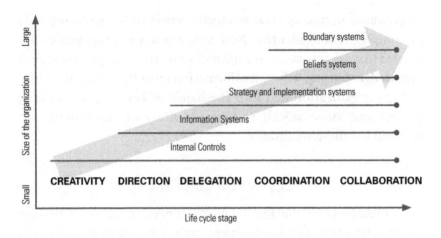

FIGURE 2: LEVERS OF CONTROL

Figure 2 illustrates various control systems commonly in use to overcome challenges in the difference phases.

Internal controls to free up creativity. In the creativity phase of start-up companies, there is little need for formal control systems. The founders' vision, purpose and passion are transferred to employees through personal presence and interaction. The newly formed organization is generally small, so employees are in constant face-to-face contact, communicate with each other, freely exchange critical knowledge and share a passion that rubs off from the founders. There is no need for formal controls because everyone is physically and emotionally connected and on the same page. Key assets of the business are protected through informal internal control systems formed by a common bond and purpose. People ensure that assets are secure, and that accounting information reliably reflects the business operations, because doing so helps secure their own livelihood. The success of the business and the careers of people are intertwined with a shared purpose and vision.

Performance indicators to clarify direction. When a start-up grows into the direction phase, people become physically and emotionally removed from direct contact with the founders or top executives. Direct, daily interaction with all employees is no longer possible. To compensate for less personal interaction, managers must institute systems to see what is going on. Information systems with key performance indicators (KPIs) are introduced that create shared observation points. This allows managers to see what is going on and helps employees focus their attention on the things that matter. Feedback mechanisms based on the KPI results provide sufficient managerial control.

Performance indicators with regular feedback provide support for self-responsible people with knowledge that is distributed throughout the organization. Regular feedback provides clarity, so people know what is expected of them and how to get things done. Appropriate and relevant metrics act as a diagnostic instrument, giving managers insight into where the organization is and where it is going. Relevant KPIs help leaders focus on critical interactions, and then provide feedback that helps employees make sense of what they are doing and why. The entire process creates a collective awareness that promotes a culture with a shared understanding and purpose at its roots.

Delegation through strategy, performance plans and reports. In the delegation phase, with increasing size and complexity, decision authority is delegated to lower-level managers and employees who interact directly with customers. Formal strategy development processes and implementation initiatives become increasingly important. Communicating strategic objectives, both long- and short-term, throughout the organization strengthens alignment of people at all levels toward achieving objectives. Employees and channels must have a clear understanding of the goals, so decision-makers can take actions that reinforce the goals. Strategy implementation must also include regular reviews to help shape alterations in strategy if conditions change or unanticipated opportunities arise.

Strategy tools, such as frequent communication and regular reviews, enable effective thinking in ambiguous environments. In a VUCA world, a strategic plan that makes sense today may be obsolete only a few months later. Published plans, reports and reviews initiate critical thinking and evaluation of the strategy. Strategy implementation should not be a fixed series of actions. Rather, it should be a continuous learning process that allows key decision-makers to make mid-stream course corrections as conditions change. Effective leaders in this ambiguous environment interact with people at all levels and offer strategic insights that create a shared awareness of where the organization is and where it is going. Additionally, personal interaction allows people to share their observations with the leaders, which help leadership sense when changes are happening. In combination, this creates a culture based on a shared intent, so that people with delegated authority have a common, connected way of thinking. Like a rowing team with a crew of eight, all must be pulling in the same direction, with the same force, and tightly coordinated by the team captain.

When uncertainty is high, frequent reports showing results of critical functions enable self-organized teams to evaluate performance and take reinforcing or corrective action. At this stage, resources are allocated on demand, when needed, with flexible plans and regular decentralized business reviews to support strategy implementation. Leaders interactively challenge teams. Together, these methods help create a culture where people have a shared agenda that facilitates collaboration.

Coordination through vision, values and contributions. Businesses in the coordination phase operate in multiple markets and locations, which makes coordination across physical, organizational or marketplace boundaries more difficult. It becomes impossible to formulate and enforce rules to cover every possible situation. Global organizations must consider and comply with legal and cultural differences that vary from nation to nation. Formal, rigid command and control methodologies emanating from the home office become ineffective and cumbersome. Coordination at this level demands that managers share a common purpose and freely share critical information with people inside their organizations, as well as other business units. Headquarters can assist business unit executives by developing and disseminating tools that communicate basic beliefs. It becomes necessary for people throughout the company to believe in and follow mission and vision statements to align business units, engage the workforce and help employees maintain focus on what matters.

Collaboration through mission, risks and structure. In large, mature companies, leaders rely on collaboration, creative knowledge, and opportunity-sensing capabilities of employees for innovation and new business ventures. At this stage, personal interaction complements management tools. Information and knowledge sharing, strategic direction toward a common purpose, effective implementation, shared common beliefs and clearly defined boundaries combine to balance entrepreneurial action with the need for control that limits risks. Leaders of large, mature companies must evolve their thinking to be what organizational theorists Charles O'Reilly III and Michael Tushman described in a 2004 *Harvard Business Review* article as 'ambidextrous' thinking. This means that leaders must exploit current strengths while simultaneously leveraging core competencies to explore new opportunities to continue growing. They referred to the Roman god Janus, who had two sets of eyes — one for focusing on what lay behind, and the other on what lay ahead. The list of companies where leaders focused energy inwards to exploit current capabilities, to the exclusion of exploring new opportunities, is long. It includes iconic has-been names we cited earlier, like Sears, Kodak and Bethlehem Steel. Exploring new opportunities for large, mature companies demands that leaders shape a common culture that encourages knowledge sharing and collaboration. This stimulates creativity while finding the right balance between control and a willingness to take risks and adapt the structure as needed to promote growth.

Dynamic beliefs (vision, values and contributions) and boundary tools (mission, risks and structures) enable employee engagement, knowledge sharing and creativity. People must share common aspirations and norms in an environment where knowledge and decision-making are distributed throughout the organization. Leaders of businesses in the collaboration stage must interact and engage in dialogue on contribution and risks. People need to know what their contribution is and what level of risks the organization is willing to accept. Shared aspirations and norms create a strong and unified culture at scale.

CONTROL SYSTEMS

Figure 3 provides a summary of how the management style, organizational structure and systems must adapt as the organization grows and advances through the various growth stages.

	CREATIVITY	DIRECTION	DELEGATION	COORDINATION	COLLABORATION
Management	Make and sell, individual, entrepreneurial	Operational efficiency, directive	Market growth, delegative	Consolidation control	Problem solving, innovation, participative
Organization	Informal	Centralized, functional	Decentralized, geographical	Line staff, product units	Matrix, network
Systems	Internal controls, market results	Standards, cost centres, information	Implementation, business reviews, profit centres	Strategies, plans, resource allocation, beliefs	Mutual goal setting, beliefs and boundaries

FIGURE 3: CONTROL SYSTEMS

WRAPPING IT UP

A solid understanding of the growth life cycle framework enables leaders to proactively manage the development of their organization. They need to prepare their organizations to successfully make the transition from one stage to the next.

Refer to Figure 3. Here are several questions for you to reflect on, regarding the organizational growth life cycle:

- What is your current growth life cycle stage?
- What are the managerial challenges in your current life cycle stage?
- What must be done to lay the foundation to advance to the next stage?
- What are you actually doing about it?
- What resources or capabilities does your organization need to move forward?

Chapter 3 introduces three managerial ecosystems needed to solve the evolution – revolution challenges.

THE GROWTH LIFE CYCLE

According to Greiner, the growth of an organization follows five life cycle stages. Roots from the past, with a distinct management approach, organization structure and management systems, characterize every stage. Growth stalls unless managers learn how to overcome inherent crisis patterns.

KEY CHAPTER IDEAS

- Creativity, direction, delegation, coordination and collaboration are the five life cycle growth stages of an organization, according to Greiner.
- Crises of leadership, autonomy, bureaucracy, complexity and identity are the inherent inhibitors of growth.
- Past actions, decisions, processes and behaviours characterize your current life cycle stage more than anything else.
- Leaders must find the right balance between the need for control and the need for knowledge sharing and creativity.
- They should be proactive in preparing their organizations to transition from one stage to another.

ACTION AGENDA

- Know your organization's history.
- Know your current life cycle stage.
- Prepare for and manage life cycle transitions.

FURTHER READING

Management perspective on levers of control:
Michel, L (2013). *The Performance Triangle: Diagnostic Mentoring to Manage Organizations and People for Superior Performance in Turbulent Times.* London: LID Publishing.

Expert perspective on the choice of management systems:
Michel, L (2021). *Diagnostic Mentoring: How to Transform the Way We Manage.* London: LID Publishing.

Ambidextrous thinking:
O'Reilly III, C. & Tushman, M. (2016). *Lead and Disrupt: How to Solve the Innovator's Dilemma.* Stanford, CA: Stanford University Press.

Related research on the management control:
Nold, H; and Michel, L (2016). The Performance Triangle: A Model for Corporate Agility. *Leadership & Organizational Development Journal,* 37(3).

THE MANAGERIAL MODES & ECOSYSTEM

Over the past 20 years we have analysed survey data and helped executives from more than 400 organizations decipher the information and understand what it means for their company. Through the decades, very clear managerial patterns have emerged. These patterns allow us to identify important characteristics of various general management styles. The resultant models are useful tools in helping leaders understand the current management state of their organization and what needs to be done to improve, by accessing the vast body of knowledge and people-centric capabilities that exist in their company. A basic starting point for understanding the managerial ecosystem is four general operating modes of management that are common in today's digital economy.

Every organization has one dominant management mode or style that aligns with the life cycle growth stage. Three dynamic and interconnected ecosystems frame the structural and behavioural patterns within the five life cycle stages. Understanding the characteristics of the three ecosystems — people-centric management, agile organization and dynamic operating systems — helps leaders chart a course to design or redesign the organization to maximize its dynamic capabilities. Where you are designing, or redesigning, depends on the life cycle growth stage you are in. Creativity and growth stages might require leaders to design the initial management framework, while leaders in the delegation, coordination and collaboration phases must redesign the organization to advance to the next growth stage. We have observed that over time unseen viruses creep into most organizations, interfering with day-to-day performance and inhibiting growth. For example, employees will never tell the top executives that they do not have confidence in them because they are not perceived to be credible. Or, decision-making is guided by data that was meaningful five years ago, but is no longer relevant, leading to flawed choices. When this happens, the crisis of growth is near, and leaders should try to identify these viruses and eliminate them before initiating disruptive change projects.

Chapter 3 introduces management modes and three ecosystems, with their respective capabilities.

FOUR OPERATING MODES

Understanding the characteristics of four general operating modes helps managers succeed in different business environments and life cycle stages. The dominant management mode needed for superior performance in a fast-moving VUCA environment differs greatly from what's called for in a stable environment. In an industry or environment where the rate of change is slow, command and control styles often dominate, and they can be successful. However, in the VUCA world that characterizes the 21st century, where knowledge is key, an operating mode that enables people to effectively apply their knowledge is essential. A knowledge-based environment is fundamentally different from one where work is highly standardized and managers can take control. Human beings, specifically knowledge workers, are really good at most complex, collaborative and creative activities. They are much better at this than machines. Adapting to a VUCA environment is hard for both machines and people in highly controlled, standardized organizations. However, leaders must actively and aggressively work to create an environment that allows people to use their knowledge and be creative. In a VUCA world, teams, networks and ecosystems of people, working together toward a common goal, can create immense value. In fact, these become fundamental and necessary conditions for superior performance.

Figure 4 introduces four operating modes relative to the contextual setting in which the organization operates. The left side (y-axis) represents the context in which the organization operates, ranging from a stable, slowly changing environment at the bottom to a dynamic or rapidly changing one at the top. The bottom (x-axis) represents the management style, ranging from traditional command and control to people-centric styles. The combination results in four quadrants: rules-based, engagement-based, change-based and capabilities-based operating modes that are the dominant management styles. Results of our survey data indicate that all organizations can be placed into one of these four quadrants, according to the dominant management style.

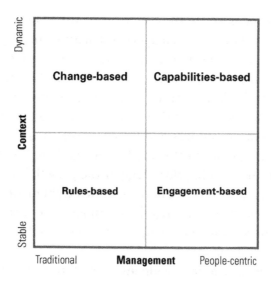

FIGURE 4: FOUR OPERATING MODES

Rules-based management works well in a stable environment where knowledge is concentrated with managers at the top, with them organizing, planning, coordinating and controlling all decisions and employee activities. Bureaucratic control procedures promote efficiency and help establish consistency, quality and reliability of products and services. People are there to follow orders. When things change, executives typically address specific gaps by adding more rules or systems to tighten efficiency and improve quality. The rules-based methodology is often combined with other modes in organizations that require a hybrid approach. A hospital emergency room is such an example. Teams normally follow standard procedures. When a special situation occurs, the staff's capabilities allow them to find creative solutions to the problem. Rules-based management dominates in the direction stage of the growth life cycle. We have identified eight distinct features of rules-based management: command, procedures, targets, change, efficiency, bureaucracy, power and standards.

Change-based management styles dominate in highly regulated industries when volatility, uncertainty and ambiguity in the internal or external environment increase. In response to rapid change, management focus shifts from control to the change needed to adapt to new conditions. Managers restructure the organization, reallocate resources and refine processes in response to the environmental changes. Executives tend to be reactive rather than proactive, with limited learning from prior actions, leading to a never-ending series of disruptive change initiatives of questionable value. The financial services and telecom sectors are examples of industries that operate in this mode. Change-based management dominates in the coordination stage of the growth life cycle with segmented organizations. We have identified eight distinct features of organizations in the change-based mode of operation: command, procedures, targets, change, emergence, self-organization, delegation and options.

Engagement-based management is preferred by knowledge-driven organizations that operate in a stable environment. In a modern people-centric environment where knowledge sharing is key for success, traditional, formal command and control approaches become less effective. Self-responsibility and personal recognition are key motivators for knowledge workers to perform. Engagement-based methods combine informal and formal controls on knowledge inputs, behaviours and outputs to align individual interests through visions, beliefs, boundaries and values. Modern public administration of cities or states is a good example. People are encouraged to fully engage their talent. Engagement-based management dominates in the delegation stage of the growth life cycle for decentralized organizations. We have identified eight distinct features of engagement-based management: self-responsibility, teamwork, attention, capabilities, efficiency, bureaucracy, power and standards.

Capabilities-based management dominates when knowledge is widely distributed throughout the organization as complexity increases and the need for creative innovation dominates. The focus of management shifts to enabling collaboration and relationship building, paired with a deep sense of purpose. Under these conditions, management transforms organizations in support of fast decision-making and proactive, flexible action, which lead to robust outcomes. Capabilities-based management becomes the foundation for innovation in organizations. Start-up firms, research-based organizations and businesses in exploration mode operate in this manner. Capabilities-based management dominates at both ends of the growth life cycle: creativity and collaboration. We have identified eight distinct features of capabilities-based management: self-responsibility, teamwork, attention, capabilities, emergence, self-organization, delegation and options.

WRAPPING IT UP

The four operating modes illustrate the need for different managerial responses and structures in the digital economy, depending on the operating environment and the stage of development the organization is in.

Here are questions for you to reflect on regarding the dominant operating mode:

- What is your current operating mode?
- How does it align with the dominant growth life cycle stage?
- Where do you want your organization to be?
- What actions can you take to position your organization to advance to the next level?

THREE ECOSYSTEMS

The term 'ecosystem' was first coined by Arthur Tansley, an English botanist, in 1935. Tansley described it as a structural and functional unit of ecology where the living organisms interact with each other and the surrounding environment. In other words, an ecosystem is a dynamic system of interactions between organisms and their environment where both are dependent on each other.

We have adapted the ecosystem concept to business to describe how organizations interact with their environment. In our 20 years of research and observation, we have identified three organizational ecosystems that help describe the dynamic interactions between people, the organization and the external environment. We have found that these ecosystems exist in all organizations, in one form or another. The ecosystems themselves are also inextricably interconnected, making up parts of a larger complex and dynamic ecosystem that is *the organization*. Three ecosystems with their unique capabilities (Figure 5) shape the behavioural and management patterns of the five life cycle growth stages. They are extensively documented in our other books:

- **People-Centric Management** (*People-Centric Management: How Managers Use Four Levers to Bring out the Greatness of Others*, Michel, 2020)
- **Agile Organization** (*The Performance Triangle: Diagnostic Mentoring to Manage Organizations and People for Superior Performance in Turbulent Times,* Michel, 2013)
- **Dynamic Operating System** (*The Leadership Scorecard: Perspectives, Dimensions and Patterns for Mastery in the Digital Economy*, Michel and Anzengruber, 2024)

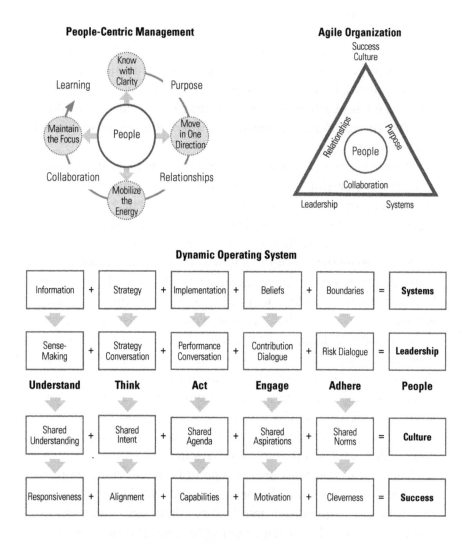

FIGURE 5: THREE MANAGERIAL ECOSYSTEMS

The **people-centric** ecosystem is one that most of us can readily relate to. People constantly interact with each other and with the external environment. When successful 21st-century executives develop ways to manage the people-centric ecosystem, the organization benefits from talented people who possess skills, knowledge and a high-performance attitude. This mode of management follows the principles of self-responsibility, delegation, self-organization and focus of attention. Such enabling management is in sharp contrast to traditional management, where authoritarian control and command prevail.

The people-centric ecosystem consists of enabling systems and supporting leadership who provide positive reinforcement and sufficient resources to balance and power the ecosystem. Effective leadership and systems enable people to achieve a state called 'flow' that allow them to fully use their unique talents. Anyone who has played sports can relate to the notion of flow as that time in a game when a team gets *hot* and everything seems easy. To a basketball player in the hot zone, the hoop looks a meter wide, and you cannot miss. Teams get in the groove when they all move in one direction and singularly focus on winning. In an enabling people-centric organizational environment, people in a state of flow can face down greater challenges than ever thought possible. The reinforcing loop from management sets in and propels people, and the organization as a whole, to new levels of achievement. The toolbox of resources available to management provides the positive or negative reinforcing loop that sets acceptable boundaries that shape behaviours and actions.

Work *in* the ecosystem aims to support both the reinforcing loop and the balancing loop. People-centric leaders develop methods that help people quiet their minds, focus their capabilities and use resources wisely. This management style requires responsible leadership and supportive systems.

As such, people-centric management techniques also require work *on* the system. This involves making sure systems and leadership meet people's needs to help them achieve a state of flow. This enables the productive utilization of time, attention, energy and space. Doing all this effectively means that there must be room (and budget) to refuel limited resources. People-centric management enables the organization to access vast stores of experience, knowledge and skills inherent in people at all levels.

Agility is the necessary feature of organizations in support of people-centric management. Agile organizations develop a work environment where people serve their customers in ways that generate positive returns for the organization and its stakeholders. The critical characteristics of the agile ecosystem are balance between organizational culture, leadership and systems. Power for the agile ecosystem is generated by the people ecosystem, through the release of vast stores of energy in the form of knowledge and experience.

The agile ecosystem consists of an organization with a shared culture, interactive leadership and an effective operating system. Effective operating systems include not just the information technology, but the processes or rules that govern the exchange of critical information to and from decision-makers. Effective operating systems provide relevant information to the right people, at the right time, facilitating informed decisions. People in agile ecosystems have a shared culture, embodying common beliefs and values. Leaders in the agile ecosystem practise interactive leadership that engages and supports people at all levels, with a supportive operating system. The critical characteristic of value-adding agile ecosystems is balance. If one of the main attributes becomes overly powerful or weak, the entire ecosystem becomes less effective. Overbearing dictatorial leadership, lack of trust or comments like 'The system won't allow me to...' are all indicators that the ecosystem is not functioning effectively. None of these three components come for free. Leaders must continuously invest time, effort and financial resources to balance the reinforcing loop to attract customers and promote efficient operations that add value.

Dynamic operating systems are an ecosystem unto themselves, enabling people to cope with the challenges in the VUCA world. Dynamic operating systems comprise many unseen and rarely discussed elements that can enable or interfere with the agile ecosystem. The ability of people, the organization, work, operations and management to address a challenging environment better than the competition drives growth and considerably reduces costs and operational risks.

The dynamic feature of an operating ecosystem (Figure 5) consists of rules, routines and tools that facilitate interactive leadership. Meaningful interaction within the people-centric ecosystem and the agile ecosystem are enabled through the shared purpose, strong relationships and collaboration. The dynamic feature of systems enables people to deal with greater challenges. Dynamic systems come with tools that can handle volatility, routines that deal with complexity, interactions for uncertainty and flexible rules that define boundaries for dealing with ambiguity. Leaders must engage with people to help them make sense of what is going on, so they can drive strategy with a clear understanding of how their performance contributes to success and what the acceptable levels of risk are. The culture helps ensure that people have a shared understanding of what needs to be done, and the intent to get things done, with a shared agenda and aspirations, along with accepted norms of behaviour. Designing an effective dynamic operating ecosystem must be deliberate and ongoing. Investment of time, effort and money in a dynamic operating system that enables people, the organization, operations and management to handle adversity better than others is a true competitive advantage.

WRAPPING IT UP

In the VUCA 21st-century environment that every organization operates in, the understanding and proactive design of complex ecosystems becomes essential for long-term success. In people-centric, agile and dynamic operating ecosystems, people can reach their flow state more often if there is no undue interference from overbearing bosses, restrictive rules and processes, and their own minds. They can play the game easily and perform at their peak. Effectively designing and guiding dynamic ecosystems requires a high level of managerial fitness, agile maturity throughout the organization and the development of dynamic operating system features. Making it so is a deliberate choice every manager must make.

Three ecosystems, with their capabilities, aim at mastery through better management. Recognizing and developing them becomes part of the evolution through an organization's life cycle growth stages.

Here are a few questions for you to reflect on concerning the ecosystem's capabilities:

- What are your current people-centric, agile and dynamic system capabilities?
- Where do you have strengths to leverage and weaknesses to address?
- How do both strengths and weaknesses impact your organization's ecosystem?
- How do these capabilities fit your current life cycle growth stage?
- What can you do to leverage strengths or eliminate weaknesses to advance to the next level?
- What specific actions can you take now?

WHEN VIRUSES INTERFERE

Many events or conditions can disrupt living ecosystems, causing damage or even destruction. Organizational ecosystems are susceptible to the same threats. In our work over the past 20 years, we have observed many interferences that act like viruses in living organisms. These viruses cannot be seen, but they disrupt various systems, causing the patient (the organization) to become sick... or worse. When viruses interfere in organizations, the crisis of growth will not be far off. In *Levers of Control* (2005), Professor Robert Simons stated: "To unleash this potential [knowledge workers] managers must overcome organizational blocks. Management control systems play an important role in this process." Over the years, viruses creep into most organizations, in the forms of faulty leadership, irrelevant or ineffective systems, or an infected culture where people share a limiting belief that prevents them from performing at their peak. As coaching and performance improvement author Timothy Gallwey (2000) observed, "The greater the external challenges accepted by a company, team or individual, the more important it is that there is minimum interference occurring from within."

When viruses creep into an organization, it is time for spring cleaning. Some of the most common organizational infections we have observed include toxic culture, flawed leadership and broken systems.

Toxic culture. Examples of a toxic culture include unclear or vague operating procedures, business values that are not clearly linked to outcomes, cynicism, upward delegation, outdated reasons for centralized decision-making, a technocratic view of decision-making and a lack of shared assumptions. When these factors are in play, people lack trust in each other, and management is viewed as not credible. Culture generates much talk, and blame, from corporate executives, but rarely much in the way of effective action. Organizational culture — that shared set of beliefs, values and assumptions — cannot be seen or touched. It emerges gradually, beginning when an enterprise's founders start working together. As such, culture cannot be changed directly. A toxic culture creates subtle dissonances that are hard to detect. For example, employees will never go to the CEO's office and state that they do not trust him or her, or their immediate supervisor. These underlying beliefs and values are shaped by perceptions of leadership, and in response to forces from systems, and become embedded in the minds of people as *how we do things around here*. Changing people's beliefs and values is a difficult challenge. Everyone knows that changing a culture demands time and serious effort, focused on the 'right' beliefs. Fixing culture requires altering systems and leadership behaviours in a way that people are positively affected. It is possible to change people's behaviours through punitive action or rewards, but when the incentive is removed, they return to their original behaviour because the underlying beliefs have not changed. Change can happen through workshops, mentoring or corporate programmes that are well crafted and professionally orchestrated, which can yield positive results via different ways of thinking. The root of a defective culture always lies in flawed leadership or broken systems. So, the task is to fix leadership and systems first.

Flawed leadership. Examples of flawed leadership include excessive control, busyness, lack of time, disproportionate attention to detail, micromanagement, senselessness, obsessive focus on numbers, and saying one thing and then doing another. Normally, organizations try to hire the best and brightest, and train them to stay that way, or compel them to fit pre-established templates for behaviour or processes. Bad leadership normally begins with one manager, who can ultimately infect an entire organization that is below him or her on the organization chart. People adapt their leadership style to survive, or to be perceived as effective and eligible for promotion. Consequently, one bad apple can infect an entire leadership team. At that point, the only viable fix is to replace them all. If caught soon enough, the infection can be isolated and 'treated' with effective counselling, as it will initially reside with a single person, or within a small group. Replacing a leader is an option, but that normally comes too late, after the infection has spread and the damage is done. Fixing a leader takes time, and lingering toxins might still spread for a while, making it even more difficult to reverse the damage. Fixing a leader is expensive and the likelihood of success is questionable, despite the promises of a huge 'leadership-fixing' industry. Coaching or training flawed leaders is ineffective. Performance problems can be fixed where there is a will to learn, but in our experience that will decreases the higher up managers are on the organization chart. Ego and the need to not be perceived as weak create behavioural problems (or a mixture of performance and behaviour problems) that require a different course of action.

Broken systems. Examples of broken systems include bureaucratic or non-existent routines, burdensome formality, faulty design, failure to revisit past decisions, slow delivery of critical information that hampers decision-making, rules infected with the viruses and ineffective tools that fail to get the right information to the right people at the right time. A set of system flaws can plant the seeds for flawed leadership. Common culprits include management by objectives, poorly conceived incentive programmes, burdensome and inflexible budgeting processes, fights over resource allocation and poor communication. When any one of these is present, it is likely to infect the entire organization. Systems viruses have a huge impact on the entire ecosystem and degrade performance throughout. Managers in human resources, finance, operations, risk, governance and other support functions are often the cause. We have observed the impulse to focus and optimize performance in their own domain, which may not integrate or align with other functional areas. Fixing systems is critical and affects the entire organization, so it is often a risk. However, doing nothing is not an option. Compared to changing culture or fixing leadership, fixing broken systems is relatively cheap and easy. Implementing systems is a free choice, with many alternatives to choose from, and it can be done relatively quickly when the will is there. Yet, simply fixing the systems toolbox might not be good enough. Integrating the various ecosystems might require a new systems design to fundamentally rethink the way you lead the organization.

The symptoms of a broken operating system can be seen everywhere. The causes often lie with the tools, routines or rules that govern the prevailing management model. All of these are signs of a toxic culture that is missing energy or lacking in flow experiences. The result is crippled growth and stagnation. Broken operating systems are the root-cause of managerial crisis in organizations at every life cycle growth stage.

Here are a few questions for you to consider when thinking about viruses in your organization:

- What are the viruses that interfere with your performance?
- How do they limit the development of your organization?
- To what extent do viruses cause the next crisis of management?
- What specific actions can and should you take to eliminate the viruses?

Part II introduces mastery in better management to set the standards for life cycle transitions.

THE MANAGERIAL ECOSYSTEM

The environment (stable vs. dynamic) and the management style (control vs. people-centric) determine the operating mode of an organization. The dominant management mode can be categorized as one of four general modes: rules-based, change-based, engagement-based or capabilities-based. Organizations contain multiple interdependent ecosystems with people-centric relationships, agile management characteristics and dynamic capabilities. Over time, viruses creep into the ecosystems, interfering with their health and degrading performance. Viruses infect the organizational culture, leadership and operating systems, and must be eliminated to advance to the next stage of growth.

KEY CHAPTER IDEAS

- All organizations have a dominant operating mode that is influenced by the environment and the approach to handling people.
- Within the operating modes, people-centric, agile and dynamic capabilities ecosystems drive operations and growth.
- Every life cycle stage comes with a dominant operating mode.
- Viruses creep into ecosystems and degrade the health, performance and growth potential of the organization.
- When viruses interfere, the crisis of growth is just around the corner.
- Viruses must be identified and eliminated for the organization to advance to the next life cycle growth stage.

ACTION AGENDA

- Determine your dominant operating mode.
- Reflect on your managerial ecosystems.
- Pay attention to potential viruses that limit your growth.
- What actions can and should you take to eliminate the viruses?

FURTHER READING

Management perspective on operating modes:
Michel, L (2020). *People-Centric Management: How Managers Use Four Levers to Bring Out the Greatness of Others*. London: LID Publishing.

Expert perspective on people-centric, dynamic, and agile capabilities:
Michel, L (2021). *Diagnostic Mentoring: How to Transform the Way We Manage*. London: LID Publishing.
Nold, H (2018). Dynamic Capabilities for People-Centric Management in Turbulent Times. In M F Brandebo & A Alvinus (Eds.), *Dark Side of Organizational Behavior and Leadership (pp. 109-124)*. London: IntechOpen.

Insight into organizational culture:
Nold, H; and Michel, L (2021). Organizational Culture: A Systems Approach. In Alsharari, N (Ed.), *Accounting and Finance Innovations*, London: IntechOpen.

Related research on operating modes:
Michel, L; Anzengruber, J; Wolfe, M; and Hixson, N (2018). Under What Conditions do Rules-Based and Capabilities-based Management Modes Dominate? *Special Issue Risks in Financial and Real Estate Markets Journal*, 6(32).

PART II

MASTERY IN MANAGEMENT

Mastery of management techniques that are suited for the 21st-century digital economy is needed to successfully guide the organization through the six life cycle growth stages. We have identified four levers needed to separate people-centric managers from traditional command and control managers. The Performance Triangle provides a framework that defines the dynamic capabilities of agile organizations. The Leadership Scorecard was developed as a complementary management tool that provides insight into whether an organization has a traditional or a dynamic operating system. Together, these visual aids define the capabilities needed for better management in a digital, VUCA world. People-centric management is a competitive advantage if it gets work done, creates value, is specific to the organization, is hard to copy, limits short-cuts and is deeply embedded in the organizational culture.

Part II outlines what is needed for mastery in management to guide organizations as they transition through the life cycle growth stages.

PEOPLE-CENTRIC MANAGEMENT

Four people-centric levers provide a roadmap of dynamic capabilities that are needed to advance from traditional to people-centric management style, which is more effective when leading knowledge workers in a digital world. Effectively navigating the transition from one lever to the next requires high levels of awareness, freedom of choice, trust in yourself and those around you and focus of attention. These attributes enable people to know with clarity, move in one direction, mobilize the energy and maintain the focus on getting things done that matter. All of these are the essential ingredients for effective management in a decentralized organization with delegated authority.

Chapter 4 outlines four people-centric management levers.

PEOPLE-CENTRIC LEVERS

In Chapter 1, The New Business Context, we explored the tensions between external challenges and the demands on management and work. We explained the need to establish an operating system that helps businesses successfully identify and generate value from opportunities. Context and the operating system take centre stage with the four people-centric levers.

In this chapter, we will explore the people-centric management framework (Figure 6) and the principles behind it, the means to make it work and triggers needed to advance from one lever to the next. These levers will guide the development from traditional to people-centric and dynamic management styles, which are better suited to knowledge workers and operating systems in a digital environment. The people-centric levers framework prompts leaders to ask essential questions regarding better management in decentralized organizations with delegated authority.

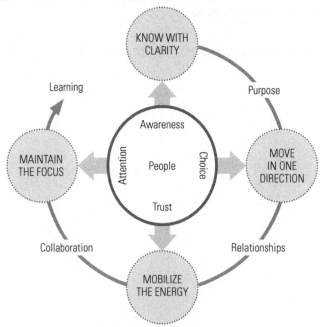

FIGURE 6: PEOPLE-CENTRIC LEVERS

People-centric management revolves around complex inter-actions among workers, managers and the environment. It is dynamic in nature and constantly changing. We start in the centre of the diagram (Figure 6), with the people-related con-textual triggers that generate power for the levers in the outer game. The four inner-game principles (awareness, choice, trust and attention) help people perform effectively, and simultane-ously address the challenges of the outer game. The outer game — defined by clarity, direction, energy and focus — identifies the challenges people face when they do work. Transferring the energy created by people in their inner game to power the levers of the outer game requires four elements (purpose, relationships, collaboration and learning) that put people-centric management into action. These actions effectively connect the inner with the outer game to generate value for the organization. We will offer insight into how people apply inner-game attributes to address outer-game challenges. In combination, as illustrated by Figure 6, these people-centric levers describe a dynamic system that stands in stark contrast to the traditional command and control styles that dominated 20th-century management.

INNER-GAME PRINCIPLES

We have already provided the clues to reconciling the tensions that either enable or prevent people from maximizing their inner game potential. These are the four principles of the inner game. People are best equipped to cope with and resolve these tensions by following four inner-game work principles:

1. **Awareness** helps individuals cope with complexity because they are aware of what is going on around them and can make decisions that fit the situation.
2. **Choice** allows people to handle ambiguity. They must have the opportunity to choose the most effective option. With that comes the freedom to say *no* to an arbitrary rule or procedure.
3. **Trust** is critical when people address uncertainty. Without trust in themselves and others, it becomes impossible to share essen-tial information that is needed to deal with a specific situation.

4. **Attention** is necessary when people deal with volatility. They need to be able to focus all their attention and capabilities on one decision, in order to make the most effective choice.

The inner game is a mental technique developed by Timothy Gallwey that enables people to cope with the outer game — the challenges encountered when they perform work. Gallwey suggested that mental interferences prevent people from performing at their peak. The mental difference is 'I hope I make this putt' versus 'I will make this putt.' Most of us who have played competitive sports can relate to the difference between 'I hope the balls goes in' and 'That ball is IN!' The inner game depends on people's ability to block out negative external mental interferences and focus on the positive. Simultaneously, the inner game helps them learn and perform at their peak by applying their knowledge, skills, experience and talents. These four principles form the foundation for people-centric management.

THE MEANS OF WORK

People-centric work requires purpose (the ability to find meaning); relationships (the ability to connect and interact); collaboration (most work requires more than one person to complete the task); and learning (the ability to adapt to changing customer needs). Here is why these are so important:

- **Purpose** is the foundation for motivation and self-responsibility. People need answers to questions like, 'What is my purpose?' and 'How do I find meaning?'
- **Relationships** connect people. They need an answer to, 'Who can I rely on?' and 'Who can I trust?'
- **Collaboration** coordinates the work of people. They need an answer to, 'What support do I get?' and 'How can others contribute?'
- **Learning** refers to the ability to perform, innovate and grow. People need an answer to, 'How do I stay on track?' and 'What have we learned from prior attempts?'

In combination with the inner game, these four means function as the unseen driving forces that connect the entire system to create value, provide organizational resilience, offer stability and drive positive outcomes. These, along with four people-centric principles, provide answers to essential questions on providing the means for work.

PEOPLE-CENTRIC LEVERS

The four people-centric levers offer a clear choice between traditional and people-centric management. They are:
- How do we know with clarity?
- How do we move in one direction?
- How do we mobilize the energy?
- How do we maintain focus?

Traditional management favours bureaucracy, power, command and control, and targets. People-centric management techniques, on the other hand, are about self-responsibility, self-organization, delegation and focus of attention.

The people-centric style is about identifying, selecting and transforming opportunities into value. With people in mind, leaders can apply these four principles as the means to deliver value with their teams in a dynamic environment. They should employ the key levers for people-centric management and apply the following principles with their teams to add value to the organization:

1. **Know with clarity: raise awareness.** Help people find purpose. People-centric managers know that motivation stems from self-responsibility. A common higher purpose replaces incentives as a motivating factor. All managers need to do for people is help them make sense of what truly matters and the societal purpose their work serves. People naturally want to do good, so defining a higher purpose is the best way to identify opportunities and deal with the complexity in your business.

2. **Move in one direction: enable choice.** People-centric managers relate with people in ways that enhance both the personal and organizational knowledge base. People-centric managers delegate decisions and engage with employees to enhance their skills and knowledge. Giving people choices, along with direction, are managerial means to bundle the energy that is inherent in the

group, help people pursue the right opportunities that add value and move in one direction as the way to deal with ambiguity.

3. **Mobilize the energy: build trust.** Facilitate collaboration at all levels, both horizontally and vertically, in the organization. People-centric managers facilitate self-organization based on trust as the means to deal with uncertainty. People must trust in themselves, co-workers and managers to freely share knowledge and collaborate effectively. Trust is essential to mobilize resources in ways that enable teamwork across organizational boundaries, which turns opportunities into value.

4. **Maintain the focus: focus attention.** Enable learning by eliminating non-value-adding interferences that distract people from paying attention to things that matter. People-centric managers identify common beliefs and set reasonable boundaries to keep attention centred on what truly matters. They know that focus enables learning, which unlocks creativity and persistence to pursue chosen opportunities, despite the turbulence of higher volatility.

People-centric management is work *in* the system. People-centric leaders follow these four principles, and encourage subordinates to do the same, to institutionalize the enabling management approach into the DNA of the organization, which treats the people as valued individuals. Creating an environment where people can express and use their unique talents is what distributed people-centric leadership is all about.

Here are a number of questions for you to consider when thinking about people-centric management:

- Do you have an environment that enables people's inner game to dominate? If not, why, and what can you do about it?
- Does your working environment provide the means for effective work? If not, why, and what can you do about it?
- What are your people-centric levers?
- How does your organization perform on these levers?
- What levers require your attention, and what can you do about it right now?

Chapter 5 introduces the features of an agile organization.

PEOPLE-CENTRIC MANAGEMENT

People-centric managerial levers describe a choice between traditional and people-centric management in decentralized organizations operating in a VUCA environment.

KEY CHAPTER IDEAS

- The inner game principles — choice, awareness, trust and attention — provide the basis for effectively releasing the vast body of knowledge and expertise inherent in the organization.
- Developing effective means of work, encompassing purpose, relationships, collaboration and learning is the vehicle that channels the inner game capabilities of people into innovation and creativity.
- Answers to the four people-centric levers — How do we know with clarity? How do we move in one direction? How do we mobilize the energy? How do we maintain the focus? — help channel the inner game of people who have an effective means of work into value for the organization.

ACTION AGENDA

- Do we have management structures that enable the inner game?
- Have we imposed command and control processes or procedures that interfere with the inner game? If so, what non-value-adding processes can be eliminated?
- Do we have an environment where people have healthy relationships and collaborate effectively to share their individual and collective knowledge? If not, what can be done to facilitate better teamwork?
- Do we have effective people-centric levers that unleash the creative and innovative potential of those in the organization? If not, why, and what can be done to change the situation?
- What can we do to utilize the people-centric management model to delegate decision-making in your organization?

FURTHER READING

Management perspective on the model:
Michel, L (2020). *People-Centric Management: How Managers Use Four Levers to Bring Out the Greatness of Others*. London: LID Publishing.

Expert perspective on the design of the levers:
Michel, L (2021). *Diagnostic Mentoring: How to Transform the Way We Manage*. London: LID Publishing.

CHAPTER 5

AGILE ORGANIZATION

The Performance Triangle (Figure 5) describes a framework for a dynamic system of capabilities for an agile organization. It is important to recognize that 'agile organization' refers to the ability to adapt to change in an orderly manner, without experimenting with disruptive, largely unsuccessful change initiatives. It is not a matter of agile software development. We are talking an entire organization's ability to adapt to changing internal and external environments. The dynamic Performance Triangle system illustrates the complex interactions among individuals, operating systems and the work environment. The external environment determines the key agile elements that enable the organization to perform, innovate and grow. Each industry has unique dynamics, and every organization is at a different growth stage, so no two are alike. The critical capabilities of agile organizations are speed, agility and resilience. Agile capabilities are required to operate in a dynamic and people-centric environment with complex structures, where coordination and collaboration are essential.

Chapter 5 describes the attributes of the agile organization, using the Performance Triangle model. This model provides executives with a reference point to help them understand their current structure and what needs to change to move to the next life cycle growth stage.

THE PERFORMANCE TRIANGLE

The Performance Triangle describes the overarching operating system and environment necessary for people to perform at their peak, and the organization to maximize inherent capabilities (Figure 7), with culture, leadership and systems at the angles and successful outcomes on top. Effective agile actions require a culture of shared beliefs, values and assumptions. People must be on the same page. Leadership is interactive with people throughout the organization to facilitate conversations around purpose, direction and performance. Everyone must understand what is expected, how to get things done and how they are doing. Systems should have a diagnostic quality, with focus on activities that have the greatest impact on performance, while simultaneously allowing for self-directed action for deviations from the chosen path. Systems should provide relevant information to people at all levels, so that they can make informed decisions in response to unexpected events. Shared culture, effective leadership interactions and diagnostic controls make up the capabilities of an agile organization. Together, these dynamic capabilities help people detect weak signals in the environment that indicate something has changed, allow for fast interpretation of that information and facilitate timely action.

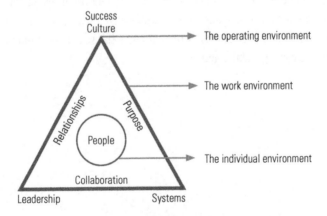

FIGURE 7: THE PERFORMANCE TRIANGLE

The individual environment. People are at the centre of the triangle. Awareness of what is going on, freedom of choice, trust in themselves and others, and focus of attention are the essential ingredients that allow people to perform at their peak. These are the capabilities that enable organizational speed, in the form of fast and effective decision-making at all levels. When the environment and management style help people cultivate these four capabilities, leaders can delegate work and decision-making close to the front line. As a result, decisions are made where the work is being done, by people with the most knowledge of the situation or customer, which improves the effectiveness of decisions and accelerates decision-making and action.

The operating environment. The angles of the triangle with leadership, systems and culture enable organizational agility. Interactive leadership is about the personal interaction between leaders and employees. Communication that promotes effective dialogue helps everyone understand what their role is, what they are expected to do, how they should do it and how they are performing. Diagnostic systems establish the rules, routines and tools needed to get work done quickly and effectively. It is important to recognize that diagnostic systems are more than the information management computer systems that organizations spend billions on implementing. Diagnostic systems include the rules, processes, procedures and routines that provide relevant data and information to the right people at the right time, so that decision-makers can make informed choices. Culture represents an invisible guide and a glue that binds the organization and other parts of the triangle together. Organizational culture is made up of many unspoken and rarely discussed beliefs, values and assumptions that tell people, 'This is how we do things around here.' Agile capabilities are at their peak when leaders connect and interact with employees throughout the organization, diagnostic systems offer guidance and feedback, and culture establishes strong bonds among all stakeholders.

The work environment. Purpose, relationships and collaboration establish resilience. Resilience is a key organizational attribute that enables it to absorb a shock or significant rapid change, and then regain balance and recover without panic or catastrophic upheaval.

When people share a common purpose that is greater than just making money, collaborate across organizational or functional boundaries, and connect to build healthy relationships that promote knowledge sharing and new knowledge creation, businesses can resist any external shocks. They are resilient.

THE INDIVIDUAL ENVIRONMENT

For effective organizational agility, people need to be the centre of both leadership and management attention. Focus on the unique qualities of individuals began in Italy in the 14th century and spread as the European Humanism movement of the 18th century. Humanism held that people were rational, self-responsible, critical thinkers and self-developing individuals. One of the many underlying philosophies of humanism was that people naturally want to contribute, learn and grow. However, there is no such thing as *the* perfect image of mankind. We are all different, unique and, for the most part, irrational beings. This generalization of human nature helps us understand the gap between what people need to perform well and the management need for control in most organizations.

In 1960, the academic Douglas McGregor's influential book, *The Human Side of Enterprise*, summed up much of the prior work on employee motivation and managerial perceptions of human nature. Based on how managers viewed typical workers, McGregor grouped managerial styles into two general categories, which he called Theory X and Theory Y. He suggested that these fundamental assumptions about human nature and what motivates workers shape the manager's style when organizing work and dealing with employees.

Theory X-style managers assume that the typical worker has little ambition, avoids responsibility and is more interested in achieving individual goals than those of the company. In general, Theory X-style managers believe their employees are less intelligent, lazier and work solely for the money. This type of manager fundamentally believes that employees' work ethic and motivation are based on their own self-interest. Managers who believe that employees operate in this manner are more likely to implement strong command and control structures, using rewards or punishments as motivation.

Theory Y managers have a more humanistic view and assume that people are internally motivated, enjoy their job and work to better themselves and the organization without a direct reward in return. These managers view their employees as among the company's most valuable assets, and structure the organization and shape the culture around this fundamental assumption. Under Theory Y, they tend to take full responsibility for their work and do not need close supervision to generate a quality product or service.

The differences in how managers view human nature result in very different, almost diametrically opposed, management styles. Theory Y managers tend to relate to employees on a more personal level and view them as responsible individuals who come to work motivated to do a good job and can be trusted to make the right decisions. Conversely, the Theory X manager tends to have more directive or incentive-based relationships with employees, believing they must be told explicitly *what, when and how*, and then either bludgeoning or providing a carrot to motivate them to work.

Our view draws from McGregor's work and is built on the belief that humans engage with others and the work environment through a self-control mechanism, called self-responsibility. Awareness, choice, trust and focus of attention are the elements of how people activate their own unique and personal control mechanism. Self-responsibility and personal control are always present, and managers can only interfere with it. In order to deliver peak performance, people require an environment that allows them to control the mechanism. The micromanager, who feels the need to control every aspect of the work environment and the workers, becomes a killer of organizational agility by stifling independent thought and creativity.

Performance and creativity require degrees of freedom, self-responsibility and the ability to focus on tasks that are important. These characteristics are not typical in organizations built and managed by classically trained managers, using complex command and control techniques developed in the last century. Classically trained managers will insist that 'everything is under control.' However, the word control reflects a lack of understanding of what performance is all about. Humanism, expressed by the 18th-century Enlightenment philosopher Immanuel Kant, promoted the view of 'Humans as the end, not the means.' This means that people should not be used to reach solely materialistic goals. Creativity, freely interpreted, requires fairness (equality), individualism and an elevated sense of the purpose of work. Kant called these the attributes of a modern society.

Translated into the reality of today's organizations, this means that self-responsible employees require freedom of choice, trust and purpose to perform at their peak and be creative. The enabling mode of management assumes that people are self-motivated and want to get things done fast.

PERFORMANCE AND SPEED

Four elements of the people-centric enabling mode (Figure 8) provide insights into the individual environment, with *speed* as the dynamic capability and *performance* as the outcome. These factors are:

- **Awareness**, to understand what is going on, why and to know with clarity.
- **Choice**, to move in one direction by making consistent and common-sense decisions.
- **Trust**, in each other and managers, to act responsibly and mobilize the energy of the group.
- **Focus**, on tasks that add value to stay on track.

Employees need observation points to focus their attention on tasks that add value to the organization. Greater awareness means they sense early signs of change and have a significant degree of freedom to react to them. Choice is the foundation for self-responsibility. Once people have made their choices on actions to take, they must be trusted to maintain the right focus to follow through. The inner-game principles require an enabling work environment to help people translate knowledge into action.

FIGURE 8: THE INDIVIDUAL ENVIRONMENT

Awareness, choice and trust help people focus their attention on what counts and adds value. In his 1960 book, *Flow: The Psychology of Optimal Experience*, Hungarian-American psychologist Mihaly Csikszentmihalyi described a state in which learning, performance and creativity are at their peak. Flow shifts control to the knowledge worker and redefines the role of the manager or supervisor as a mentor or coach, rather than a taskmaster.

KNOWLEDGE WORK

'Knowledge work' means that people distributed throughout the organization — not just leaders — have unique insight and the authority to make decisions and act on the spot. Distributed decision-making requires an agile operating environment in which people can apply their full potential. The agile operating environment stands in sharp contrast to the traditional command and control principles of the 'rules-based mode' of operating, where management interference prevents people from using their knowledge and experience to seize opportunities. In the enabling operating mode, thinking and doing are united.

Knowledge work is made up of five control elements:

1. **Understand.** Relevant and timely information with immediate feedback raises awareness of what is important. This helps

people understand and evaluate potential outcomes, and then focus their attention on what matters to find the best outcome. Superior understanding requires that sensors are finally tuned, not muted, so people can sense what is going on.

2. **Think.** Knowledge workers have a set of mental maps gained from training and experience that help them make sense of situations and make decisions. The benefits for an organization come from both individual and collective thinking. Critical thinking requires that people have an unobstructed opportunity to create meaning and asks them to make a deliberate choice for focused action.

3. **Act.** Acting is the process of translating ideas into doing. The management challenge is to create an environment that enables knowledge workers to mobilize resources to get things done. People put their energy into things they care about, and energy requires action channelled into meaningful objectives. Meaningful contribution toward meeting meaningful objectives requires that people can apply knowledge with management support that balances freedom of choice with managerial constraints. Superior contributions are built on a foundation of trust in people, and in them sharing valuable knowledge.

4. **Engage.** Focus of attention is a limited resource. Mental and emotional energy is required to maintain it at a high level. Knowledge workers' attention must be focused on the task at hand to prevent distraction from competing demands. Too often, particularly with traditionally trained managers, interference in the form of non-value-adding rules, paperwork or daily distractions prevents employees from being able to focus on and become engaged with the primary task. A high level of engagement requires conscious management effort to develop a common set of shared beliefs, motives and purpose.

5. **Adhere.** Physical, emotional and mental energy creates pull and a positive tension with the boundaries of an organization. Energy helps knowledge workers find the right balance between safely staying inside the lines and searching for opportunities outside the boundaries. This natural tension between the need for control and individual creativity requires

a balance between efficiency and entrepreneurship. A high level of adherence to the organization's purpose, mission, beliefs and boundaries maintains a good balance.

Figure 9 contrasts a traditional command and control management style with agile, people-centric enabling approaches to knowledge work, according to these five elements.

	Understand	Think	Act	Engage	Adhere
In an agile environment workers...	Use information to get work done	Make decisions	Are motivated by a sense of purpose	Have clear priorities	Are empowered and clear about norms
People use their potential	Unlimited and relevant information	Unlimited opportunities; encouraged to take risks	Focus energy on meaningful tasks driving decisions	Focus attention, which is a limited resource	Use creativity to challenge boundaries; find the right balance
In a traditional context...	Information is limited to the top	Managers make decisions	Managers motivate performance with rewards	Employees follow orders...	...and management controls what gets done
People are bound by limitations	Lack of information	Lack of opportunities; avoidance of risk	Lack of common higher purpose	Conflicting goals and tasks; lack of resources	Too many rules and restrictions or unclear boundaries

FIGURE 9: CONTRASTING KNOWLEDGE WORK

Agile management assumes that it is human nature to want to contribute to the organization, develop personally and professionally, and work in a goal-oriented way that is emotionally rewarding. This is in sharp contrast to traditional-mode management assumptions, which hold that people are motivated by money or fear, need to be controlled in every aspect of their job, and should be trained or conditioned to do just one thing well. Figure 10 illustrates the differences in fundamental assumptions about work for employees and managers.

Agile assumptions	Traditional assumptions
Knowledge employees...	*As compared to...*
Want to contribute	Don't do anything on their own
Want to do things right	Need to be developed
Want to achieve	Need to be directed
Want to be creative and develop	Do what they are told
People-centric managers...	*As compared to...*
Ask questions and focus	Motivate and decide; tell people what to do
Shape the environment	Judge and review performance goals
Support creativity	Sit at the top; provide instructions
Establish relationships	Are responsible; have the power to change and set the rules

FIGURE 10: ASSUMPTIONS ABOUT WORK

In an agile context, managers have a new role: to create an environment where people can unlock their full talent.

Here are some questions for you to consider, concerning the individual environment:

- What is your dominant environment — command/control or people-centric?
- How does the dominant environment impact your ability to perform?
- Would the emergence of creative new ideas or solutions to problems add value?
- Are you tapping into the vast knowledge base of your knowledge workers to encourage creativity?
- What elements require your attention?
- What actions can you take to create a people-centric, agile work environment that maximizes individual and organizational potential?

THE OPERATING ENVIRONMENT

Greater agility requires an operating environment that enables people to perform and act fast. The operating environment shapes the behaviours, decisions and, ultimately, the performance of individuals and the entire organization. The Performance Triangle offers a model operating environment for superior agility and innovation.

Culture, leadership and systems frame the angles of the triangle. Superior decision-making and effective actions require a culture that creates a shared set of beliefs, values and assumptions. Leadership must interact with people at all levels, inside and outside the organization, and then facilitate constructive dialogue around purpose (Why are we here?), direction (Where are we going?) and performance (How do we get there? What is my role?). Systems that work diagnostically direct attention to the issues that matter most to the business and allow people to act in a self-directed manner based on timely, relevant, reliable data to make informed decisions.

In our view, there are three basic ways to influence what people do and how they do it:

1. **Culture** works like a compass that points people in the right direction. As we've been saying, culture embodies the values, beliefs and norms that shape behaviour. It tells people, 'This is how we do things around here.'

2. **Leaders** directly influence people internal and external to the organization through interaction and interference. Leaders can tell them what to do and how to do it, or they can outline what needs to be done and let individual creativity and innovation take over. Leadership interaction is heavy work. It requires energy and time commitments from top to bottom on the org chart to covert discussion to constructive dialogue.

3. **Systems** reflect governing strategies, mission, objectives and the like. Systems direct activity and influence people's behaviour and the decisions. Systems work like autopilot, providing relevant and timely data that supports critical decision-making. Once in place, systems serve their purpose and

influence people, but should be critically and objectively evaluated as times and the environment change. What worked nicely yesterday may not necessarily be useful today.

All three ways of influencing human behaviour must be in balance for organizations to be agile. We have observed many instances where one part of this intricate and delicate system dominates, which inhibits the organization's ability to adapt. Many people have experienced 'The system won't let me,' which would indicate an environment where systems are inordinately dominant.

A shared culture, interactive leadership and dynamic systems make organizations agile. They help people detect weak market signals early on (from feedback data) allow for the interpretation of that information and facilitate timely action to adapt to change. These are the features of an agile organization and the foundation for innovation.

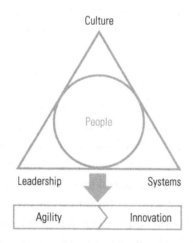

FIGURE 11: THE OPERATING ENVIRONMENT

The Performance Triangle contains three dimensions (Figure 11) that describe the operating environment. A balanced operating system creates organizational **agility** as the dynamic capability that enables and encourages **innovation**. Creativity and innovation are essential for the agile organization to identify, develop and implement solutions to problems that had never been anticipated. In a VUCA world, where today's comfortable status quo is threatened tomorrow in ways never anticipated, reacting quickly and effectively to threats or opportunities becomes an essential quality for success. It is likely that someone in your organization sensed what was coming and has an answer. The challenge is to get this person's observations and knowledge to the decision-makers, and quickly. We have identified attributes that shape and drive each of the three primary dimensions of the Performance Triangle. These are:

- **Culture.** The shared understanding, intent, agenda, beliefs and norms of behaviour that exist in the collective minds of people.
- **Leadership.** The sense-making conversations around strategy, performance, contribution and risk, with people throughout the organization.
- **Systems.** The generation of relevant, timely information to support strategy formulation and implementation, and then shape distributed decision-making effectiveness by establishing boundaries, rules, routines and tools.

As noted, culture represents the invisible guide and glue that holds the entire organizational system together. Interactive leadership is about personal relationships between leaders and employees that enable healthy interaction based on trust. Dynamic systems establish the rules, routines and tools needed to make informed decisions and get work done quickly and effectively. Organizational agility is at its peak when leaders connect and interact with employees, and systems provide guidance and feedback in a culture founded on trust.

The following sections on culture, leadership and systems create awareness of the critical organizational dimensions — the operating environment of an agile organization.

Culture is the single most powerful dimension that determines whether work gets done. A common culture creates shared context, enables or inhibits knowledge exchange, and defines the invisible boundaries of collaboration. Simply stated, if you do not trust me, you will not share what you know. Period. A vibrant culture establishes a shared context as the common ground for understanding, with a mutually shared agenda, language, thought models, relationships and purpose. Shared context is all about a shared mindset. This shapes the behaviour of individuals based on common ways of thinking and shared norms that facilitate knowledge exchange and define approaches to problem solving. The organizational culture becomes the invisible force that, like gravity, shapes all interactions within the universe of people in which the organization exists.

We agree with the assertion that culture has both visible (climate) and invisible (ethos) components. The climate consists of manifestations that can be observed through the decisions, artefacts, behaviours and actions of the people in the organization. By observing the visible climate, we can understand the underlying beliefs, values and shared assumptions that shape collective thoughts that make up the culture. The prevailing ethos has a stabilizing effect on the organization and helps people interpret what is going on, give actions or events meaning, and generate predictable outcomes.

It is important to note that changing culture is more than changing individual mindsets or behaviours. It is about altering the underlying collective mindset that shapes behaviours as a sort of habit system. We also know that behaviours can be changed with rewards or punitive management actions, but when the reward or punishment is removed, people return to their original state. Systems can only be changed by action, experience and feedback, attained through experience, rather than the cognitive abstractions of new values. Therefore, culture is both an outcome and a strong influence, with systems and leadership as its triggers.

The five culture elements, which establish a shared mindset, include:
1. Shared **understanding**, to know with clarity what is going on and why.
2. Shared **intent**, to move in one direction as a unified group.
3. Shared **agenda**, to mobilize the energy by synergizing the talents of people.
4. Shared **aspirations**, to maintain the focus on key tasks.
5. Shared **norms**, to maintain the focus using a common language.

Leadership is a key component of the Performance Triangle. In today's organizations — whether a small, highly energetic, creative group like a start-up, or a giant ecosystem like a century-old multinational

— leadership is exercised wherever it influences other people's thinking, behaviours, decisions and actions. Leadership is not necessarily tied to traditional positions of power in hierarchies, due to titles. Effective leadership comes from many people in organizations with no official title. We all know this.

Leaders in agile organizations form healthy relationships, allowing them to interact with others on a personal level. They engage with employees to facilitate meaningful dialogue and collaboration that establishes a supportive work environment based on a culture of trust. In the broadest sense, leadership is communication and interaction with others, at all levels, vertically and horizontally, throughout an organization. We suggest that leaders in any organization develop effective communication and interaction skills that are natural and unique to them. This takes time and effort.

The traditional notion is that the culture of an organization is shaped at the top of the management hierarchy and cascades downward. We generally accept this belief, but as we suggested earlier, the culture begins to form as soon as two or more people start to interact in the organization's most formative stage. However, in many companies, we have seen a huge disconnect between what top executives think is going on and what the rank-and-file employees actually perceive. This disconnect becomes a significant roadblock when the need for change arises.

Leaders and managers at all levels must recognize that their actions and behaviours are being observed and interpreted by employees through the lens of their own beliefs and values. Many leaders, perhaps inadvertently, fail to connect with employees, and they communicate conflicting values and beliefs by their actions. Employees will rarely approach the CEO and say, 'You said this, but the company actually did that. Which is it, and what's going on?' The result is that people are left to develop their own interpretation, which is in many cases inconsistent with organizational goals.

Leading requires fluency on topics or in situations that are probably unnatural for most of us. Very few people welcome conflict or enjoy giving someone bad news. Effective teaming and personal interaction mean that leaders must take interpersonal risks. They will have to step outside of their comfort zone on occasion.

True teaming requires a group-wide sense of psychological safety and stepping back to see and appreciate others' perspectives. People-centric leadership is about losing traditional control, which is superficial and involuntary, to gain real control, through intrinsic motivation and voluntary participation.

Leadership is a complex and indefinable quality, but we have identified five unconscious (and rarely discussed) leadership attributes that contribute to strengthening the culture and performance of the organization.

Mapping to these attributes, people-centric leaders routinely engage with people at all levels in five conversations, as interaction to exercise leadership control. They are as follows:

1. **Sense-making discussion**, to help people understand what is going on around them and know with clarity the reasons why.
2. **Strategy conversation**, to help people understand where the organization is going, and then think and move in one direction.
3. **Performance conversation**, to help people understand what is expected to support organizational goals, so they act and mobilize the energy of the group.
4. **Contribution dialogue**, to help people understand their personal contribution toward goals and objectives, to engage and maintain the focus.
5. **Risk dialogue**, to help people understand the level of risk the organization is willing to accept, which helps them maintain focus on tasks that matter.

Systems are located at the lower-right angle of the Performance Triangle. They represent the institutional toolbox, with rules, routines and resources that set the stage for rigorous and disciplined leadership. Effective systems support implementation of management decisions and strategy by striking the right balance between freedom to act and constraint. Interaction between people and systems provides the fuel to power the formation of beliefs that shape decisions. This fuel is essential for helping people identify a common and higher purpose for doing what they do. In addition, systems set behavioural boundaries needed to achieve the desired balance between entrepreneurship and efficiency.

Systems are both influenced by and influence the culture and leadership practices that shape the decision-making process, through millions of complex interactions. As noted earlier, when we talk about systems, we are not just talking about IT systems, but the rules and routines that shape the input and output from computerized tools. Everyone reading this chapter is familiar with the phrases 'garbage in, garbage out' and 'what gets measured gets done.' However, we contend that such thinking is just scratching the surface of the complex dimension we call systems. What managers and employees do with the output from IT systems, and how that output shapes decisions and behaviours, is rarely considered. Similarly, as mentioned previously, we have witnessed many examples of systems developed in prior decades being used to drive decisions today, even though the business dynamic — and the wider world around us — have changed dramatically. We have seen instances where managers created systems to generate relevant data needed to solve some problem or give the organization an edge 20 years earlier. The problem was solved, partially with the aid of the data, and the company gained an edge over competitors, but managers continue using legacy data that no longer effectively supports today's important decisions.

Managers making decisions based on information that is no longer relevant leads to regrettable decisions, without them realizing the damage they have caused. The 'We have always done it this way' mindset becomes dangerous when critical decisions are needed. It therefore becomes imperative for leaders to constantly evaluate whether the old rules, routines and tools being used to drive decision-making are still relevant, and whether they shape positive behaviours and yield desired outcomes.

We have identified five characteristics of effective systems. Leaders should continuously question whether their systems do these things. The answers provide insight into unconscious and rarely examined beliefs, values and shared assumptions that either inhibit or enable the effectiveness of systems. Leaders must remain objective and unemotional because responses to these questions may be unexpected and personal. It is important to recognize that the system of work and the system of management are interconnected and constantly changing. Either can have a significant impact on the other, so asking the right question is essential. Changing the system of work will not yield performance if the operating system that governs it remains flawed because of flawed decision-making.

Five diagnostic attributes of systems support the effectiveness of people to get work done, with the benefit of:

1. **Information.** To get the right knowledge to the right people at the right time, to increase clear understanding of possible outcomes.
2. **Strategy.** To help people align actions by thinking and moving in one direction.
3. **Implementation.** To help them mobilize their energy and act proactively, focused on organizational goals.
4. **Beliefs.** To help people become personally engaged and maintain their focus on tasks that matter.
5. **Boundaries.** To shape the limits of behaviour, to help people maintain focus.

Success stands at the top of the Performance Triangle, representing the ultimate goal of management. Successful firms meet or exceed expectations by making performance visible, in the form of socially accepted outcomes.

Over the years, we have observed attributes that are common to successful organizations of all kinds, sizes and industries, and profit is NOT one of them. We have identified attributes and yield outcomes demonstrating success regardless of whether the organization is for-profit, not-for-profit, a governmental agency, an NGO or another form of enterprise. In the Performance Triangle model, five attributes determine success: Responsiveness, which is the ability to sense opportunities and react to them; Alignment of the organization with strategy, which is a prerequisite to creating value; Organizational core competencies that are the foundation for sustainable competitive advantage; Motivation of the team to get things done; The wisdom of how the organization defines and uses its boundaries.

These attributes define the primary, tangible and intangible value-creating elements of an organization. Here's more on each of them:

1. **Responsiveness.** Of people who understand and appreciate the concerns and expectations of customers with clarity and take quick and effective action. This is a commitment to customers for effective action.
2. **Alignment.** For people to take actions that move the company in one direction to support its mission, vision and strategic goals. People must be attracted to and buy into the strategic vision.
3. **Capabilities.** Of people and the organization to mobilize the energy of their combined capabilities. Synergistic recombination of individual capabilities generates core capabilities and competitive advantage for the organization.
4. **Motivation.** For people to maintain focus regardless of complexity or stress from an unexpected situation. This reflects aspirations of the entire team.
5. **Cleverness.** Of people to remain in focus and apply their inherent creativity to solve problems or innovate. This encourages innovation and defines the boundaries of entrepreneurship.

Here are some questions you should consider relative to the operating environment:

- What is your dominant environment?
- Do your people share a common set of beliefs that support organizational vision and mission?
- Do they share a culture that promotes knowledge sharing and innovation?
- Would a more balanced operating environment improve success?
- When was the last time you critically reviewed your systems? Are they appropriate for today's environment?
- Do leaders engage people in dialogue, as opposed to issuing edicts or commands?
- Do people really understand their contribution and part in the organizational puzzle?
- Do legacy systems inhibit or enable innovation?
- Do you have the basic elements for success? If not, why not, and how can you develop them?
- What elements require your attention?

THE WORK ENVIRONMENT

Purpose, collaboration and relationships make up the three sides of the Performance Triangle (Figure 12). Their configuration describes the attributes of a resilient organization supported by an operating system that has the potential to enable growth from within. Resiliency describes the ability to absorb shock and continue to operate and grow. In the VUCA world, unanticipated shocks come in many forms, like a disruptive technology, governmental regulations, rapidly changing consumer preferences, adverse economic conditions or even a pandemic. Resilient organizations withstand the impact, quickly make changes or adjustments, and then continue operating successfully.

When unanticipated disruptions occur, we have found that people need three things to continue performing at their peak. They must find purpose in what they do, have healthy relationships based on trust and collaborate with others to share valuable knowledge. Purpose, relationships and collaboration are the bonding elements of every organization that links the operating environment with the individual environment. For superior decisions, knowledge work requires people to believe that their efforts are for a higher purpose than just profits or stock price. Higher purpose is the driving force behind intrinsic motivation.

FIGURE 12: THE WORK ENVIRONMENT

Knowledge workers use both internal and external relationships to share and expand their knowledge, which unleashes creativity and innovation to create value for clients. Only knowledge that is shared and applied has value for any organization, so the trick when an unanticipated shock hit is to share knowledge as quickly and efficiently as possible to develop and implement an effective response. New technologies facilitate the sharing of information in a way that generates new knowledge, provided people have embraced a common purpose, developed healthy relationships and collaborated in an environment of trust. The name of the game is to accelerate the rate of knowledge sharing, which will accelerate the pace of innovation needed to react to the shock.

Most knowledge-related tasks in complex organizations require more than one individual for their completion. Solutions or innovative ideas require knowledge from different viewpoints or disciplines. It is the combined knowledge and the shared experiences, through productive collaboration, that stimulate creativity, innovation and growth.

Resilience results from a deep sense of purpose, trusting relationships among stakeholders and collaboration to share critical knowledge. With these capabilities embedded within the organizational DNA, companies have a better chance of withstanding external shocks and change.

Three characteristics make up the work environment, with **resilience** as the dynamic capability supported by the operating system's dynamic capability. The outcome is innovation and growth. These characteristics are:

1. **Purpose.** The meaning people attach to work that answers the questions 'Why are we here?' and 'How does what we do benefit society?'
2. **Relationships.** Based on trust, establishing connectivity among people opens them to sharing what they know for the common good.
3. **Collaboration.** Is the ability to work across diverse teams to accelerate knowledge sharing, generating synergy for knowledge work.

Successful organizations shape their work environment propelled by people with deep understanding of why they are there, strong connectivity built on trust and effective cooperation.

The following sections on purpose, relationships and collaboration describe the elements of the people-centric work environment that enable organizational resilience, along with strategies to establish a resilient organization for better management.

Purpose connects systems and cultures to people who generate energy to power the dynamic system. However, as the philosopher and sociologist Jürgen Habermas said, "There is no administrative production of purpose." What we often hear when the world changes is that when people lose sight of the purpose of their work, leaders begin to question motivation of the people. When employees view their work as meaningful and socially beneficial, they contribute with greater energy. They become fully present, physically, mentally and emotionally. Leaders rarely, if ever, look at their own actions to question why this is happening. Purpose is created individually and is unique for every person. Individuals provide purpose to the world, and everyone sees the world differently as they try to make sense of what is happening. This characteristic is called sense-making, not 'sense-giving.' Purpose cannot be delivered, dictated or decreed by management. It needs to be found individually as people assimilate experiences through their own lens. Individuals search for purpose. Importantly, in tough times, purpose needs reinforcement. People need reassurance that the purpose they are working toward aligns with their personal values. Agile techniques enable purpose at scale.

Relationships are the cornerstones of every interpersonal transaction. In individualized, people-to-people business, relationships with both internal and external stakeholders, trust and agreement between employees and the organization are essential. As such, 'relationship capital' is central to the success of a company. However, healthy relationships come at a price. They take time and concerted effort to develop and impose a challenge on every leader of an organization. Relationships also facilitate interpersonal connectivity. The greater the number of connections among people in an organization, the more restrictions and boundaries they place on one another. These boundaries limit their freedom of movement and ability to perform. As a result, relationships and connectivity must be tuned to the optimum level well before a crisis hits. You cannot wait until an unexpected disruption occurs, and then send out emails with a 'Call to Action.' It will be too little, too late, and will fall on deaf ears.

Relationships are an important means for addressing the challenges in an ambiguous context. Connected people with diverse knowledge make better decisions in any situation than one lonely manager might on their own. Individuals connect and build relationships. Agile techniques enable relationships at scale.

Collaboration is an issue because of complexity, which increases with size and scope of the organization. Out of necessity, leaders keep adding functions, geographies, departments, services, client groups and other structures to our organizations. In a complex and networked world, where knowledge matters, collaboration is more important than ever. Every structure creates barriers between people who need to work together, such as limited or distorted information flows. In some companies, we have seen informational silos that limit knowledge sharing and cooperation. Some of these silos appear to be hardened against nuclear attack; one could almost be fired for talking to accounting. Agile, people-centric organizations must resolve the fundamental cooperation problem between employees and organizations with different, often conflicting, goals.

Collaboration is an essential capability to address challenges in an uncertain environment. The synergy of collective knowledge and many diverse minds is better than individuals at dealing with uncertainty. Individuals who sense what is happening naturally collaborate to find solutions if for no other reason than self-preservation. Engage agile techniques to scale collaboration in organizations.

Here are some questions about the work environment for you to consider:

- What is your dominant work environment?
- Do your people share a vision attached to a common purpose that goes beyond earnings or stock price? If not, why?
- Do you have an environment where people trust each other, and management?
- Do various departments or business segments collaborate effectively to propose innovative solutions? If not, why?
- How do these characteristics impact your ability to grow?
- What dimensions require your attention and what action can you take?

DYNAMIC CAPABILITIES AND OUTCOMES

The Performance Triangle combines elements of the individual, operating and work environments into a dynamic operating system that drives the business. All organizations, regardless of size, form, for-profit or not-for-profit status, or maturity have these components in some form or fashion. Managers work in and shape these to develop the operation's dynamic capabilities, which deliver the expected outcomes.

In a rapidly changing environment, dynamic capabilities help groups of people align their beliefs, behaviours and actions to achieve common objectives. Dynamic capabilities become an invisible force in the complex operating system of an organization, aligning employees around a central core with information, direction, plans, beliefs and boundaries.

Speed, agility and resilience are the three central elements of dynamic capabilities. Dynamic capabilities are configurations of resources (talent, routines, rules, competencies, structures, etc.) that enable organizations to continuously adapt to rapid changes in the environment. These capabilities, embedded in the operating system, allow people to perform at their peak inner game and develop the abilities needed to cope with a volatile environment — the outer game. With increasing variety and interdependent dynamics in the VUCA environment, organizational dynamic capabilities become a true competitive advantage.

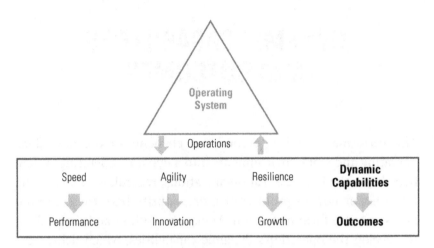

FIGURE 13: DYNAMIC CAPABILITIES AND OUTCOMES

The organizational operating system — with the individual, operational and work environments — determines the nature of operations. However, generating positive outcomes is what matters to all stakeholders. Figure 13 illustrates how dynamic capabilities connect with and compliment the operating system to yield positive outcomes.

These capabilities help organizations navigate changes in the environment without the negative effects of traditional change programmes. Effective dynamic capabilities assist executives in finding the most effective balance between speed and control, agility and stability, and resilience and renewal. Balance is the key here, because the need for speed, agility and resilience changes over time in a VUCA environment. Executives should be constantly evaluating the operating system and capabilities; this is a truly dynamic situation. Constant and continuous evaluation will help ensure that reinforcing loops and balancing loops are in tune with each other.

Performance, innovation and growth are key indicators for organizational outcomes in virtually all organizations. Awareness, choice and trust help people focus on what counts. The result is flow, that special creative state we've talked about, where learning, performance and joy combine to deliver superior results. In an environment where people can unlock their creativity and generate new knowledge, innovation is the outcome. The way managers set goals and deal with stakeholders determines much of the internal growth capacity of a company. We have observed many organizations where well-meaning executives set so-called 'stretch goals' or respond to stakeholder demands in ways that are counterproductive, because they stifle knowledge sharing and innovation.

When speed does not match performance, managers need to look at the individual environment. When agility and innovation do not correlate, the operating environment needs work. When resilience does not lead to growth, managers should search for clues to root causes within the work environment.

SPEED

The inner game describes the attributes people need to effectively translate knowledge into action. The result is speed as a dynamic capability in organizations.

Self-responsibility is the people-centric principle by which individuals have control over what they do and how they do it. Employees have the freedom of choice to make decisions and act on the spot to avoid cumbersome detours that come with traditional hierarchy. They assume accountability for delegated responsibilities.

Trust is the most critical and most difficult (and easiest to lose) people-centric attribute to achieve. When people trust each other, they freely share knowledge and rely on one another for support and assistance when needed. Mutual respect reduces the need for complex, detailed rules of engagement between people to get things done. Trust replaces the need for systems such as target setting or management by objectives, which slow things down by shaping behaviours that may not be natural for people and tend to yield unintended consequences.

Learning quickly and sharing what is learned with relevant decision-makers is the solution for time-critical action in dynamic situations. In the 1980s, best-selling management guru Tom Peters said that the secret was to "test fast, fail fast, adjust fast." This could also be applied to learning and decision-making when dealing with time-critical situations. Inner-game attributes of awareness and focus of attention are necessary for accelerating learning, rapid decision-making at all levels and, ultimately, performance when the unexpected happens.

Speed is strongly correlated with superior performance. Our research confirms that people mastering the inner-game techniques far outperform those who lack these capabilities. We therefore conclude that people who master the inner-game in an environment that allows for self-responsible action are the real drivers of speed in organizations. As such, speed is the most essential dynamic capability that helps organizations succeed in a volatile environment.

However, speed also needs the balance of control. Mario Andretti, the Formula 1 racing world champion, once said: "If you have things under control, you simply don't go fast enough." Managers must recognize that organizational speed involves risk. They must have a positive view of human nature, like McGregor's Theory Y. Self-responsible people who master the inner game deftly master the accelerator pedal, and instinctively know the right balance between speed and taking too much risk. The intelligent release of their collective knowledge and skills — and awareness of their resource limitations — are the controls that naturally counter-balance speed.

PEAK PERFORMANCE

Helping executives identify conditions that inhibit performance is a major objective of the Performance Triangle. People who perform at their peak require a work environment that enables them to play the inner game and use their knowledge and resources wisely and quickly.

Superior performance results from people engaging and focusing their full potential in what they do. This requires minimum interference from both the internal and external environments. That is why the individual environment, populated by people, is in the centre of the triangle. People-centric management requires an agile organization designed with an environment with minimal management interference that could impede individual potential.

People are, or should be, every manager's first priority. When management priorities make people number one, superior performance is the outcome. Chapter 5 demonstrated how the inner game drove speed and superior performance, enabled by a supportive, agile work environment and organization. Mastering the inner game releases the vast creative energy inherent in people and drives top-notch performance.

AGILITY

Interactive leadership, dynamic systems and a shared culture with delegated decision-making as a primary management principle are the enablers of agility in organizations. The starting point for organizational agility is the ability to sense threats or opportunities early, take rapid and effective action, and then make continuous changes as the situation changes throughout an integrated organization. Dynamic systems with key performance metrics and feedback processes enable flexibility and adaptability because managers know what is going on, and then provide continuous guidance to subordinates. In this way, the organization — through the interpersonal network, with people playing the inner game — can make minute adjustments as needed. This process reduces the need for disruptive change initiatives, which have a low success rate.

Agile organizations promote self-organized work in teams with delegated decision-making, for greater flexibility, fast and effective adaptation to external change, and accelerated and enhanced problem solving. Thus, the agile organization benefits from intensive innovation.

Effective leadership is characterized by frequent personal interaction with people at all levels in the organization, and with external stakeholders. Next to systems, leadership is the most important managerial control mechanism. Leaders who see the need to change, and decisively act on it, can directly influence employee behaviour and internal systems. Engaging, proactive leadership enables effective, nimble responses to changes in the environment.

A shared culture gives people the ability to act based on broad direction, without strict management command and control mechanisms. Organizational agility is enhanced because people share a common set of values, beliefs and norms. Agility therefore requires proactive leadership that facilitates knowledge sharing, seeks consensus, trusts people, delegates more and builds an environment for people to maximize inherent tacit knowledge (Nold, 2021).

Organizational agility must also be balanced with stability. Imagine a coiled spring. It can only be effective if it is fixed on one end. That anchoring is like stability in an organization. For agile capabilities to work effectively there must be a balancing mechanism that anchors the organization and provides needed stability. Stability is anchored in the shared culture, interactive leadership and an operating system that enables people to perform and act flexibly.

INNOVATION

Agile characteristics enabled by a shared culture, interactive leadership and effective operating systems set the stage for knowledge workers to use their creativity as a means of achieving higher levels of innovation. There is a strong linkage between knowledge work and innovation. Furthermore, innovation is directly related to value creation in organizations.

Innovation is greatest when the environment promotes the characteristics of a people-centric enabling mode of operation (see Figure 8) where awareness, choice, trust and focus of attention dominate daily interactions. People freely share what they know, and outcome results, in innovative ideas for new offerings, product enhancements or process improvements. Furthermore, our research confirms that organizations operating in a people-centric capabilities-based mode, with a dynamic operating environment (see Figure 4), far outperform those in rules-based, change-based or engagement-based modes of operation. Organizations operating in the people-centric capabilities-based mode favour self-responsibility, delegation, self-organization and focus of attention over traditional command and control management techniques. Thus, people align and become creative within an operating environment where culture provides the invisible compass, where leaders interact to influence (not dictate) what is being done, and where systems offer choice. Decisions and resulting innovative ideas are outcomes from mutual trust among people with great awareness of what is going on, who are allowed to focus their attention and creative energy on the issues.

RESILIENCE

Resilient organizations have dynamic characteristics that enable them to absorb a shock or unexpected events and continue operating efficiently and growing. From our research, we have identified three main attributes that resilient organizations possess. We view purpose, relationships and collaboration with self-organization as the principal dimensions for resilience of organizations. These form the sides of the Performance Triangle (see figure 7). Organizations with high levels of resilience can reinvent themselves and find new business models that preserve and build on core competencies. Healthy relationships bring new knowledge to the firm and facilitate sharing across the organization. Collaboration expands the knowledge base beyond traditional organizational boundaries so it can be utilized in the form of new ideas. Companies populated by people with a shared purpose create an environment that inspires entrepreneurial behaviour. This combination strengthens organizational resilience and promotes growth opportunities, for individuals and ultimately the entire organization.

Organizational resilience relies on the robustness of operating systems. Resilience provides a stabilizing effect on the organization, through social controls and absorptive capabilities. Organizations reach greater levels of resilience by cultivating a higher shared purpose, promoting healthy relationships and encouraging cooperative strategies that transcend organizational boundaries and facilitate knowledge sharing.

The 'work environment' defines how organizations establish goals as a bonding element in relationships (see Figure 7). The work environment is the trigger that nurtures collaboration and provides clues to the meaning of work, to help answer the question, 'Why are we here?' Arbitrarily set too narrowly, targets established by upper management limit the options available to people to do their jobs effectively. Alternately, broad direction from upper management opens multiple avenues for people to connect, cooperate and find meaning.

Resilience requires the balance of renewal. By itself, resilience is a conserving capability, looking primarily at current core capabilities that can be adapted or changed in response to a threat or opportunity. Only through its counterpart, renewal, can the organization maximize its growth potential. Renewal means gathering or creating new knowledge through intense collaboration among people with a deep sense of common purpose. Both resilience and renewal require this collaboration and knowledge sharing. The difference is that resilience is more defensive in nature, while renewal is more offensive. Success in warfare requires a solid defense to ward off an enemy, followed by an aggressive counterattack to win the battle. As on the battlefield, organizations must find the right balance between defense (resilience) and offense (renewal) to be successful.

GROWTH

Purpose, relationships and collaboration give the organization the capacity to absorb unexpected shock and grow by exploring new opportunities. Our research for the book *Diagnostic Mentoring* confirmed a strong relationship between resilience and renewal.

An organization where people find common purpose in what they do, collaborate effectively across internal boundaries and gain new knowledge is likely to weather any storm. Employees find new ways to adapt to unplanned events and take advantage of new business opportunities that contribute to growth. They become personally and emotionally engaged and grow when purpose and self-responsibility are the sources of intrinsic motivation. They can gain knowledge and learn from others, both inside and outside the organization. Complex 21st-century organizations exist in a VUCA world where there is almost no work or change effort that can be completed solely by one person. Work happens in teams, where people collaborate and contribute their valuable knowledge to help everyone adapt and grow.

Here are the questions for you to consider when thinking about dynamic capabilities and outcomes:

- What are your dynamic capabilities and outcomes?
- Look closely and objectively to assess whether your environment has the attributes necessary for speed, agility and resilience. If they are not present, why not, and how can you improve?
- How do your dynamic capabilities impact your ability to perform, innovate and grow?
- What elements require your attention and what action can you take? (The fix is not an overnight thing, so think long term.)

Chapter 6 introduces the dynamic operating system with the Leadership Scorecard.

AGILE ORGANIZATION

The Performance Triangle frames the attributes of an agile organization. Organizational agility is essential to operate in a VUCA environment with network-type organizations and structure that require collaboration and flexibility.

KEY CHAPTER IDEAS

- The individual environment comes with awareness, trust, choice and focus of attention — the skills necessary for performance and speed.
- The operating environment frames systems, leadership and culture elements that establish agility and innovation.
- The work environment is about purpose, collaboration and relationships — the capabilities needed for resilience and renewal.
- In combination, these are dynamic capabilities required for complex organizations to be successful in the VUCA 21st century.

ACTION AGENDA

- Use the Performance Triangle model as a roadmap to help identify strengths and weaknesses to be leveraged or improved, in order to advance to the next growth stage.

FURTHER READING

Managerial perspective on the Performance Triangle:
Michel, L (2013). *The Performance Triangle: Diagnostic Mentoring to Manage Organizations and People for Superior Performance in Turbulent Times*. London: LID Publishing.
Nold, H (2021). *Agile Strategies for the 21st Century: The Need for Speed*. Newcastle upon Tyne: Cambridge Scholars Publishing Ltd.

Expert perspective on the Performance Triangle:
Michel, L (2021), *Diagnostic Mentoring: How to Transform the Way We Manage*. London: LID Publishing.
Nold, H (2018). Dynamic Capabilities for People-Centric Management in Turbulent Times. In M. F. Brandebo & A. Alvinus (Eds.), *Dark Side of Organizational Behavior and Leadership* (pp. 109-124). London: IntechOpen.

Related research on the Performance Triangle:
Nold, H; and Michel, L (2016). The Performance Triangle: A Model for Corporate Agility. *Leadership & Organizational Development Journal*, 37(3).

THE DYNAMIC OPERATING SYSTEM

Chapter 6 builds on and expands the concept of four operating modes introduced in Chapter 3 (see Figure 4). Our research has led us to identify four general categories, with characteristics that are dynamic and suitable for specific environments. Each dynamic operating system is characterized by different ways of engaging people, decision-making, coordinating work and performing. Leaders should be very aware of the style of management that currently exists, and then question whether the current operating system will help with or hinder moving to the next level of growth. The Leadership Scorecard we have developed is a tool to give leaders insight into the attributes of their current operating system, allowing them to make conscious decisions on what needs to be done if the system does not fit the environment, or if they want to grow to the next level. The choice of operating system is, or should be, an intentional and thoughtful management decision. The Leadership Scorecard provides the visibility needed to knowingly create the dynamic capabilities required to operate in a variety of environments and organizational structures. Essentially, leaders must know where they are today to plot a course for tomorrow.

Chapter 6 describes the four dynamic operating systems and the environments where they are most effective, and then introduces the Leadership Scorecard as a tool to help evaluate the current operating system.

FOUR OPERATING SYSTEMS

Better management requires a dynamic operating system that fits the needs of people, and both the current and future environments. The key features of operating systems revolve around people-centric management techniques, agile attributes and dynamic capabilities. Before we dig into the details of design, we must distinguish between the four dominant operating systems. While they never exist in pure form, one set of management styles typically becomes dominant. Clear understanding and appreciation of the strengths and weaknesses of the dominant system helps leaders make conscious decisions on actions needed to take the organization to the next level.

Domestication is a distinctive feature of operating systems, as well as a barrier to changing them. Domestication in the organizational sense (rather than biological) is the process of translating explicit processes and systems into implicit values, capabilities and behaviours that become deeply embedded in culture. We define organizational domestication as the behaviours and actions of leaders and employees who unconsciously follow the habits and patterns dictated by the organization's rules, norms and values. Culture works like glue and becomes the DNA of the organization. Because culture exists in the minds and experience of people, it becomes virtually as difficult to reconfigure operating systems as it is to alter the DNA of a living organism.

It is no surprise that managers and employees are expected to make quick decisions, and then focus their actions on what matters most, while demonstrating entrepreneurial behaviours in everything they do. However, the reality of dealing with specific situations typically interferes with these expectations.

In our information-rich, dynamic environment, the requirements and expectations heaped upon employees are difficult, if not impossible, to live up to. People are distracted, struggle with decisions and miss opportunities. The unintended result is that managers and employees often have no choice but to act in their own self-interest. Consequently, talent is not effectively used, and companies perform far below their potential. This tug of war between and self-interest is endemic in the dynamic, knowledge-driven environment, in which we have become comfortably uncomfortable.

In many organizations, systematic information overload, analysis paralysis, endless meetings, bias toward rationality, risk-aversity and blindly following rules dominate ways of thinking and doing. This comes at the expense of effective decision-making, deliberate actions and behaviours suitable for a specific situation, or aligned with company beliefs and boundaries. We know that this is the result of domestication that has become the DNA of the organization susceptible to viruses.

As with living organisms, over time viruses creep into organizational culture. Ultimately, these viral infections lead to faulty leadership and misplaced and ineffective managerial systems, resulting in flawed decisions, missing action and undesired behaviours. This creates a negative domestication spiral that accelerates over time, because of a deteriorating operating environment.

On the positive side, a vibrant culture with interactive leadership and supportive systems enables fast and effective decisions, actions with impact, and desired behaviours. These are the outcomes of an operating system with a deliberate design, leading to positively domesticated behaviours. Such companies enable a high degree of individual effectiveness where talent is used well.

People naturally follow given rules. They intrinsically want to do well. That is why the operating system is so important. It determines how people decide, act and behave. It is deeply embedded in the organization's culture. Therefore, changing the operating system becomes a particularly challenging task. It means changing the rules, routines and tools that tell people how to think and act. Taking all of this into account, how can leaders identify viruses in the organizational DNA, and then take action to eliminate the infection and jump-start positive domestication?

The idea of positive domestication starts with every individual's *return on management* (ROM). Harvard Business School Professor Robert Simons developed the ROM concept in 1995. The notion is that time, attention and energy are scarce resources for everyone. In order to achieve a high ROM, it is necessary to carefully invest time and focus attention on tasks at hand, to generate a maximum amount of productive energy. We know that many leaders and employees struggle with both time management and focus of attention. Simons' simple equation illustrates the relationships.

ROM = Productive energy released / time and attention invested

An effective operating system must yield a high ROM (Figure 14) at both individual and organizational levels. In the corporate strategy context popularized by academics Charles O'Reilly and Michael Tushman, the strategic mindset of 'exploitation versus exploration' describes the difference between exploiting current capabilities and seeking entirely new approaches. Exploitation describes a strategic mindset that seeks new opportunities for growth by leveraging core capabilities through innovation. We adapt these terms to describe a management approach that focuses on exploiting individual and organizational capabilities to become more efficient and productive. Conversely, management approaches that create an environment that builds on core capabilities to pursue creative new avenues for growth, both personally and organizationally, are explorative in nature. Organizations with high ROM support individual effectiveness through time utilization and focus of attention to generate high levels of energy. Organizational effectiveness increased through efficiency and innovation, resulting in superior value creation. Finding the right balance between exploitation and exploration is the key to generating positive outcomes.

Effectiveness	Exploitation	Exploration	Outcome
Individual	Time	Attention	Energy
Organizational	Efficiency	Innovation	Value creation

FIGURE 14: RETURN ON MANAGEMENT

Figure 15 describes four operating systems that align with the four operating modes introduced in Chapter 3: rules, engagement, change and enabling. Each has a different purpose and outcome that spans a range of traditional and people-centric approaches to management.

The operating systems are not mutually exclusive; all systems contain elements of the other approaches. However, one style tends to dominate. Managers can consciously choose to mix and blend four operating systems, depending on the specific managerial needs dictated by the environment in which the organization operates.

Context	Traditional ← Management → People-centric	
Dynamic	**Change** Management action	**Enabling** Learning, development and cooperation
Stable	**Rules** Hierarchy and power	**Engagement** Individual knowledge

FIGURE 15: FOUR OPERATING SYSTEMS

The left side (y-axis) represents the general business context or environment in which the organization operates. Stable environments change slowly, or very little, while dynamic environments are characterized by rapid or disruptive change. The bottom (x-axis) represents the general management style being employed. Traditional management is characterized by tight controls, beginning with micromanagement, while people-centric management emphasizes individual responsibility, with a wide range of freedom to act. The rapidly changing environment characteristic for most businesses in the VUCA 21st century — along with the tech-savvy generation's access to information and talent — forces companies to be clear about the operating system.

The answers to four questions help us distinguish between the four operating systems:

1. How do we engage people so they know with clarity what is going on around them?
2. How do we make timely and effective decisions, and then move the entire organization in one direction?

3. How do we coordinate work to release the potential energy in people?
4. How do we maximize performance while simultaneously maintaining the focus of attention?

In rules-based operating systems, decisions are deferred to senior management, at the top of the organizational hierarchy, and people work in an environment dominated by rules and procedures. Engagement-based systems facilitate collective debate and intrinsic motivation, but decisions and actions are slow. With change-based systems, management maintains control through traditional command and control techniques, and then takes corrective action in response to changes. Capabilities-based operating systems require self-responsible people and managers, and speedy, collective decisions, with a focus on learning and development to release the potential energy of people. Figure 16 summarizes the features of the four generic operating systems.

Operation	Rules	Change	Engagement	Capabilities
Culture, leadership and system	Hierarchy and power	Management action or reaction	Emphasis on individual knowledge	Emphasis on learning and development
Context or environment	Relatively stable environment; slowly changing	High uncertainty and rate of change; highly disruptive	Knowledge- and technology-intensive	High complexity and ambiguity
How we understand and engage	Leaders direct and motivate with extrinsic rewards	Stretch goals with extrinsic incentives	Encourage personal mastery and meaning	Encourage self-responsibility and shared purpose
How we think and decide	Through structured hierarchy	Managers make decisions	Debate and reason	Collective wisdom
How we act and coordinate	Rigid processes and operating procedures	Continuous change projects	Projects, workshops and meetings	Self-organization, mutual adjustment
How we behave and motivate	Top-down goals and control	Forced aligned action	Self-interest	Common goals, shared mindset

FIGURE 16: FEATURES OF OPERATING SYSTEMS

Operating systems come with a toolbox for leaders and employees that helps them assess which style of operating system is currently in use. The toolbox helps evaluate whether the system helps people know with clarity what is going on, align and move in one direction, mobilize the potential energy of people and maintain focus on value-adding tasks.

The dominant operating system varies, depending on the business environment in which a company operates. Often, companies unwillingly or unknowingly operate with mixed (or multiple) operating systems that may vary within the organization. Our research, based on a sample of more than 400 companies, confirms that 45% of them still operate with the rules-based operating system as the dominant management style.

Mixing operating systems may be necessary because of the unique demands of various functions. For example, a global pharmaceutical company we worked with used engagement-style systems for the research and development function, while the manufacturing operations applied the control-based system. This makes sense, since R&D demands high levels of creativity and problem-solving capabilities, while the emphasis in manufacturing should be on quality and productivity. The selection and design of the toolbox for each system of operations is a senior executive task that requires experience, with deep understanding of the demands of specific functions.

In a highly regulated, safety- or quality-first context, the rules-based operating systems may still be most effective. Change-based operating systems are the norm in transaction-oriented and heavily technology-supported industries, such as insurance, banking and telecom. Engagement-based operating systems do well in knowledge-driven environments, such as educational institutions or professional services businesses. Capabilities-based systems can be effective in high tech, media and other industries requiring high levels of creativity, or when responding to disruptive events like the Covid pandemic.

Counterintuitively, hybrid operating systems can be effective in a variety of settings that require both a high degree of flexibility and a rigorous set of operating procedures. This is certainly the case in the cockpit of a commercial airliner, a hospital emergency room, a military unit in a combat situation or a firefighting company. In life-or-death occupations such as these, finding the right balance between control and flexibility is both a science and an art, because it is impossible to anticipate every potential situation and have a rule or procedure designed for that specific circumstance. These examples do not illustrate normal, everyday business operations, but looking at the extremes helps to make the point.

In an emergency room, we trust the exceptional skills of highly trained doctors, nurses and technicians who follow detailed protocols, and then intuitively do what is right in that specific instance. They are trained to follow strict protocols and standards, but when the situation requires, their intuitive skills or instinct, rather than established routines, save lives. Agility and dynamic capabilities beat rigorous routines in situations requiring immediate action and innovative solutions.

In military combat or firefighting, leaders can only provide broad guidance on how to go about handling a specific emergency. On the battlefield or at the scene of a blaze, well-developed skills and intuition are required to do what is necessary. No command from above could ever be better at reacting quickly and flexibly to fit the situation. Soldiers and firefighters respond in the best way their training, experience and intuition allow. Through years of training, practice and conditioning, they have absorbed rigorous procedures for dealing with emergencies that become automatic, and they can simultaneously exhibit flexibility and resilience in the trenches.

Well-developed dynamic operating systems facilitate intuitive decision-making (the agile elements) and well-practiced routines (the stable elements) rather than rigid authority, decision paralysis-by-analysis or knee-jerk reaction. Such highly developed operating systems allow for fast responses, permit flexible action and promote robust solutions.

ENGAGING SELF-RESPONSIBLE PEOPLE

Rules-based operating systems are what most of us know well. For the past 100 years, industrial-style leaders have been trained to motivate and control people. Despite the wealth of research proving that there is no meaningful relationship between bonuses and performance, extensive extrinsic and monetary rewards continue to dominate people-management practices. Stretch goals tied to incentives — intentionally ambitious performance targets that 'stretch' one beyond his or her designated work objectives — remain a popular motivational strategy in change-based operating systems.

The fact is that rules-based systems achieve exactly what they intend to: fulfilment of detailed objectives, and not one bit more. As management expert Peter Drucker once said: "Management by objectives [MBO] works — if you know the objectives. Ninety percent of the time you don't." Our experience with so many companies confirm Drucker's observation. We have seen countless unintended consequences and counterproductive behaviours resulting from misguided attempts at MBO or establishing stretch goals.

The engagement-based operating system demands personal mastery and meaning to engage people. We know from the philosophers of 17th-century European Humanism that self-responsible people are, by definition, intrinsically motivated people. The engagement-based operating system is built on the assumption that people are fundamentally internally motivated. As such, the overriding management task is to help employees find purpose in what they do, and then channel natural motivation to advance organizational goals. As we noted earlier, this is called sense-making, not sense-giving.

High-performance athletes around the world know that engaged people need four things to perform at their peak:

1. They must be able to focus their attention on what matters now.
2. They need a high degree of awareness of what is going on around them.
3. They trust their own skills, and the skills of the team.
4. They require freedom to instantaneously choose what play to make.

Choice is a prerequisite for self-responsible behaviours. If you cannot say no, then you have no choice and therefore cannot be self-responsible. Managers are well advised to give this careful thought.

As an example, a renowned leadership think tank we worked with decided to invest in 'people engagement' activities, as recommended by well-known mainstream consultants. No doubt, management's efforts resulted in a more welcoming workplace. However, the company lost on speed, agility and robustness. Meetings, town halls and more personal conversations augmented the sense of purpose, but what truly mattered to the organization was whether employees could fully apply their talent and focus their attention on priorities, to get things done. Management applauded themselves for increasing employee engagement, which was good, but they missed an opportunity for more significant results.

We provided deeper insights from our diagnostic mentoring tools, which revealed this organization's need to complement engagement activities with a toolbox for 21st-century working practices. Less than two months after these practices were implemented, collaboration became a natural way of working, and relevant knowledge was more widely shared and accumulated. This resulted in increased creativity and performance.

Promoting self-responsible action and a deep sense of purpose enables people to use their time most effectively. As a result, organizations that embrace this approach get things done faster, and more effectively, while still maintaining control, despite a more dynamic and ambiguous environment.

MAKING DECISIONS BASED ON COLLECTIVE WISDOM

With rules-based operating systems, decisions are made by people higher up in the hierarchy. Delegated decision-making that requires the manager's signature actually means that the boss always makes the decisions. We know that most leaders understand that this type of top-down control makes organizations slow, inflexible and fragile, yet they commonly do little about it.

In change-based operations, it is always the manager who decides, assuming that they are the most qualified and most knowledgeable in the organization. The academic and influential business management author Henry Mintzberg suggested than in such organizations, people are seen as (re)movable human resources, costly human assets, and human capital. Hence, the overused phrase 'Our people are our most valuable asset.' People are not seen as human beings who add value to an organization, but more like a tool that just happens to be breathing.

In contrast, engagement-based operations favour debate, reasoning, and committees. People are valued for the knowledge and experience they contribute. The result is calendars filled with endless meetings that slow the decision-making process. Decision-making by committee has the advantage of facilitating knowledge and more effective decisions. The disadvantage is that the process slows to a crawl and the company loses agility.

Capabilities-based operations favour decision-making through collective wisdom. Decisions are delegated to the most knowledgeable, experienced, and skilled person. Rapid feedback loops sharing methods and results throughout the company ensure that individuals, and the bigger organization, learn quickly and continuously improve their decision-making and implementation of decisions. Treating people as intrinsically motivated, self-responsible individuals and facilitating rapid knowledge sharing increases agility and adaptability.

A high-tech utilities provider we work with successfully transformed from a CEO-driven decision-making style to a collective approach, taking advantage of the inherent capabilities of its employees. The challenges of the energy sector — with decreasing investment in traditional energy sources and increasingly risky new sources — demands that companies continuously sense what is politically acceptable and technologically feasible, judge what is possible and then decide what is achievable. As such, energy companies require ongoing sensing of political and technological winds, followed by constructive debate leading to productive action, without being bogged down by paralysis-by-analysis.

With the help of diagnostic mentoring techniques, the CEO of this company was able to change his approach and began to mobilize and harness the knowledge and experience of his executive team. Adopting more people-centric approaches quickly transformed his team into a body that used its collective wisdom to accelerate and improve the decision-making process. The example of the people-centric approach adopted by senior executives was adopted by lower-level managers, and eventually flowed throughout the organization. This prevented the company from becoming locked into decisions without choices that hindered growth and success in a very volatile and ambiguous industry.

COORDINATING SELF-ORGANIZED WORK

Each style of operating system requires different approaches to organizing and coordinating work among individuals and across functions. Managers should be aware of the unique characteristics inherent in each type of system.

With rules-based operating systems, work is organized and coordinated with detailed processes, guided by work instructions, standard operating procedures or rules. When difficulties emerge, the natural reaction of managers is to create more detailed procedures. Through time, the body of procedures grows, until the focus of people's attention and energy is just *not to break any of the rules.*

With change-based operating systems, managers continuously initiate change projects in response to issues that arise. Over time, it becomes necessary to initiate change projects just to reconnect parts that have become disconnected through recently added structures and accountabilities. Adapting to constantly changing expectations becomes a way of life for employees and managers.

With engagement-based operating systems, people are encouraged to engage with each other and motivated to share their unique knowledge to add value to the organization. However, decisions are made by upper-level managers, which slows the decision-making process. A relentless number of workshops, committee meetings, realignments and role clarifications are required to coordinate work with the engagement-based operating system. The unintended consequence is that people spend an inordinate amount of time in meetings, debating the issues, which takes away their ability to focus on actually getting things done.

The capabilities-based operating system supports companies by decentralizing decisions. Self-responsible knowledge workers create self-organized work groups and ad-hoc project teams to solve problems and come up with innovative ideas. These self-organized groups are exempt from following detailed plans or budgets set by the boss. The team is empowered to make a wide range of decisions without generating masses of paperwork or seeking approval from above. People are able to focus their talents on the issue at hand and decisions are made quickly, which adds to the agile capabilities of the company.

Pharmaceutical firms we work with have long-established project teams that develop assets from research, development, distribution, marketing and sales, as essential parts of the business. People in the various functions contribute specific knowledge and expertise throughout the course of ongoing and temporary projects. They mutually adjust in a self-organized and purpose-driven manner to release their productive energy. In this way, they help the company remain flexible yet grounded, with a stable backbone. Self-organized work and mutual adjustment helps employees focus their attention on what matters most. A high degree of agility and flexibility comes from the ability of people with a shared purpose to quickly shift focus onto tasks that add value.

DRIVING PERFORMANCE THROUGH BROAD PURPOSE

One of the primary attributes of people-centric management techniques is instilling in people a shared sense of purpose. As we have mentioned, employees become highly motivated and dedicated when they commit to working toward some goal that serves a higher purpose for humanity. They willingly commit their energy and talents to achieving something other than a simple pay check, or to drive up earnings and stock price.

Rules-based operating systems apply rigorous individual management by objectives, with top-down goals and frequent performance appraisals. The underlying view of human nature fits McGregor's, where people are motivated by basic self-interest and lack sufficient mental capacity for self-responsibility, so they must be told what to do. The perception of people in this operating system is that they focus on meeting the minimal expectations that drive the performance review. Managers typically dedicate inordinate effort to getting agreement on goals and conducting reviews of the performance objectives.

Change-based operations favour action orientation. In other words, valuable management time is dedicated to aligning value-adding projects and coordinating actions. These companies argue that implementation is what makes or breaks performance, but they are saddled with rules and procedures that force them to commit valuable energy to changing the rules or processes to improve performance.

In engagement-based organizations, knowledge-driven employees follow their self-interest. People willingly contribute their special talents to the task at hand, with an underlying expectation of what is in it for them. This makes it difficult for management to find balance between individual self-interest and corporate goals.

People working in capabilities-based operating systems collaborate on teams with a shared mindset and clarity, based on broad direction, with a strong, shared purpose. Managers spend their valuable energy helping employees understand the intricacies of an issue so they can focus their energy and talent on resolving the issue.

The public transportation company we recently worked with had transitioned from government agency to independent entrepreneurial business unit. One of the legacies it brought along was a rigid management-by-objectives system that dominated most management conversations. As a governmental entity, it was good practice to be very detailed and concrete when it came to target setting. A review of the organization's toolbox revealed that rigorous and detailed routines made it slow, inflexible and fragile, like every other bureaucratic public administration. This was not a good fit for the now-independent business, which needed an injection of entrepreneurship. The answer was to change the purpose from meeting objectives to serving clients and striving to offer the city's residents the world's best public transportation system. This change in mindset was not easy, and it took time and effort by the senior leaders, but it unlocked the energy and talent inherent in the workforce. The energy released led a transformation into an entrepreneurially-driven organization that was no longer weighed down by the negative effects of detailed targets. All stakeholders benefited from this significant change in belief systems.

Organizations with capabilities-based systems are able to release employees' latent productive energies by embedding a broad sense of purpose, cooperation and high connectivity into the DNA of the organization. These are the features of highly resilient businesses.

Here are a number of questions for you to consider regarding your operating system:

- What is your dominant operating system?
- How does it impact the organization's ability to operate in your current context?
- Is your dominant operating system an appropriate fit with your industry and environment? If not, why?
- What elements require your attention?
- Do you need to change your dominant operating system to advance to the next stage of growth? If yes, what areas need work and what specific actions can you take today? (Remember that changing people's mindset takes time.)

THE LEADERSHIP SCORECARD

To assist executives in evaluating their operating system, we developed the Leadership Scorecard. It asks questions, the answers to which will be unique to every organization, but the answers offer insight into the critical attributes of operating systems. This will help executives identify which quadrant their organization is currently in, so they can make an informed decision about where they want to take it. We created a matrix that merges the key attributes of operating systems (clarity, alignment, energy and focus) with the dimensions of the Performance Triangle (systems, leadership, people, culture and success). Then, we broke each intersection down into elemental components with questions, the answers to which collectively stimulate introspective dialogue and help executives identify the core attributes that define the operating system.

With the Leadership Scorecard, the four levers combine with five systems and five leadership interactions to help develop people-centric management attributes. People understand, think, act, engage and align with the direction of the firm. 'Know with clarity' helps people understand and raises their awareness of what is going on around them. 'Move in one direction' guides the thinking as one group, while providing individual choice of action. 'Mobilize the Energy' refers to individual responsibility to take actions that deliver value based on trust. 'Maintain the focus' defines an environment that promotes engagement and helps people refocus their attention on what matters when it gets interfered with.

The Leadership Scorecard (Figure 17) combines 20 elements as observation points into a table intended to stimulate introspective dialogue, which helps leaders identify the dominant system needed to help them work *in* the system to make changes. The horizontal view of the scorecard for systems identifies the management attributes (information, strategy, implementation, beliefs and boundaries) that define the system. The vertical view represents the organizational dimensions illustrated by the Performance Triangle (systems, leadership, people, culture and success).

Notice the arrows beneath the elements making up the operating system. They direct you down to the most fundamental questions that drive the entire dynamic system, and ultimately success. These elements become context-related and specific through the answers to the questions. Each organization will be unique. Executives will have context-specific perspectives combined with honest and objective dialogue surrounding the answers to these questions, which can provide significant insight.

To summarize, dynamic operating systems comprise multiple sets of interrelated systems. Effective information systems help raise awareness of what is going on and help employees make sense of what is important. This increases the agility of the organization as people can react to changes in the environment. Clarity of strategy supports leaders by providing direction and establishing a shared intent throughout the organization. Clear direction enhances the overall alignment of employees, who become focused on value-adding actions. Rigorous implementation and performance conversations, with healthy two-way dialogue, help establish the shared agenda needed to mobilize the core capabilities of the company. Strong beliefs promote constructive conversation about the contribution of every employee, who must know his or her place and what is expected. Frequent and thorough contribution discussions help establish shared aspirations and purpose, which increase intrinsic motivation. Clear boundaries that define what is acceptable and what is unacceptable action, with a conversation about risks, help set norms of behaviour. The result of all of this is that the organization becomes smart about how it mobilizes and uses its inherent capabilities. In combination, systems, leadership and culture define the intangible capabilities that determine success: responsiveness, alignment, core capabilities, motivation and cleverness.

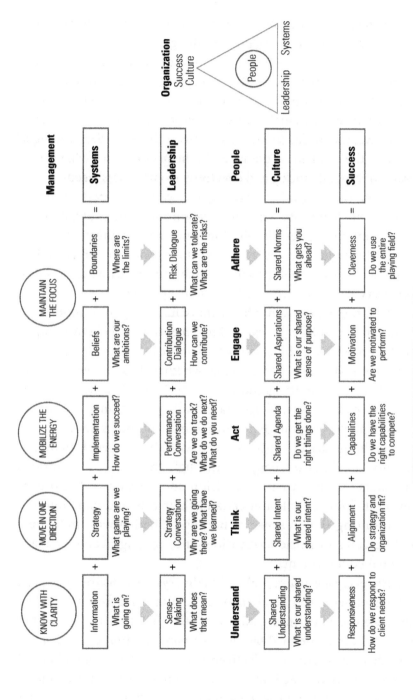

FIGURE 17: THE LEADERSHIP SCORECARD

To illustrate the points we are trying to make, imagine driving a car. Doing so safely involves five primary things.

First, you need a dashboard that indicates how the car is operating and lets you know how fast you are going. In organizations, rapid distribution of relevant information lets people know what is going on, which helps them make sense of decisions and actions, and arrive at effective, timely decisions. This creates a shared understanding of how well the company is doing, which helps people see what is necessary to respond quickly and effectively to customers' needs.

Second, the navigation system guides you to the destination via the most efficient route. The conversation about the strategy creates a shared intent and agenda with the team on what direction to take. The strategy must be widely shared throughout the organization, enabling self-responsible people to think and be creative as they deal with every-day issues with customers or suppliers.

Third, the engine and wheels translate energy into motion. In organizations, this equates to implementation. Effective implementation begins with performance conversations that help people understand what needs to be done, whether they are on track and what their role is in the grand scheme of things. This helps convert the strategy into a shared agenda, providing a roadmap for how to get from point A to point B by getting the right things done.

Fourth, the driver controls speed with the gas pedal. In organizations, acceleration happens through frequent conversations on beliefs that align with the vision and mission of the organization, helping people understand their role and contribution. The resulting shared sense of purpose, aligning with individual goals, creates intrinsic motivation, encouraging people to make personal commitments.

Fifth, every car needs brakes. Braking systems ensure that speed remains under control and enables the proper reaction to sudden, unexpected events. In organizations, this function resides within clear boundaries, defined by the governance and procedural structures that set risk limits, effectively clarifying what is in and out of bounds. Clearly defined and effective boundaries that are neither too restrictive nor too vague support the ability to grow and adapt quickly, while maintaining adequate management control.

Here are some questions for you to consider when thinking about your Leadership Scorecard:

- What is your current Leadership Scorecard?
- How well can you answer the 20 questions? (Be objective and honest.)
- What are your answers, and those of your team, to the questions on the scorecard?
- How do the answers impact your ability to manage in your current growth stage and environment?
- What elements require your attention to advance to the next growth stage?
- What specific actions can you take to drive your organization ('the car') more quickly to your destination?

Chapter 7 outlines management as a competitive advantage for success in every life cycle stage.

THE DYNAMIC OPERATING SYSTEM

Thorough understanding of the four operating systems defined by the Leadership Scorecard tool equips executives to make informed decisions on how to operate in a variety of environments and clarifies what is needed to get where they want to go.

KEY CHAPTER IDEAS

- Operating systems for rules-based, engagement-based, change-based and capabilities-based management systems define the dominant operating system in all organizations.
- The key elements needed to mobilize the core capabilities of organizations, regardless of operating system, are engaging, self-responsible people who make decisions based on collective wisdom, coordinating self-organized work and driving performance through broad purpose.
- The Leadership Scorecard, with 20 elements and probing questions, promotes self-reflection that helps create awareness for critical organizational attributes needed to promote controlled growth and change.

ACTION AGENDA

- Identify your dominant operating system.
- Answer the questions on the Leadership Scorecard with your team. Be honest and objective.
- If the answers are surprising, continue to probe by engaging in productive dialogue with key people.
- Develop and implement action plans to engage self-responsible people to help make decisions based on their collective wisdom.
- Develop and implement methodologies that encourage and coordinate self-organized work groups that share a broad purpose that drives superior performance.

FURTHER READING

Managerial perspective on the operating system:
Michel, L (2020). *People-Centric Management: How Managers Use Four Levers to Bring Out the Greatness of Others.* London: LID Publishing.

Managerial perspective on the Leadership Scorecard:
Michel, L; and Anzengruber, J (2024). *The New Leadership Scorecard: Perspectives, Dimensions and Patterns for Mastery in the Digital Economy.* London: LID Publishing.

Expert perspective on the design of the operating system and Leadership Scorecard:
Michel, L (2021). *Diagnostic Mentoring: How to Transform the Way We Manage.* London: LID Publishing.

Related research on the requirements for the operating system:
Michel, L; Anzengruber, J; Wolfe, M; and Hixson, N (2018). Under What Conditions do Rules-Based and Capabilities-based Management Modes Dominate? *Special Issue Risks in Financial and Real Estate Markets Journal,* 6(32).

CHAPTER 7

A COMPETITIVE ADVANTAGE

Better management is a distinct competitive advantage. In today's hyper-competitive VUCA environment, corporate executives must seek out and take advantage of every capability in their organization. Traditional ways of viewing competitive advantages, popularized by business strategy theorist Michael Porter's Five-Forces and Value Chain models, or the resource-based view, look primarily at physical capabilities that might differentiate an organization from a competitor.

We have identified six attributes that signal whether management qualifies as a competitive advantage. A careful and honest appraisal of these qualities can help executives identify strengths to be leveraged or weaknesses that should be addressed. The management index helps evaluate the dynamic capabilities of an organization and compares them with a reference portfolio of hundreds of companies, in many industries, that we have worked with over the years. As any coach knows, the starting point for developing a championship team is to understand how you compare to the competition, what skills can be used to gain an advantage, and what skills need improvement. The management index helps establish this starting point.

Success at every stage in the growth life cycle requires the development and implementation of management standards that fit the current stage, while simultaneously laying the foundation needed to advance to the next stage of growth. Better management becomes essential for growth and organizational maturity.

Chapter 7 identifies the attributes of better management that can be leveraged into a competitive advantage and provides a useful tool to help 21st-century executives start developing a championship team.

MANAGEMENT IS A COMPETITIVE ADVANTAGE

Identifying and then cultivating a competitive advantage is at the heart of maximizing performance in competitive markets. Most 20th-century strategies centre on achieving an advantage by providing a product or service that appeals to a specific target market through cost leadership, differentiation and/or focus. The traditional approach to implementing the general strategy has been to dedicate management efforts to making operations more efficient and productive. As such, executives dedicate an enormous amount of time, effort and money to streamlining the value chain or managing the resources of the company.

In today's disruptive and hyper-dynamic global markets, traditional competitive advantages based on the value chain or resources can dissolve quickly. New business models powered by new technologies or innovative application of existing technologies can rapidly alter the strategic position of a company. Just look at how Uber has changed the taxi business, Amazon changed retail shopping or Airbnb changed the hotel business. These types of disruptive business models are constantly emerging, in nearly all industries. New business ecosystems create new and different value propositions, in ways that were never envisioned just a few short years ago. Additionally, globalization has turned narrow segments into huge market opportunities that permanently dilute product focus. More than ever, traditional competitive advantages based on product attributes and the value chain are hard to maintain in ways that yield sustainable, above-average returns.

After more than a century of continuous process and productivity improvements, one of the last remaining opportunities to gain a competitive advantage can be found in developing new and improved management techniques. Our work with hundreds of executives worldwide indicates that while the environment, people, technology and interests of stakeholders have changed, companies continue to manage people and segments with 20th-century techniques. The underlying management model and the operating systems remain rooted in the industrial age. Management techniques were developed to align with and coordinate what Porter described as primary activities and support activities. Coordinating the various activities is the critical task that drives all other action. Our research shows that developing new and better management techniques is one of the few remaining opportunities to create a sustainable competitive advantage.

To be a true differentiator, management mastery needs to fulfil the criteria of a competitive advantage. In line with strategic management professor Jay Barney's resource-based view of the firm, and the VRIN criteria for competitive advantage (valuable, rare, inimitable and non-substitutable), our research has revealed six components that signal whether management qualifies as such an advantage. The resulting model, illustrated in Figure 18, identifies six criteria that must be mastered for management processes to so qualify.

FIGURE 18: MANAGEMENT AS A COMPETITIVE ADVANTAGE

Executives should be objective, and ask the right questions, to determine if their management generates a competitive advantage. The key questions are as follows:

1. **Does the work environment enable people to get work done?**
   Our model uses culture, purpose, relationships and collaboration to describe and evaluate the work environment. An engaging work environment contributes to a competitive advantage because it motivates and enables people to get work done.

2. **Does your organization keep promises and create value?** Our model looks at performance, innovation, growth and success (see definition of success in Chapter 5) to determine organizational outcomes and reveal whether management creates value. Credibility (saying what you do and doing what you say) along with keeping promises is a competitive advantage because it establishes trust with all stakeholders, which is critical for knowledge sharing.

3. **Does your management create unique value?** Our model uses ten questions to evaluate whether management applies a command and control-based (traditional management) style and structures, or an enabling-based (people-centric management) approach to leading people. A people-centric approach is a competitive advantage because it releases the latent potential in human beings in ways that focus their creative energy on tasks that add value.

4. **Do people use their talent to exceed expectations?** Our model uses awareness, trust, choice and focus of attention as the means for people to experience flow, which allows them to perform at their peak and learn. Achieving flow — the state of high performance that we've referenced several times here — is a competitive advantage that is hard to copy.

5. **Is your operating system ready for VUCA?** Our model helps executives identify what the dominant operating system is and evaluate whether it is designed for a stable, traditional environment or a dynamic one. A dynamic operating system is a competitive advantage, as it prevents short-cuts while offering flexibility.

6. **Is your culture deeply embedded in the toolbox?** Our model visualizes systems and leadership as highly interactive, with diagnostic features that are glued together by the culture. Survey data tells us whether the culture is rooted in the toolbox, and is a competitive advantage, or an invisible anchor holding the organization back.

If the answer to these six questions is yes, management can become a competitive advantage. Our research confirms that executives who adopt management processes that have agile, people-centric and dynamic capabilities outperform others by a huge margin. Once developed, these capabilities permeate the entire organization and become deeply embedded in the culture. They become part of the organizational DNA and a true competitive advantage that is difficult for rivals to copy. That is why every executive should strive for better management based on developing dynamic people-centric capabilities. The Leadership Scorecard provides a guide to help put the concepts into practice.

Here are some questions for you to reflect on concerning your management as a competitive advantage:

- Have you asked the right questions and can you be objective when you get answers?
- Which questions indicate that your management qualifies as a competitive advantage?
- Which questions indicate that it does not qualify as a competitive advantage?
- What actions can you take today to begin developing better management techniques that give the company a competitive advantage?
- How does developing better management as a competitive advantage impact performance in your current life cycle stage?
- Could adopting better management techniques help propel your company to the next life cycle stage? If so, how, and what do you need to do?

MANAGEMENT MATURITY

Analysis of data gathered from clients participating in our Executive Survey reveals patterns that allow us to group companies into general categories based on the management index on a Maturity Scale. This scale is a useful gauge for comparing organizations' dynamic capabilities. When executives know their current maturity level, they can chart a course to advance to the next level. The maturity level is calculated using the dynamic capabilities and outcome scores from the Executive Survey. The Maturity Scale groups organizations into a six-level ranking, from contestants at the bottom to pioneers at the top. That top level reflects companies that have demonstrated strong dynamic capabilities, resulting in superior positive outcomes.

The six maturity levels shown in Figure 19 indicate where organizations are in their shift from traditional management to better management: contestants, exploiters, changers, enablers, performers or pioneers.

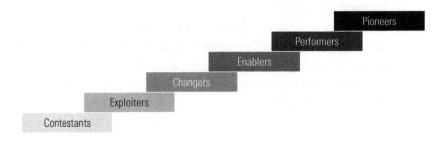

FIGURE 19: SIX MATURITY LEVELS

This scale is the result of 15 years of research with the Performance Triangle model and survey tool, encompassing data from more than 400 organizations worldwide. The large sample includes companies in many industries, of varying sizes, both public and private, as well as governmental agencies, all in many stages of development.

They ranged from start-ups to mature global powerhouses. The Maturity Scale has proven to be a valuable tool, offering a benchmark for organizations and helping executives realize what can be achieved by adopting more people-centric management techniques. Our research indicates that there is a strong correlation between dynamic capabilities and success (see Chapter 5) that translates directly into superior traditional operating results (income, stock price, return on assets, customer service) compared to organizations lacking these capabilities.

Contestants are organizations that inherited an organizational design based on operating in a stable environment. Often, environment and current capabilities do not match because the environment is no longer stable. This mismatch may result from an infected culture, faulty leadership or misguided systems. Typical but ineffective and expensive attempts to resolve the situation include fixing the culture, people, leaders or systems, in isolation. Contestants are stuck in the mud of bureaucracy and executives fail to visualize the dynamic, interrelated nature of the operating system.

Exploiters are organizations designed to exploit physical and human assets. Managers seek to optimize processes that increase efficiency to maximize utilization of both human and physical assets. Many organizations are quite successful in doing so. Consequently, the leaders are largely satisfied with the current situation, focus attention on exploiting current capabilities and overlook potential growth opportunities. However, in dynamic markets, exploiters lack the capabilities to adapt quickly. They are limited to trying to fix the current situation by squeezing results, through tightening performance management (MBO or stretch goals) and embarking on disruptive, expensive, and largely ineffective change initiatives.

Changers are organizations designed to implement disruptive change. Whenever the leaders believe that change is required, they alter the organizational structures and reallocate resources. They keep restructuring as the environment changes due to emerging threats or opportunities. The result is an endless series of reorganizations and change initiatives that disrupt the various dynamic systems, generating unintended consequences and leading to still more reorganizations. The fix for changers is always to add more control and direct managerial influence, hoping to create relentless customer focus and improve operational performance.

Enablers are organizations designed to promote employee engagement in a stable environment. Managers attempt to intrinsically motivate people based on self-responsibility, purpose and social control. The environment favours action-orientation and knowledge work. However, management implementation of the people-centric approach is insufficient to cope with a dynamic setting. The typical fix for enablers is to implement radically decentralized decision-making.

Performers are organizations designed to be effective in a dynamic environment. They have developed dynamic capabilities to help navigate a VUCA world, balancing people's needs and organizational objectives. Coordination across boundaries, self-control and connectivity help them outperform their peers, even in a turbulent world, in performance, innovation and growth.

Pioneers are organizations designed in a way that promotes continuous evolution in response to change, but in small bites that prevent wholesale disruption. Highly developed dynamic capabilities deliver superior outcomes even as the world changes. Decentralized decision-making, teamwork and active engagement of self-responsible people, instead of rigid command and control, are the trademarks of a new way to manage. This is the agile way of operating in the 21st century, with guided self-organization as one of the fundamental principles.

Here are some questions about your organization's agile maturity for you to ponder:

- What is your current maturity level? (Be honest.)
- Are you satisfied with the outcomes you are currently producing?
- Could you benefit from adopting management techniques that would advance the organization to the next level? If yes, what actions can you take now to begin the process?
- How does your organization's maturity impact performance in your current life cycle stage?
- Would advancing to the next level of maturity help your organization advance to the next life cycle growth stage? If yes, what areas need your attention?

With the ideas introduced in the Parts l and ll as a basis for your thinking, Part lll outlines the detailed patterns of five life cycle growth stages.

A COMPETITIVE ADVANTAGE

Developing better management techniques is among the few remaining opportunities for companies to gain a competitive advantage over peers. We have identified six attributes that signal whether management qualifies as a competitive advantage. The Maturity Scale describes multiple levels, with specific dynamic capabilities in each level. It is a tool that helps executives visualize the dynamic capabilities in their organization so they can chart a course to better management.

KEY CHAPTER IDEAS

- Six key questions about competitive advantage that executives should ask are how does the organization: Get work done? Create value? Target specific markets? Become hard to copy? Take no short-cuts? Have deeply embed shared values and goals?
- Management is one of the few remaining opportunities for organizations to gain a competitive advantage. Such an advantage is needed at every stage of the growth life cycle.
- The Maturity Scale sets the standards, with characteristics of contestants, exploiters, changers, enablers, performers and pioneers.
- Advancing up the Maturity Scale requires executives to develop the right dynamic capabilities in the work environment that yield intangible value.
- Leaders should be very aware of their current state on the Maturity Scale and be proactive in preparing to advance to the next stage.
- The executive toolbox helps identify strengths and weaknesses with people-centric management, people performance and the operating system.

ACTION AGENDA

- Recognize that management can be a competitive advantage, and then evaluate the components that are needed.
- Identify the maturity level of your organization.
- Take immediate action to remake management from a necessary evil into a competitive advantage. The Maturity Scale provides the standards.

FURTHER READING

Managerial perspective on competitive advantage:
Michel, L (2022). *Better Management: Six Principles for Leaders to Make Management their Competitive Advantage.* London: LID Publishing.

Expert perspective on the components:
Michel, L (2021). *Diagnostic Mentoring: How to Transform the Way We Manage.* London: LID Publishing.

Related research on the diagnostic measurement:
Nold, H; Anzengruber, J; Michel, L; and Wolfle, M (2018). Organizational Agility: Testing Validity and Reliability of a Diagnostic Instrument. *Journal of Organizational Psychology,* 18(3).

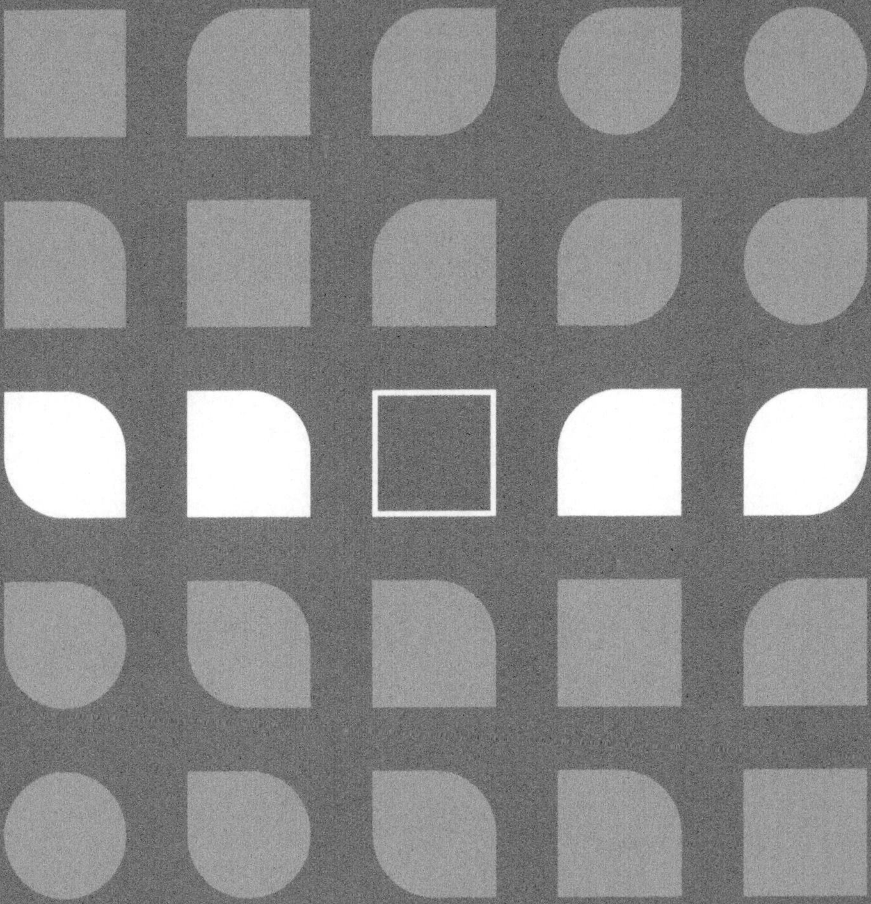

PART III

FIVE
LIFE CYCLE
STAGES

Organizational growth as outlined by Greiner follows five life cycle stages, We have touched on several times already: creativity, direction, delegation, coordination and collaboration. Every stage comes with specific evolutionary and revolutionary attributes, followed by a crisis or organizational challenge that must be overcome to advance to the next stage. We evaluate organizations by looking at their structure through the lens of viewing management as a competitive advantage. Mapping management patterns using the Leadership Scorecard tool allows us to identify the dominant management style for each life cycle stage. The first step in any journey is to know where you are today. Only after establishing your current position can you plot a course for the future.

Part III describes the dominant management patterns typical of organizations in all five life cycle stages.

Chapter 8 explores Stage 1, creativity, in the entrepreneurial organization.

CHAPTER 8

CREATIVITY

Entrepreneurial start-ups create innovative new products or create new markets. The founders are typically technical experts or highly creative, innovative people who see opportunities missed by others. Entrepreneurs typically have an informal management style that works just fine with a small group of highly motivated people who work closely together every day. As the organization grows and becomes more complex, however, this style creates the crisis of leadership.

THE ENTREPRENEURIAL ORGANIZATION

The creativity life cycle stage consists of entrepreneurial organizations, including start-ups. The early stage of an organization tends to be informal, with the focus on creating new products and markets. Innovation and informality dominate the business and the management model.

Founders who run these new companies are typically visionaries who are technically or entrepreneurially oriented and see opportunities that are overlooked by others. They often have a distain for traditional, formal managerial activities. Their minds and energies are focused on making and selling the new product or service, with backroom or support activities viewed as more of a nuisance.

In the early phase of an organization, a powerful sense of purpose dominates the culture. Employees are motivated by their enthusiasm about the business idea and opportunities. The focus is on growth and early profitability as key measures. With an attractive new product or strategy, the business grows in size and complexity as new employees are hired to fill specific needs. Challenges are acted upon quickly and informally, with personal involvement by the founders. Everyone pulls together, sharing roles and responsibilities. People commonly wear multiple hats.

So, what is the dominant profile of entrepreneurial organizations?

Our sample group of start-ups and early-stage companies that have participated in the Executive Survey, operating in the *creativity* life cycle stage, tend to score at the *enablers* maturity level (Management Index of 70) and operate in the *engagement-based* management mode. Figure 20 illustrates the survey scores that are typical of companies in the creativity stage, which give the start-up a competitive advantage. Figure 20 also shows the average, or standard, of more than 400 organizations in our population as a reference point.

Competitive Advantage
*>75 = top tier standards, 60-75 = medium tier standards, <60 = bottom tier standards
**>50: people-centric/dynamic standards; <50: traditional standards

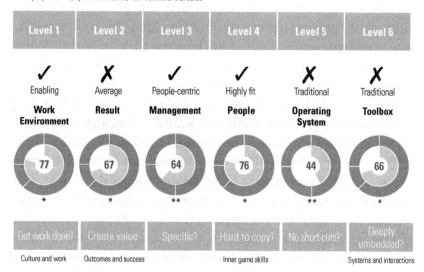

FIGURE 20: CREATIVITY AS A COMPETITIVE ADVANTAGE

Innovation, creativity and speed are the hallmarks of entrepreneurial organizations. Our sample group has created an enabling work environment (Score of 77) where people collaborate and work closely together to get things done. Innovation at this point is predictably the highest among all life cycle stages. People can apply their full talent (Score of 76) to quickly move the company forward or adjust to unexpected changes. The organization generates results that yield superior value, compared to the standard (Score of 67). Application of people-centric management techniques (Score of 64) translates into responsiveness to customer needs, which unsurprisingly is the highest, compared to the typical pattern in the other life cycle phases. The management operating system is informal (Score of 44) and there is no, or poorly developed, structure or formal toolbox (Score of 58).

In combination, creativity-stage organizations meet the 'people' levels of competitive advantage: an enabling work environment, people-centric management and highly fit people make their management effective (get work done), specific and hard to copy.

At this stage of development, formal systems, supported by functional staff experts, are typically not necessary. External consultants or specialized service providers can provide the needed functional support, freeing the founders and the core employee group to focus on developing the business idea or market. Values and strategic direction are communicated effectively through the founders' actions and reinforced every day by discussions about beliefs, through direct intervention. Risks are mitigated by a deep understanding of client needs and wants, technological expertise and suppliers. Performance is monitored informally and without reliance on standardized reports. Formalized internal controls can be minimal and yet still be adequate to meet the standards of auditors and banks because of personal oversight by the founder. Weakness in control can be offset by the founder's personal scrutiny of transactions and activities.

Figure 21 illustrates the dominant features we have observed using the Leadership Scorecard template in companies in the creativity stage of development. Darkened boxes identify the dominant features, while outlined boxes with no shading denote features that have been sidelined or ignored.

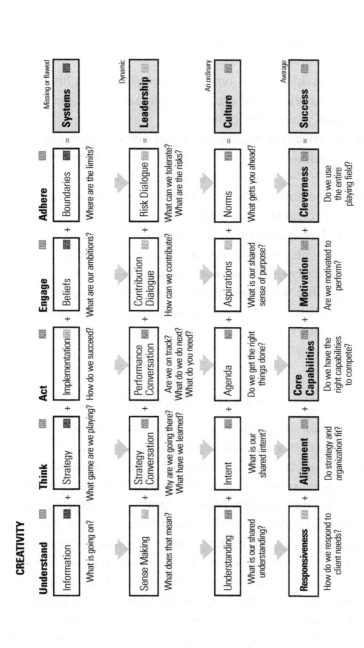

FIGURE 21: THE LEADERSHIP SCORECARD FOR CREATIVITY

In an entrepreneurial environment, informal inter-personal communication, market results and a formal business plan dominate the decision-making process:

- **Internal controls.** Driven by market information and personal intervention by the founders.
- **Sense-making.** Decisions and motivation are highly sensitive to marketplace feedback gathered by key individuals in direct contact or with direct knowledge.
- **Responsiveness.** Management acts quickly when confronted with technological or operational issues, or customer reactions, because they are close to the daily action.
- **Implementation.** Business plans are developed but can be modified quickly if new information becomes available.
- **Shared aspirations.** A relatively small, core group of employees are highly motivated by a common goal that is reinforced with frequent, informal communication.
- **Leadership with contribution and risk dialogues.** Leaders are in direct contact with people to recognize and reward them with the promise of ownership. People also know the appetite for risk.

CRISIS OF LEADERSHIP

As the organization develops, grows and becomes more complex, it becomes too large to manage personally and informally. Formal systems and procedures are required as specialized functional departments are created to manage geographic, product or market expansion. Communication between locations and the newly created hierarchies becomes increasingly difficult when turf wars erupt as managers compete for resources and recognition. The entrepreneur and founder are no longer able to engage in all decisions and personally convey direction to all employees. As complexity and size increase, the leadership style of the typical entrepreneur is no longer sufficient to manage the organization. This situation leads to the *crisis of leadership*, which must be overcome to successfully continue along the growth path. Without effective controls and responsible leaders in key positions, inefficiencies accumulate and market opportunities are missed as unseen interferences creep into and infect the culture.

Here are some questions for you to consider at the creativity stage:

- Where does your organization's fitness meet or exceed the standards of competitive advantage?
- How does your organization's Leadership Scorecard enable creativity?
- What are the implications of you overcoming the crisis of leadership?
- What specific actions should you take to prepare for the next stage of growth?

Next is Chapter 9, with an introduction to the second, or *direction*, stage of growth and the emergence of functional structures. The emergence of specialized functional departments provides direction to the organization from individuals with specialized technical knowledge. Functional structures introduce a new set of issues that must be overcome to continue growing.

CREATIVITY

Entrepreneurial organizations have a design and management style that promotes innovation, creativity and speed. Direct personal engagement between the founders and employees provides motivation and adequate management direction informally. Success and growth create the crisis of leadership, which must be resolved to continue successful growth.

KEY CHAPTER IDEAS

- An entrepreneurial organization is informal, with as little formal structure as possible.
- Enabling creativity and innovation is the dominant management style.
- People-centric management results in speed by accelerating the sharing of knowledge and decision-making.
- As the organization grows in size and complexity, the crisis of leadership must be resolved to provide more direction and control without stifling creativity and innovation.

ACTION AGENDA

- Assess your company's competitive advantage. Compare it to a similar organization at your current stage of development, and one at the next level of growth.
- Review your organization's Leadership Scorecard. Compare it with the master template.
- Manage the evolution. Anticipate the crisis of leadership and then prepare for the inevitable.
- Search for the right balance between control and creativity.
- Take measures to identify and eliminate the unseen, limiting viruses so you can continue down the growth path.

FURTHER READING

Managerial perspective on competitive advantage:
Michel, L (2022). *Better Management: Six Principles for Leaders to Make Management their Competitive Advantage.* London: LID Publishing.
Nold, H. (2018). Dynamic Capabilities for People-Centric Management in Turbulent Times. In M F Brandebo & A Alvinus (Eds.), *Dark Side of Organizational Behavior and Leadership* (pp. 109-124). London: IntechOpen.
Nold, H., (2021). *Agile Strategies for the 21st Century: The Need for Speed, Newcastle upon Tyne:* Cambridge Scholars Publishing Ltd.

Expert perspective on management:
Michel, L (2021). *Diagnostic Mentoring: How to Transform the Way We Manage.* London: LID Publishing.

Related research on the measurement of the dimensions:
Nold, H; Anzengruber, J; Michel, L; and Wolfle, M (2018). Organizational Agility: Testing Validity and Reliability of a Diagnostic Instrument. *Journal of Organizational Psychology,* 18(3).

CHAPTER 9

DIRECTION

The second stage in Greiner's Growth model is 'direction.' In the direction stage, the organization has grown beyond the creative entrepreneurial stage. The founders have resolved the crisis of leadership and the organization has grown in size and complexity by establishing functional departments with specific expertise and scope of responsibility. Functional departments engage professional managers with specialized skills to operate essential parts of the value chain (R&D, production, distribution, marketing, finance, communications, HR) under directive leadership. Over time these managers compete for limited resources and recognition, and typically feel restricted by centralized directives that limit their actions and damage sensitive egos. The second crisis of autonomy emerges, which must be negotiated to continue advancing up the growth staircase.

Chapter 9 describes the characteristics of organizations in the direction stage of development, which now has a structure with functional departments. In this chapter we will discuss the typical Leadership Scorecard pattern that we see and offer suggestions on how to overcome the crisis of autonomy.

THE FUNCTIONAL ORGANIZATION

As the pace of growth increases, new locations are added, more people are hired, and more markets are served. To reduce redundancy and increase efficiency, leaders introduce functional units populated with people possessing specific skills and managed by individuals with prior experience in the field. Product development, manufacturing and sales departments emerge, along with infrastructure units such as HR, accounting and finance that are created and managed as separate cost centres.

The new functional managers and their teams assume responsibility for setting direction within the department's area of responsibility. Lower-level supervisors are treated as functional specialists, with a focus on implementation and directing the day-to-day activities of a staff.

So, what is the dominant profile of functional organizations?

From our research, we observe that organizations operating in the *direction* life cycle stage typically have a pattern of results placing them at the *changers* maturity level (Management Index of 65) with the *rules-based* management mode, to achieve the competitive advantages seen in Figure 22.

DIRECTION   **INSIGHTS**

Competitive Advantage
*>75 = top tier standards, 60-75 = medium tier standards, <60 = bottom tier standards
**>50: people-centric/dynamic standards; <50: traditional standards

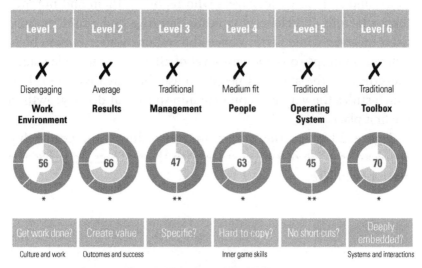

FIGURE 22: DIRECTION AS A COMPETITIVE ADVANTAGE

In the direction stage, maximizing efficiency, quality and asset utilization are central features of functional organizations. Analysis of responses from organizations in the direction stage signals that the work environment is disengaging (Score of 56). People do not feel engaged and committed to the company goals or objectives. Despite that, the business delivers average results and value (Score of 66). Handling people is more representative of an exploitation-type business model than the exploration-type model that is characteristic of companies in the creative stage (Score of 45). The rules-based management approach perfectly fits the exploitation-type model (Score of 47). People are limited in how they can apply their talents (Score of 63). The traditional toolbox is deeply anchored in the organization's culture, which makes it hard to change (Score of 70).

Taken together, the characteristics of direction-stage organizations fail to meet any of the competitive advantage standards. Their management is not sustainable.

Typical of the direction stage, senior leaders take control by directing the divisions and departments with detailed instructions and controlling the flow of information. Senior leaders set detailed performance goals, budgets and incentive programmes for divisional and functional managers who report to them and monitor them carefully. Efficiencies typically improve and profit margins rise. However, while performance and responsiveness remain high, innovation drops to the lowest level of all growth life cycle stages. Cleverness — the ability of people to use their creativity — is low, which stifles the very entrepreneurship spirit that drove growth in the first place.

Figure 23 maps the dominant traits shown on Leadership Scorecard for the direction stage with the features, to serve as a master template.

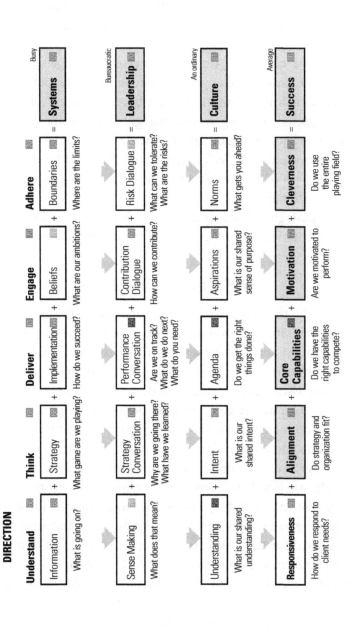

FIGURE 23: THE LEADERSHIP SCORECARD FOR DIRECTION

In a directive environment, leadership with performance targets, incentives and formal communications dominate management thinking and actions. The thinking and doing are separated as follows:

- **Internal controls.** Accounting systems, budgets, required documentation and approval procedures are introduced.
- **Sense-making.** Communication becomes more formal and impersonal, making it increasingly difficult for people to know what is going on around them.
- **Beliefs (Benefits).** Performance targets are set by the executives, with incentives for lower levels that are intended to be motivational.
- **Risk dialogue.** Work standards are adopted under the assumption that meeting predetermined standards reduces risk.

CRISIS OF AUTONOMY

Unfortunately, the success of driving functional efficiencies hampers the creativity and initiative that were the hallmarks of the original entrepreneurial business. With narrow job specialization and tight performance goals, employees find it difficult to respond to customer issues and internal interferences. Organizations lose vitality and their ability to quickly adapt to changing market conditions and opportunities is lost. Employees find it difficult to work across organizational boundaries as silos interfere with the free flow of knowledge. Central support functions find it hard to establish shared rules applicable to everyone, covering every eventuality and to bridge the inherent barriers of the organization. Frustration builds, leading to a *crisis of autonomy*. The founders and senior leaders are blamed for the loss of the entrepreneurial spirit and widespread frustration as people struggle to feel engaged.

Here are a number of questions for you to consider when in the direction stage:

- Where does your company's fitness meet or exceed the standards for competitive advantage?
- How does your Leadership Scorecard fit the pattern for the direction stage?

- Are you satisfied with the current results?
- Do you want to continue to grow and take advantage of emerging opportunities?
- What are the implications of you overcoming the crisis of autonomy?
- What specific actions can you take to overcome this crisis?

Ahead, Chapter 10 contains an introduction to Stage 3 in the growth model — delegation — which describes transition from a functionally structured organization that provides direction to a decentralized organization. Decentralized organizations introduce new issues around delegation that must be overcome to continue advancing up the growth path.

DIRECTION

The company has grown in scope and complexity thanks to entrepreneurial success. Functional organizations are created with professional managers to oversee specific functions or divisions under directive leadership by senior executives. The second crisis of autonomy mounts as functional or divisional managers compete for resources and recognition while being controlled by the directives from the cadre of senior executives.

KEY CHAPTER IDEAS

- Success and growth naturally result in a division of labour and resources, which increases complexity but maximizes productivity.
- A functional or divisional organization creates physical and psychological silos throughout the value chain.
- Direction by senior executives and managers becomes the dominant management style.
- Productivity increases at the cost of reduced knowledge sharing and creativity.
- The crisis of autonomy emerges as divisional and functional managers seek more delegated accountability.
- The crisis of autonomy must be resolved to advance to the next stage of growth.

ACTION AGENDA

- Assess your organization's competitive advantage. Compare it with that of similar organizations.
- Review your organization's Leadership Scorecard. Compare it with the master template to see how you stack up against other companies.
- Manage the evolution. Take proactive action to prevent the crisis of autonomy. Or, if you find yourself in the throes of it, take measures to resolve this crisis.
- Diagnose your organization to identify viruses that perpetuate directive management styles.
- Take proactive measures to eliminate the viruses that inhibit growth and advancement to the next stage.

FURTHER READING

Managerial perspective on competitive advantage:

Michel, L (2022). *Better Management: Six Principles for Leaders to Make Management their Competitive Advantage.* London: LID Publishing.

Nold, H., (2021). *Agile Strategies for the 21st Century: The Need for Speed,* Newcastle upon Tyne: Cambridge Scholars Publishing Ltd.

Expert perspective on management:

Michel, L (2021). *Diagnostic Mentoring: How to Transform the Way We Manage.* London: LID Publishing.

Nold, H (2018). Dynamic Capabilities for People-Centric Management in Turbulent Times. In M F Brandebo & A Alvinus (Eds.), *Dark Side of Organizational Behavior and Leadership* (pp. 109-124). London: IntechOpen.

Related research on the measurement of the dimensions:

Nold, H; Anzengruber, J; Michel, L; and Wolfle, M (2018). Organizational Agility: Testing Validity and Reliability of a Diagnostic Instrument. *Journal of Organizational Psychology,* 18(3).

CHAPTER 10

DELEGATION

As organizations overcome the crisis of autonomy and emerge from the direction stage, decentralized structures with delegated decision-making and accountability are established. Professional managers are assigned to sub-units, plants, market areas or geographic territories and given expanded decision-making responsibility, with processes in place to hold them accountable to the home office. Trouble arises when top management at the headquarters level feel they lose control. This is the beginning of the crisis of control.

Chapter 10 describes Stage 3 in the growth life cycle, delegation, which is characteristic of the decentralized organization. Decentralized organizations present a new set of issues and problems to be overcome. We will describe the unique attributes of decentralized organizations in our models, with data collected from the representative population.

THE DECENTRALIZED ORGANIZATION

To restore responsiveness and growth, the authority to make key decisions must be pushed to lower levels, where managers are closer to the customers and issues. Creating decentralized structures and delegating important decision-making responsibility closer to street level reduces the need to run routine decisions up the chain of command. In this way, the organization can be responsive to customers' needs. In many companies, profit centre managers in market-based business units are given wide discretionary authority. They are held accountable for the profitability and performance of their unit. They typically have the freedom to run their own business, to meet local needs and expectations. This type of organization is particularly important to businesses trying to expand into new countries with unique cultures, demographics and resources. Business unit or profit centre managers become responsible for setting strategy, staffing and acquiring assets to support local product development, production, marketing and sales. Empowered profit centre leaders enable the organization to respond quickly and effectively to local market needs, restoring flexibility and improving responsiveness.

What is the dominant profile of decentralized organizations?

Those we have worked with and collected data on that operate in the *delegation* life cycles stage tend to be at the *changers* maturity level (Management Index of 68) with the *engagement-based* management mode. Figure 24 illustrates the typical pattern that delegation-stage companies exhibit to achieve a competitive advantage.

DELEGATION   **INSIGHTS**

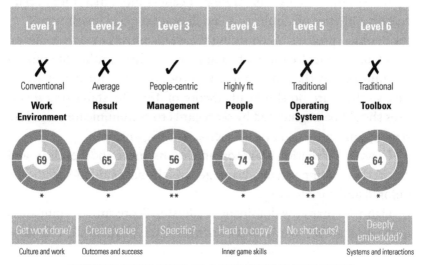

Competitive Advantage
*>75 = top tier standards, 60-75 = medium tier standards, <60 = bottom tier standards
**>50: people-centric/dynamic standards; <50: traditional standards

Level 1	Level 2	Level 3	Level 4	Level 5	Level 6
✗	✗	✓	✓	✗	✗
Conventional	Average	People-centric	Highly fit	Traditional	Traditional
Work Environment	Result	Management	People	Operating System	Toolbox
69	65	56	74	48	64
*	*	**	*	**	*
Get work done?	Create value	Specific?	Hard to copy?	No short-cuts?	Deeply embedded?

Culture and work   Outcomes and success   Inner game skills   Systems and interactions

FIGURE 24: DELEGATION AS A COMPETITIVE ADVANTAGE

Profit centres or business units in decentralized organizations function quasi-independently. Independence and freedom to act represent an opportunity for people-centric managers to demonstrate their effectiveness (Score of 56). Creating a somewhat healthy work environment (Score of 69) in an engagement-based approach to handling employees allows and encourages people to apply their unique talents (Score of 74).

Delegated authority distributes power to business units to develop and maintain their own systems that support the decision-making process. This allows business unit executives to focus their attention on results that create value and success (Score of 65).

As profit centre leaders are given a high degree of autonomy, several additional controls are needed. Leaders must communicate their values and establish mission and vision statements to motivate, empower and provide direction. Formal beliefs become critical in instilling shared values among increasingly dispersed employees. Furthermore, leaders must create and communicate strategic boundaries. All these characteristics are more typical of traditional management styles (Score of 64).

With increasing delegation of decision-making comes the risk that employees will squander scarce resources on opportunities that do not support the overall strategy. Leaders must therefore declare certain activities off-limits to avoid distraction, bad investments or doomed projects. Accounting measures must not only focus on profitability, but also on assets that generate these profits. Stabilizing the unit means that there must be processes that formalize activities, so there are no short-cuts (Score of 48). The stabilizing measures should be augmented by scorecards to communicate corporate strategy, initiatives and results across the organization.

Overall, delegation-stage organizations meet the Levels 3 and 4 criteria of competitive advantage, which makes them specifically tailored and hard to copy.

Figure 25 maps the dominant Leadership Scorecard for companies in the delegation stage, with the features to serve as a master template.

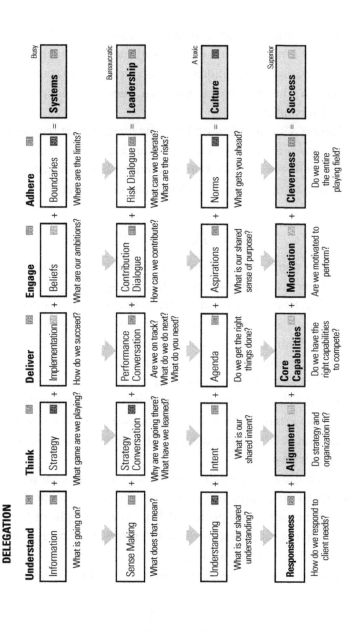

FIGURE 25: THE LEADERSHIP SCORECARD FOR DELEGATION

In the delegation environment, value creation (success) becomes dominant, guided by performance management and incentive plans, as follows:

- **Implementation.** Internal and headquarters profit centre plans and performance reports are created and maintained. The home office manages exceptions based on reports from units.
- **Beliefs.** Incentives are used to motivate people in the business units.
- **Success.** Communication from the top comes at regular intervals but is infrequent. Headquarters intervention is by exception and remote, based on outcomes, alignment with topline strategy, unit capabilities and employee motivation.

CRISIS OF CONTROL

To maintain sophisticated controls, a variety of specialized corporate support functions are installed. The purpose of these is to govern delegation by setting the rules of engagement for decentralized structures, and then monitoring the decisions to be sure that the rules are being followed. For example, HR establishes common risk-reducing policies and performance management strategies, finance/accounting drives profit and performance measurement, strategists develop and maintain a unified planning system, and corporate governance prescribes the boundaries. The CEO's support staff coordinates the management system through a corporate cycle and calendar.

However, growth through delegation creates its own problems. Decentralized structures too often become independent fiefdoms whose unit managers are protected from the oversight of the head office. When this happens, coordination suffers, resources are wasted and profitability declines, leading to a *crisis of control.*

Here are questions for you to consider if your company is in the delegation stage:

- Where does your organization's fitness meet or exceed the standards of competitive advantage?
- How does your Leadership Scorecard enable delegation?
- Do you want to advance to the next stage of growth?

- What are the impediments to you overcoming the crisis of control?
- What specific actions can you take to overcome this crisis?

Stage 4 of growth, coordination, is discussed in the next chapter. We will describe the attributes segmented organizations in our representative population demonstrate using our models, with results gathered from companies in this stage. Gaining a clear understanding of the current patterns helps executives plan for advancing to the next growth stage.

DELEGATION

Decentralized organizations delegate accountability to managers of sub-units, plants, markets or geographies. This independence and freedom to act encourages unit managers to employ people-centric methodologies and improves responsiveness to the customer or market. Business unit managers develop and implement processes and systems to measure performance and report to headquarters. Top management at the home office begins to sense a loss of effective oversight, and the crisis of control has arrived.

KEY CHAPTER IDEAS

- A decentralized organization delegates decision-making and accountability for entire plants, markets, and geographies, setting them up as sub-units.
- The decision-making power for local issues is with the managers of these units.
- Business unit managers customize processes and products for the local market and employees, but report results to the home office.
- The home office manages by exception, with regular performance reviews.
- As business units grow in size and influence, the crisis of control emerges, spotlighting a need for better alignment with headquarters-level strategies or policies.

ACTION AGENDA

- Assess your organization's competitive advantage. Compare it with similar organizations.
- Review your Leadership Scorecard. Compare it with the master template.
- Identify areas of strength to leverage and weaknesses to work on fixing.
- Manage the evolution. Be proactive to prevent the crisis of control.
- If this crisis emerges, take measures to eliminate the viruses that limit growth and got you in trouble in the first place.

FURTHER READING

Managerial perspective on competitive advantage:

Michel, L (2022). *Better Management: Six Principles for Leaders to Make Management their Competitive Advantage.* London: LID Publishing.

Nold, H (2021). *Agile Strategies for the 21st Century: The Need for Speed,* Newcastle upon Tyne: Cambridge Scholars Publishing Ltd.

Expert perspective on management:

Michel, L (2021). *Diagnostic Mentoring: How to Transform the Way We Manage.* London: LID Publishing.

Nold, H. (2018). Dynamic Capabilities for People-Centric Management in Turbulent Times. In M F Brandebo & A Alvinus (Eds.), *Dark Side of Organizational Behavior and Leadership* (pp. 109-124). London: IntechOpen.

Related research on the measurement of the dimensions:

Nold, H; Anzengruber, J; Michel, L; and Wolfle, M (2018). Organizational Agility: Testing Validity and Reliability of a Diagnostic Instrument. *Journal of Organizational Psychology,* 18(3).

CHAPTER 11

COORDINATION

Continued growth leads to the emergence of segmented organizations with specialized functions and lines of businesses that require coordination by top management. Sophisticated control mechanisms are introduced that allow leaders to understand what is going on in segments that are increasingly distant, organizationally and physically. Senior executives are able to take action when needed to keep all parts of the organization on track. Increased distance between leadership and business segments typically results in an environment that reduces trust between headquarters and business segments. In this coordination stage, the crisis of red tape arises as management introduces processes and procedures intended to keep them in the loop with organizations that have become too big and complex.

Chapter 11 describes the typical characteristics of organizations in the segmented coordination (or Stage 4) growth phase, as observed in our representative population. Executives in this stage can use this information to help assess their current situation and chart a course to the next stage.

THE SEGMENTED ORGANIZATION

The organization is now large, mature, and complex. The company has sizeable specialized functional departments, several divisions and competes in multiple product markets. To align the span of control, executives typically group the disparate units into larger market-based sectors that cluster similar business by product, region or customer. New staff groups are created to manage the increasingly important management system for planning, asset deployment and resource allocation. Staff specialists ensure that strategic criteria are consistent across the organizations, and that appropriate performance hurdles are being consistently met. Over time, a complex web of procedures requiring approval from upper-level executives or powerful headquarters specialists is created. Business unit managers must now obtain approval before embarking on any major strategy commitment or allocation of resources. The resulting procedural hurdles — frustrating, energy-sapping red tape — typically have the unintended consequence of slowing down the decision-making process, which inhibits the organizational ability to react quickly to opportunities or threats. Innovation may be limited and opportunities missed, while potential problems become real threats.

Having said that, what is the dominant profile of segment organizations?

Organizations operating in the *coordination* life cycle stage have patterns in our model indicating that they are at the *enablers* maturity level (Management Index of 70), operating in the *change-based* management mode. Figure 26 shows the pattern that companies in the coordination stage of growth display to achieve a competitive advantage.

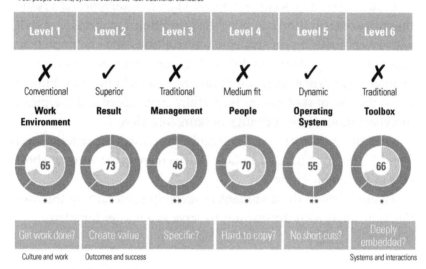

COORDINATION INSIGHTS

FIGURE 26: COORDINATION AS A COMPETITIVE ADVANTAGE

Segmented organizations operate in an enabling-based environment with a conventional work environment (Score of 65), medium fit with people (Score of 70) and traditional management toolbox (Score of 66). At this stage of development, segment managers have typically earned their positions by having formal education (an MBA) and years of experience. They have been taught and used methodologies that were initially absorbed from textbooks and adapted to the specific segment. Applying widely accepted, conventional methods lead senior executives to approach problems by constantly reorganizing and changing the structure of the organization.

At this stage, formal systems are put in place by headquarters staff for greater coordination by top management. These conventional systems become embedded in the culture, establishing a shared agenda, shared aspirations and shared norms throughout the organization (Score of 65).

In a large, mature firm, leaders must rely on the opportunity-seeking behaviour of employees for innovation and new strategic initiatives. At this point, they need to develop dynamic operating systems with interactive control processes (Score of 66). These inter-active practices and procedures point top executives to where debate and learning should occur, as well as when to intervene. As a result, the entire organization takes on a very traditional management style, with levers focusing on strategic uncertainties and the implemen-tation of strategy (Score of 46). Staff groups assist in gathering and facilitating information flows. However, to avoid unneeded bureau-cracy, the role of staff groups is carefully constrained and is typically in a continuous state of change or reorganization.

Overall, coordination-stage organizations meet the criteria Levels 2 and 5 of competitive advantage. They create value with no short-cuts in a dynamic context.

Figure 27 maps the dominant Leadership Scorecard for the coor-dination stage, with the features to serve as a master template.

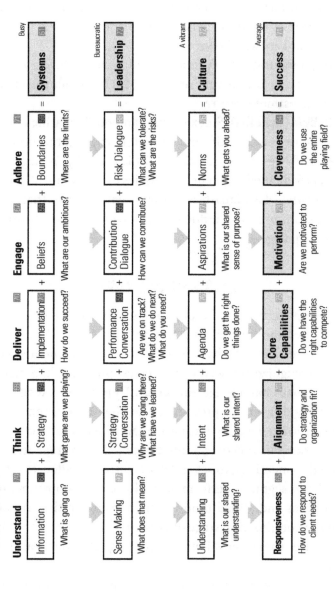

FIGURE 27: THE LEADERSHIP SCORECARD FOR COORDINATION

In the coordination stage, culture becomes a powerful common denominator that unifies the organization like a glue. The company develops centralized implementation of clear boundary systems that are supported by common beliefs. The characteristics of the Leadership Scorecard are as follows:

- **Implementation.** Formal planning procedures are established and intensively reviewed. Each segment is viewed as an investment centre.
- **Beliefs (Benefits).** Stock options and profit sharing encourage employees to identify and commit to the organization.
- **Boundaries.** Resource allocation is carefully managed across clearly defined segment boundaries by the home office.
- **Culture.** Headquarters grows with staff that initiate programmes to influence behaviours and control for line managers.

CRISIS OF RED TAPE

Over time, as central staff groups at the home office become more powerful, yet another crisis occurs. This time, it is the *crisis of red tape*. Most readers who have worked for large, segmented companies will recognize the web of processes, procedures, policies and approvals that characterize this crisis. Upper-level executives feel a need to add layers of procedures, so they have a sense of control, while lower-level operating managers feel that the decision-making process has become burdensomely slow. A great deal of time is devoted to meetings, to set and review strategy, allocate resources and evaluate segment performance. Slowed reaction time, missed opportunities and stifled innovation characterize the crisis of red tape in the coordination stage of growth.

Here are some questions concerning coordination for you to consider:

- Where does your organization's fitness meet or exceed the standards of competitive advantage?
- Do you really need all these processes and procedures?
- Should you reevaluate the need and effectiveness of all the processes and procedures on a regular basis?

- What is the effect of constantly changing structure on the culture, the mental health of employees and, ultimately, performance?
- How does your organization's Leadership Scorecard enable or hinder coordination?
- What are the major challenges you will encounter in working to overcome the crisis of red tape?

Next up is Chapter 12, covering Stage 5, collaboration, in which the networked organization emerges in various forms.

COORDINATION

Segment organizations require coordination by top management through a sophisticated control mechanism. Complex webs of processes, procedures and policies evolve, intended to keep headquarters executives informed on what is going on in the segments, so they can step in with corrective actions if the segment wanders from the corporate strategy. Burdensome approval processes degrade responsiveness and stifle innovation. The crisis of red tape arises with increasing size and complexity as the home office attempts to coordinate the various segments through processes and procedures.

KEY CHAPTER IDEAS

- Segmented organizations combine plants, markets and geographies into market segments.
- These segments are then coordinated by executives and functional managers at the headquarters level.
- Webs of processes, procedures and policies requiring home office approval for key decisions reduce responsiveness and innovation.
- As these organizations grow and become increasingly complex, the crisis of red tape demands network-type structures.
- The crisis of red tape must be overcome to continue growing.

ACTION AGENDA

- Assess your organization's competitive advantage. Compare it with the patterns displayed by our representative organizations.
- Review your organization's Leadership Scorecard. Compare it with the master template.
- Identify and target key areas to work on, and then implement an action agenda.
- Manage the evolution. Be proactive by anticipating the crisis of red tape, and act to prevent it.
- If you already have a crisis of red tape, take measures to identify and eliminate the viruses that limit growth and that got you into trouble in the first place.

FURTHER READING

Managerial perspective on competitive advantage:

Michel, L (2022). *Better Management: Six Principles for Leaders to Make Management their Competitive Advantage.* London: LID Publishing.

Nold, H (2021). *Agile Strategies for the 21st Century: The Need for Speed,* Newcastle upon Tyne: Cambridge Scholars Publishing Ltd.

Expert perspective on management:

Michel, L (2021). *Diagnostic Mentoring: How to Transform the Way We Manage.* London: LID Publishing.

Nold, H (2018). Dynamic Capabilities for People-Centric Management in Turbulent Times. In M F Brandebo & A Alvinus (Eds.), *Dark Side of Organizational Behavior and Leadership (pp. 109-124).* London: IntechOpen.

Related research on the measurement of the dimensions:

Nold, H; Anzengruber, J; Michel, L; and Wolfle, M (2018). Organizational Agility: Testing Validity and Reliability of a Diagnostic Instrument. *Journal of Organizational Psychology,* 18(3).

CHAPTER 12

COLLABORATION

Complexity increases as companies continue to grow with the introduction of functional departments and quasi-independent profit centres or business units. With the formation of far-flung segments, additional structures like matrix organizations, networks and ecosystems of all types may be introduced to facilitate collaboration. Interaction among widely disparate components is needed to solve problems and promote innovation and efficiencies that drive further business growth. The need for flexible controls grows as complexity increases. The potential loss of organizational identity creates the crisis of collaboration that must be resolved to continue successful growth.

Chapter 12 describes Stage 5 of growth, collaboration, which becomes an essential capability for networked organizations to distribute valuable knowledge among the many component-parts to facilitate further growth. Networked enterprises increase complexity by including multiple independent organizations with different attributes. Merging and blending these disparate organizational characteristics presents a new set of challenges to executives attempting to coordinate the segments in the network.

THE NETWORK ORGANIZATION

To overcome the barriers of red tape, the organization now develops a more flexible and versatile network structure. Various forms of matrices link organizationally and geographically separated business segments to facilitate the internal flow of knowledge. The management focus is on solving problems quickly in teams drawn from multiple segments. Teams are formed to handle specific issues by drawing on expertise from various disciplines. Typically, headquarters-level functional staff experts are reduced in number, reassigned and integrated into interdisciplinary teams that consult with business unit or segment teams.

- A matrix or network structure is used to assemble teams composed of people with expertise needed to address the issue the company is working to resolve.
- Conferences with key executives are held to identify complex problems and then focus essential resources and personnel on resolving them.
- Educational programmes become widely used to train managers in behavioural soft skills needed to facilitate effective teamwork and conflict resolution.
- Experimenting with new practices and technologies, particularly communication technologies, are encouraged.

And what is the dominant profile of network organizations?

Analysis of data from our representative organizations shows that those in the *collaboration* life cycles stage at the *performer* maturity level (Management Score of 72) operate in the *capabilities-based* management mode. The typical patterns of management used to achieve a competitive advantage are shown in Figure 28.

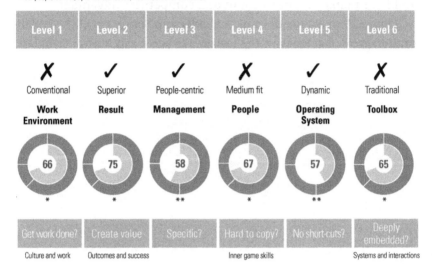

FIGURE 28: COLLABORATION AS A COMPETITIVE ADVANTAGE

At the collaboration stage of development, companies have over-come the crises of leadership, autonomy, control and red tape by institutionalizing sophisticated processes and procedures that pro-mote knowledge sharing with flexible controls. Networked organ-izations operate in a capabilities-base environment that allows people to function at their full potential. Social controls and self-responsibility replace formal, rigid command and control systems. At this most advanced stage, it's striking to note that the various components for a competitive advantage have become balanced. The scores indicate that there are no dominating or exceptionally weak components that enable these companies deliver superior results (Score of 75) in a conventional work environment (Score of 66). The company has an effective people-centric environment that encourages flow and knowledge sharing (Score of 67), with flexible operating systems that emphasize self-responsibility (Score of 57). For most organizations, the toolbox is yet to be embedded in cul-ture (Score of 65).

At the collaboration stage, balance is the competitive advantage that yields superior results. These organizations meet Levels 2, 3 and 5 for management to count as a competitive advantage.

Figure 29 maps the dominant Leadership Scorecard at the collaboration growth stage with the features to serve as a master template.

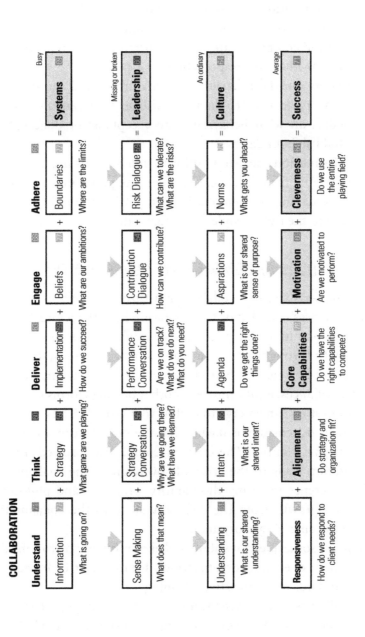

FIGURE 29: THE LEADERSHIP SCORECARD FOR COLLABORATION

In the collaboration stage, behavioural systems for social control focus on information, beliefs and boundaries, as follows:

- **Systems.** Formal command and control systems are simplified and combined into single multipurpose systems that rely on individual self-responsibility.
- **Beliefs and boundaries.** Rewards are geared more toward team performance than individual achievement. Shared beliefs on what behaviours are acceptable or unacceptable establish boundaries.
- **Information.** Real-time information systems are constantly evaluated for relevance, and then integrated into daily decision-making. The emphasis is on getting the right information to the right people at the right time.

CRISIS OF COMPLEXITY? SOVEREIGNTY?

At this phase, extensive collaboration through matrices and networks increases complexity. Collaboration in both face-to-face and advanced communications technology modes opens doors for further growth through cooperation and alliances in ecosystems that may extend beyond the boundaries of the original organization. Strategic alliances, joint ventures or other business forms facilitated by collaboration can emerge to fuel further growth. The emergence of alliances in ecosystems means that the organization loses some of its original identity. The crisis of complexity resolved through collaboration leads to the crisis of sovereignty. The challenge for leaders becomes retaining the identity, processes and philosophy that drove growth from the creativity stage to the collaboration stage in the emerging ecosystem.

Here are some questions about collaboration for you to consider:

- Where does your organization's fitness meet or exceed the standards of competitive advantage?
- Will these advantages transfer to the emerging ecosystem? Which may involve external organizations? If not, why?
- How does your organization's Leadership Scorecard enable collaboration across the new alliance or ecosystem?

- Do the players in the emerging ecosystem have similar or different Leadership Scorecards? If different, what would be the effect on collaboration?
- Can or should you try to integrate multiple Leadership Scorecards in the emerging ecosystem?
- What are the implications of you overcoming the crisis of sovereignty?

We have now explained our models and discussed the attributes of organizations in each of the five stages of growth, to help executives gain insight into their current stage. Gaining insight into strengths and weaknesses of the organization helps executives plot a course to continue growing into the next stage.

In Part IV we will explore and offer practical suggestions on *how* to prepare for and manage the transition, with four possible strategies. It is important to remember that these strategies are not mutually exclusive, so executives should mix, match and blend them to meet the unique demands of their organization.

COLLABORATION

Complexity increases, leading to the development of matrix and network organizations that require interaction among the members to collaborate and get things done. Members in the emerging alliances or ecosystems may be external organizations. Consequently, the crisis of sovereignty will emerge.

KEY CHAPTER IDEAS

- Matrix- and network-type organizations loosely connect parts that require collaboration.
- Strategic alliances, joint ventures or other forms create new ecosystems.
- The power is with those that own and manage the community.
- Coordinating the activities of the new ecosystem requires collaboration using face-to-face and technological modes.
- Integrating multiple organizations with different characteristics, practices, cultures and philosophies becomes a challenge.
- As these new matrices and networks grow, members may lose their unique identity, which initiates the next crisis of sovereignty.

ACTION AGENDA

- Assess your organization's competitive advantage. Compare it with the representative organizations.
- Compare your organization's competitive advantage to others in the emerging network and look for potentially damaging differences.
- Be proactive and address differences with the relevant players in the new ecosystem.
- Review your organization's Leadership Scorecard. Compare it with the master template and the Leadership Scorecard of other organizations in the new network.
- Be proactive and address differences in philosophy and the Leadership Scorecard to resolve gaps before they become a crisis.
- Manage the evolution. Prevent the crisis of sovereignty. Take measures to preserve the unique attributes that drove past growth and transfer relevant characteristics to the new business form.

FURTHER READING

Managerial perspective on competitive advantage:

Michel, L (2022). *Better Management: Six Principles for Leaders to Make Management their Competitive Advantage.* London: LID Publishing.

Nold, H (2021). *Agile Strategies for the 21st Century: The Need for Speed,* Newcastle upon Tyne: Cambridge Scholars Publishing Ltd.

Expert perspective on management:

Michel, L (2021). *Diagnostic Mentoring: How to Transform the Way We Manage.* London: LID Publishing.

Nold, H (2018). Dynamic Capabilities for People-Centric Management in Turbulent Times. In M F Brandebo & A Alvinus (Eds.), *Dark Side of Organizational Behavior and Leadership (pp. 109-124).* London: IntechOpen.

Related research on the measurement of the dimensions:

Nold, H; Anzengruber, J; Michel, L; and Wolfle, M (2018). Organizational Agility: Testing Validity and Reliability of a Diagnostic Instrument. *Journal of Organizational Psychology,* 18(3).

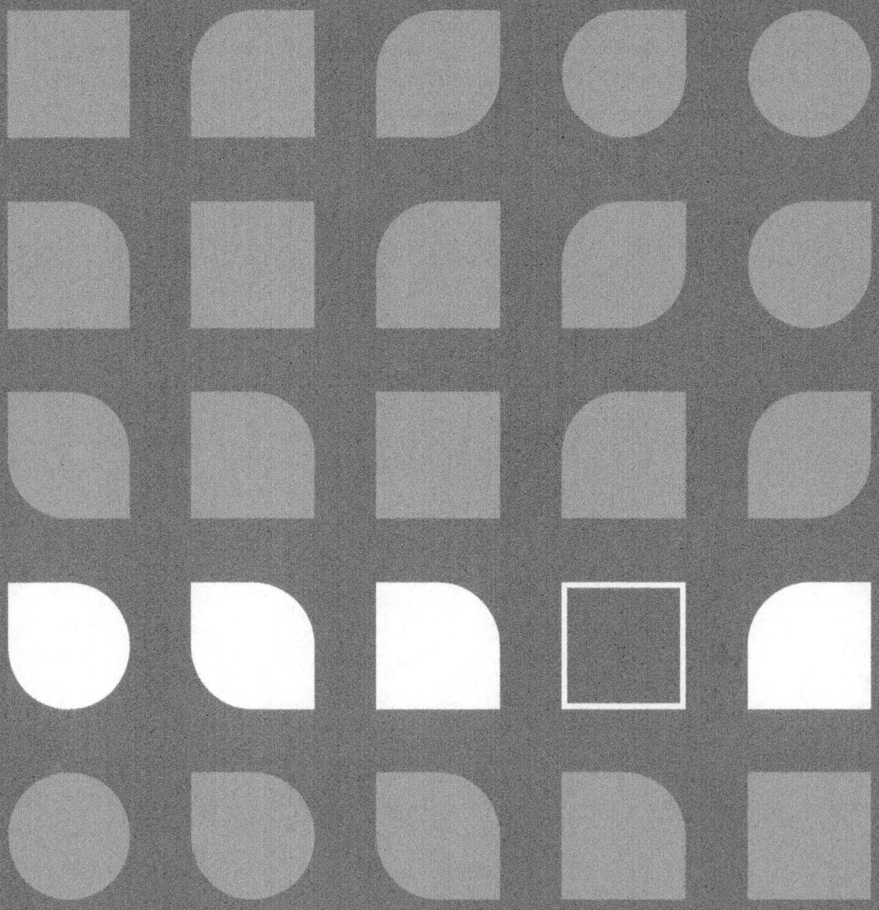

PART IV

FOUR TRANSITION STRATEGIES

Understanding the underlying attributes of the organization in its current growth stage is the first step. Identifying strengths that can be leveraged and weaknesses to be strengthened is the second step. Taking focused action, taking advantage of strengths, eliminating weaknesses and building essential capabilities becomes the key third step to advance to the next growth state. We have identified four transition strategies to help managers build essential capabilities to overcome the limiting crisis and advance down the path to growth. The four general strategies are: people first, people-centric management, dynamic operations and agile organization. These are general strategies that are not mutually exclusive. They should be blended and adapted to meet the unique needs of the organization. We offer suggestions to guide the organization through the transition with structures, systems and capabilities that help resolve the natural tension between evolution and revolution.

Part IV provides the *how* of the transitions, using four general transition strategies. Chapter 13 begins the section with people-first strategies intended to help organizations overcome the crisis of leadership.

CHAPTER 13

PEOPLE FIRST

The first growth stage transition is the move from creativity to direction. This transition requires a solution to the crisis of leadership. The challenge for executives is to create an environment that enables people to play their inner game and reach a state of flow more often. Enabling flow requires executives to put people first.

Chapter 13 offers practical suggestions on how to resolve the crisis of leadership by doing this. A people-first strategy creates the internal dynamics that facilitate the transition from the creativity stage to the direction stage.

SOLVING THE CRISIS OF LEADERSHIP

Moving from an entrepreneurial to a functional organization means putting people first in a predominantly rules-based mode of operations. This is all about enabling personal performance, which drives organizational performance. The inner game enables people to perform at their peak, such that they reach a state of flow, where time and space merge. When in the flow, work becomes easy, enjoyable, satisfying and highly motivating. People become highly engaged and want to do well, so they become responsible, productive and innovative problem solvers.

PEOPLE FIRST

Management modes introduced in Chapter 3 (Figure 30) describe four bundles of managerial principles and capabilities. Overlaying a range of traditional and people-centric management styles, operating in a range from stable to dynamic environments, produces four major quadrants representing the management modes. A people-first approach promotes the development of a work environment that enables employees to get work done and is a characteristic of better management.

To solve the crisis of leadership, enlightened management prioritizes the needs of people. Peter Drucker provided the wise guidance for management: "There is only one valid purpose of a corporation: to create a customer." Drucker saw that a company's primary responsibility is to create value for customers. Since the first line of contact that customers have with a business is with employees, your people must become a major priority. With that in mind, the question then becomes where managers set their priorities. Managers are constantly beset by challenges and pressing issues, so they must prioritize their focus and energy. We suggest that the top priority should be developing skills and capabilities. Regardless of the management style or context, people drive performance. That is why Figure 30 shows people at the centre, as THE top priority.

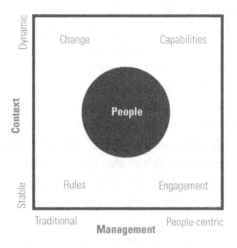

FIGURE 30: PEOPLE FIRST

The people-first priority offers the means to prevent the leadership crisis in the first place. When leaders recruit high-quality people, and then develop self-responsibility throughout the organization, these conscientious employees can take care of clients without constant supervision. The result is that the founders can focus their energy on building an organizational foundation that will propel the company along the growth path.

The most visionary leaders work hard to establish an environment aligned with four priorities. Your primary responsibility as a leader is to develop the management systems that will support growth to the next level. However, releasing the energy, skills and capabilities of self-responsible people provides the fuel for growth, so they should be your primary focus.

1. **People are the centre of your attention.** Solving the crisis of leadership demands an individualized environment where people can unlock their talent and perform at their peak. It is people who deliver value to clients. They should be able to experience flow, that special state where challenges and capabilities meet to create a positive experience. Achieving flow becomes the ultimate goal of better management. As a leader, it is your task (and your obligation) to create that kind of work environment.

2. **Your organization sets the context.** Agile capabilities described in Chapter 5 enable better management. Systems, leadership and culture form the operating environment that allows people to apply their talents and perform at their peak. It becomes important for you to recognize the inherent potential in people, and the interferences that grow over time that prevent them from reaching their full potential.

3. **Your people are the first line of contact with clients.** Better management principles enable you to practise self-responsible behaviours, and then demand self-responsibility from your team, delegate work, facilitate self-organization and lead with broad directives. This means that employees can take charge and take care of customers quickly and efficiently. Client-focus is all about your people making sure that valuable customers are satisfied, come back and want more.

4. **Success is what appeals to owners.** Owners expect growth and satisfactory return on their investment. Growth comes from satisfied customers who want to buy from you again and tell their friends about their positive experience. Returns on investment come from maximizing organizational capabilities, efficiency gains and innovations. Happy clients and satisfactory return on investment result in long-term value creation, which must be the goal of the business.

Executives who can find the right balance of these proprieties, along with seeing to the interests of major stakeholders, will create public value (Meynhardt and Gomez, 2013). Applying better management practices creates value, not only for company stakeholders but for society in general.

THE RULES-BASED MODE

Putting people first make the rules-based mode of operation a value-generating option, as professional, well-trained, experienced managers build structure and discipline that is needed to continue growing. In most industries and business situations, delivering consistent quality with high asset utilization at reasonable cost is the only way to gain the customer's trust. The rules-based mode needs to create an environment that provides management with necessary information and control, while simultaneously allowing people to perform at their peak. The right balance between rules and people drives the creation of customer value, in line with an exploitation-type business model.

In a stable environment, where power and knowledge are concentrated with a strong manager at the top, traditional management and institutional control dominate (Figure 31). The thinking and doing are separated, which justifies traditional, bureaucratic control that can be successful.

Traditional management practices promote direct control by managers through the application of narrow performance targets. The thinking by executives and managers is that desired behaviours can be shaped with incentives, with results that reinforce corporate strategy. Interactions between managers and employees focus on disseminating strategy and driving performance. Decisions are made by leaders and narrow performance targets intended to encourage people to focus their efforts on value-adding tasks.

Traditional systems consist of rules, specialized jobs and hierarchies designed to deliver predetermined outcomes. Rules and procedures support leaders' power to facilitate the assignment of resources, allocation of tasks, coordination of activities and assessment of performance. Bureaucracy governs the assignment and mobilization of resources.

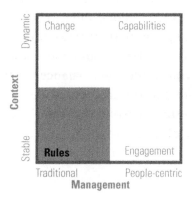

FIGURE 31: RULES-BASED MODE

Implementation of rules-based management techniques at the creativity stage builds a stable organizational platform. For example, imagine flying an airplane. No passenger would want the pilot to become creative and innovative in his job. The expectation is that he follows clear and precise standard procedures for taking off, flying and landing. Yet, in an emergency, passengers expect the pilot to apply his knowledge, gained from thousands of flight hours, to respond to the problem and land the plane safely. Standardized processes and procedures are effective if the situation is stable, but when an unexpected situation emerges, creativity and speed are necessary.

A stable control platform is in most companies a prerequisite for higher organizational agility. Without a solid foundation, with basic control and feedback routines, growing companies can lose control. As we've noted, the average life span of a start-up is about five years. A start-up may not go out of business, but the founders find themselves working harder and making less, which leads to a shakeup, with a new professional management team installed, or a merger or purchase by a third party. Consequently, companies can and should blend the rules-based mode with other approaches, as the situation requires, to build a stable platform to support future growth.

There are times when leaders want to do something that may be impossible, or even unethical or illegal. When this happens, control procedures put a constraint on command authority to prevent harmful actions. Hard work is necessary when leaders know an important task needs to get done and can be done. They will issue direct commands to get important tasks completed with the constraints of the control system. Command authority needs control procedures that achieve the right balance, as the foundation for future growth. Both control procedures and command authority are necessary, sometimes beyond the traditional control mode, to find the right blend of the two.

BUILDING DIRECTION CAPABILITIES

The inner game is the technique that enables people to perform at their peak and learn quickly. Application of inner-game principles helps create an environment that enables people to enter a state of flow. This drives performance and facilitates learning, both of which are needed to continue along the growth track.

THE INNER GAME

Executives play the inner game to cope with the challenges of the outer game. They make decisions requiring understanding, thinking, acting, engaging and adhering. They accept responsibility for decisions and are accountable for the results. Motivation for executives comes from a combination of individual responsibility and the opportunities and systems offered by the institution. The underlying features of the inner game are awareness, choice, trust and focus of attention.

Awareness, choice and trust help people focus their attention on what counts. The result is flow, with peak learning, performance and creativity. When employees operate in a state of flow, work becomes enjoyable and easy, as well as productive. Think of it as similar to when an athlete gets into the 'zone' and everything works. Flow shifts control over daily activities to the learner and redefines the role of the leader as that of coach instead of manager.

Awareness involves having access to data on what is happening, and then learning by translating observed data into information without making a judgement about it. It is about having a clear understanding of present conditions that might be relevant to deciding. Non-judgemental awareness is difficult because it requires having control over internal bias. However, it is the best way to learn and arrive at the most effective decision.

Choice is the prerequisite for responsibility. Freedom of choice allows managers to take charge and quickly take decisive action. Choice requires self-determination and self-responsibility, whereas rules that restrict choice are determined outside the manager's control. Managers are continuously confronted with the conflict of determining their own course of action or enforcing rules imposed by the organization. It is important to note that there is no freedom of choice if the individual cannot say 'No, there is a better way.' Creating an environment where people have adequate freedom of choice requires a delicate balance between self-determination and rules.

Trust generates speed and organizational agility. It is the cheapest leadership concept ever conceived and the foundation for every business transaction. A large body of research shows that trust is the single most critical factor in knowledge sharing and decision-making. We are talking about trust in yourself and in others you interact with. With trust, there is no need for any antagonistic renegotiation of contracts when conditions change. Opposing parties understand the situation and accept that the other side of the table is not attempting to gain an unfair advantage. Leaders have the choice between trust and mistrust or self-responsibility and outside control. It is common knowledge that trust must be earned and can easily be lost. The best way to earn trust is by delivering on promises. Managers must be fair, say what they are going to do, do what they say and then demonstrate respect for whomever they are engaging with.

Focus refers to self-initiated attention to what matters most. Focus of attention is a conscious act of concentration on a specific task that requires energy. The challenge is to block outside interferences, to maintain focus on key tasks. Too many times, we have seen well-meaning managers implement well-intentioned processes intended to solve a problem, leading to unexpected consequences. Unfortunately, many sincere managerial actions cause people to focus attention and energy on non-value-adding activities that degrade performance rather than enhance it. Managers must make a value choice between promoting self-initiated focus of attention tasks that add long-term benefit and short-term goal attainment or problem-solving. Sometimes, the short-term cure can be worse than the disease in the long run.

REACH FLOW MORE OFTEN

Solving the crisis of leadership relies on the executive's ability to play the inner game. The principle of the inner game defines the most important concepts and techniques that promote flow, which helps individuals learn and perform at their peak. Flow results in the organization performing better, which drives continued growth.

As we have been saying, flow is a concept that is related to the inner game. In that personal zone, a person performing a task becomes immersed in the moment, has energized focus, becomes fully engaged and feels satisfaction in completing the activity. Figure 32 illustrates this defining moment — the 'flow zone' — which is bounded on either side by boredom and anxiety.

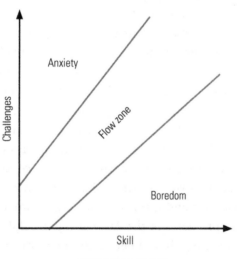

FIGURE 32: FLOW

Csikszentmihalyi (1990), who coined the term, described the phenomenon in this way:

"Flow also happens when a person's skills are fully involved in overcoming a challenge that is just about manageable, so it acts as a magnet for learning new skills and increasing challenges. If challenges are too low, one gets back to flow by increasing them. If challenges are too great, one can return to the flow state by learning new skills... The best moments in our lives are not the passive, receptive, relaxing times... The best moments usually occur if a person's body or mind is stretched to its limits in a voluntary effort to accomplish something difficult and worthwhile."

Flow is that sweet zone between boring tasks and extra challenging tasks that create anxiety.

Achieving flow is a defining moment. It is when the mind switches from the material world (matter) to the quantum world (energy). Flow is being *in the here and now,* and the past and future collapse into the present. It is where time is infinite and eternal, and space has unlimited dimensions. To reach flow, we need to leave the physical world — to step outside our body — to become a *self,* with infinite possibilities. In this state people find and use their true potential. Reaching the state of flow in the here and now requires practice. As we have described, those of us who participate in sports experience flow when they enter the 'zone,' when the game becomes easy and everything works effortlessly. Practising techniques to sharpen awareness and focus of attention helps people get there.

Flow occurs when people mentally switch from the beta state (the thinking mind) to the alpha state (the relaxed and creative mind). Most of the day, our brains are governed by the frequency of beta waves. We are awake and our senses are aware of current conditions that we react to. At times, we switch to the alpha state, during which we are quiet, relaxed, creative and intuitive, with minimum active thinking and analysing the problems of the day. During the alpha state, people are essentially dreaming. In the beta state they focus on the current conditions or problems to be solved in their immediate environment. In the alpha state the mental focus is on us, the inner self.

Creating the environment that helps people reach creative flow more often is one of the goals of the managers for the first stage transition. Creating this space starts with the manager and is intended to spread across the organization.

Here are several questions for you to answer on solving the leadership crisis:

- Do you have a crisis of leadership?
- If so, how do you solve it?
- What is your organization's dominant operating mode? Are you satisfied with the results?
- If the answer is no, what mode would be more effective?
- Do the rules and procedures that provide direction adequately balance the need for control with the need for creativity?
- Are your people performing at their peak or are they being held back by burdensome rules and procedures?
- How does your organization create the environment that enables the inner game and flow?
- What can you do to create or expand upon an environment that enables the inner game and flow?
- What can you do to transition to or build on a people-first style of management?

Ahead, Chapter 14 describes how to transition to the delegation growth stage by implementing people-centric management techniques.

PEOPLE FIRST

Direction solves the leadership crisis. The transition from creativity to direction puts people first and calls for careful balance between control and creativity. The inner game and flow are the means to enable people to perform at their peak and solve the tension between people-first management and direction.

KEY CHAPTER IDEAS

- Giving people top priority enables them to utilize their skills.
- The rules-based management mode addresses the leadership crisis by providing direction to employees.
- The inner game enables people to perform at their peak and learn.
- Flow is the mental state that people experience when they perform at their peak.

ACTION AGENDA

- Take charge as a leader. Make people your first priority.
- Review your organization's directive capabilities.
- Activate a rules-based management mode.
- Introduce or expand upon people-centric management techniques to help people to play the inner game and achieve a state of flow.

FURTHER READING

Managerial perspective on putting people first:
Michel, L (2020). *People-Centric Management: How Managers Use Four Levers to Bring Out the Greatness of Others.* London: LID Publishing.
Nold, H (2018). *Dynamic Capabilities for People-Centric Management in Turbulent Times.* In M F Brandebo & A Alvinus (Eds.), *Dark Side of Organizational Behavior and Leadership (pp. 109-124).* London: IntechOpen.

Managerial perspective on the inner game techniques:
Michel, L (2021). *Agile by Choice: How You Can Make the Shift to Establish Leadership Everywhere.* London: LID Publishing.

Expert perspective on rules-based management and the inner game:
Michel, L (2021). *Diagnostic Mentoring: How to Transform the Way We Manage.* London: LID Publishing.

Related research on the rules-based mode:
Michel, L; Anzengruber, J; Wolfe, M; and Hixson, N (2018). Under What Conditions do Rules-Based and Capabilities-based Management Modes Dominate? *Special Issue Risks in Financial and Real Estate Markets Journal,* 6(32).

CHAPTER 14

PEOPLE-CENTRIC MANAGEMENT

The second transition is the move from the direction stage to the delegation stage. Delegation helps overcome the crisis of autonomy, which emerges as the key barrier that restricts growth to the next level. The task at this point is to adapt people-centric management techniques, using the Leadership Scorecard as a guide, to delegate power and decision-making authority throughout decentralized units.

Chapter 14 describes how executives can facilitate the transition from the direction growth stage to the delegation stage by employing people-centric management concepts.

SOLVING THE CRISIS OF AUTONOMY

Moving from a functional structure in the rules-based mode of operation to a decentralized company, where key decision-making authority is distributed throughout the organization, means adopting a people-centric, engagement-based management mode. People-centric management concepts are built around self-responsibility, teamwork, focus of attention and developing individual capabilities. This is how managers delegate responsibility and accountability, engage employees, coordinate work, mobilize the energy and enable change.

PEOPLE-CENTRIC MANAGEMENT

Management modes (Figure 33) group general managerial styles into four categories, with different capabilities, depending on the context or general environment in which the organization operates. People-centric principles are the primary features of better management. People-centric techniques create an environment that offers knowledge workers the opportunity to be creative and perform at their best.

To solve the crisis of autonomy of functional managers, established in the direction phase, adopt better management techniques. These new techniques set people-centric management principles as the pre-condition for a decentralized organization with delegated responsibility. People-centric management differentiates from traditional management through a choice of four levers as the dominant management style.

FIGURE 33: PEOPLE-CENTRIC MANAGEMENT

A fundamental trait of traditional management is that knowledge is concentrated at the top of the organization. This basic assumption works fine in a stable environment with a rules-based mode of operating. Conversely, people-centric management principles assume that key knowledge is distributed through the organization, at various levels. Techniques used to access this distributed body of knowledge, to make better decisions or for innovation, dominate the mode of operating. Figure 34 identifies the four levers that define the management response that makes up the dominant management mode. The techniques or practices used as levers are all based on fundamental beliefs about human nature. There are no absolutes in the sense of right way or wrong way, or positive or negative. The levers exist in every organization on a sliding scale that approximates the degree to which traditional management techniques and people-centric techniques are applied. Every organization has unique characteristics developed over time, depending on the operating environment, the culture and other forces that drive the decision-making process.

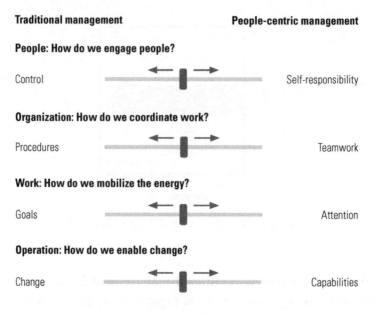

FIGURE 34: FOUR MANAGEMENT LEVERS

Each of the above levers warrants an entire volume of relevant managerial content. Much has been written about them, and many of the principles have been explored in our other books. There is not enough space here to repeat all of this. Instead, what follows is a short-version synopsis of what these principles mean.

THE PEOPLE LEVER

Control assumes that only managers have the skills and knowledge to know what and how things need to get done. As such, they tell people what to do and how to do it, and then implement performance measurement procedures to track whether it has been done.

Self-responsibility assumes that people can think, decide and act on their own. Self-responsible people have adequate knowledge to make informed decisions, are engaged, and are willing to be held accountable for their decisions. This level of freedom allows people throughout the organization, including managers, to unlock their creativity, talent and potential.

THE ORGANIZATION LEVER

Procedures are detailed routines that prescribe how a specific task needs to be performed. The fundamental belief is that people cannot, or should not, think for themselves, and must be told exactly what to do and how to do it. This increases predictability, efficiency, and the ability to reliably repeat tasks over and over, with little knowledge requirement.

Teamwork is the approach to getting work done that requires creativity and responsiveness in groups. It is needed when tasks require special or specific knowledge, and flexibility to made decisions. Effective teams are made up of diverse individuals with special knowledge, working in a trusting environment that facilitates knowledge sharing.

THE WORK LEVER

Goals refer to the attempt to force stringent alignment using detailed performance objectives and financial incentives that are paid out when people achieve specific targets. The basic assumption is that money is a primary motivational factor, rather than intrinsic rewards. The application of detailed performance objectives works well when tasks are simple and the environment never changes or is changing slowly.

Attention refers to people's ability to focus on the tasks that truly matter for them and add value to the business. The fundamental assumption is that intrinsic rewards — like the feeling of a job well done or peer recognition — is a more powerful motivator than money. Attention is a limited resource that requires careful nurturing by managers if it is to deliver full value.

THE OPERATION LEVER

Change is the process by which organizations adapt to alterations in the environment through one-time efforts. Change initiatives are a sort of replacement for management, giving poor managers cover by making it appear that they are acting. If one thing does not work, we will try something else. This approach works in a context that is relatively simple, and either unchanging or changing slowly.

Capabilities refers to management techniques that prove effective in dealing with a dynamic environment where opportunities and threats quickly emerge and demand a swift response. Effective response in such a dynamic environment requires that people apply their full talent, creativity and knowledge to address the challenges. The result is superior performance, to deal with an ever-changing environment.

In the ideal organization, the levers along the spectrum align vertically. In many, however, the levers are not aligned. This creates interferences that inhibit the organization's growth and performance. For example, if self-responsibility is on the right side of the lever, and goals is on the left side, there is a situation where management is saying one thing but doing another. Management loses credibility and the two levers neutralize each other, which degrades performance and growth. This misalignment must be resolved to achieve flow and maximize both individual and organizational performance.

THE ENGAGEMENT-BASED MODE

Engaging people is the answer to operating successfully in decentralized organizations with distributed decision-making and responsibility needed to continue growing. In a knowledge-driven industry that is stable, with little change, the engagement-based mode (Figure 35) dominates. People are tightly governed by traditional means, but with a people-centric management style that encourages creativity and teamwork. Rules and performance measures may apply to both individuals and teams.

People-centric management supports self-responsible employees in an environment that limits interferences and promotes focus of attention. People can focus their abilities on the issue or challenge of the moment, to come up with innovative solutions. Management aligns individual interests by promoting and instilling common visions, beliefs, boundaries and values. As Harvard Business School's Robert Simons (1995) put it, "In the absence of management action, self-interested behaviour at the expense of organizational goals is inevitable." Self-responsibility and focus of attention are balanced with hierarchical power and institutional bureaucracy in the engagement-based mode of operation.

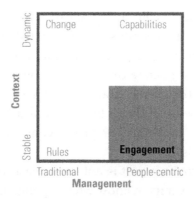

FIGURE 35: ENGAGEMENT-BASED MODE

Traditional systems suitable for a stable environment control information, provide direction, coordinate work and allocate resources. Power, hierarchy and bureaucracy tightly control and measure the results of what people do. Traditional control techniques can meet people-centric ends, provided there is a balance between the two with boundaries that do not restrict creativity or the flow of knowledge. Finding the right balance is a challenge for most managers, particularly traditionally trained MBAs.

The blend of traditional and people-centric management works in a stable environment but becomes restrictive in times of accelerated change, typical of the VUCA 21st century. Well-intended HR initiatives create a better work environment but typically fail to support an organization that competes in a dynamic market context. Too many such programmes take too long to develop and implement, while just scratching the surface of deeply rooted issues. They make HR managers and upper-level executives feel like they are doing something proactive, but the result is often the expenditure of large amounts of money and energy with little return.

Engagement requires management interaction with people throughout the organization. It is a mode where leaders must spend less time in their offices, staring at their laptops, and more time with the people who are engaged in a creative process or directly dealing with customers. Cultivating employee engagement is about helping people make sense of what they are asked to do. Managers must clearly and personally communicate what must be done and how that fits with the overall strategy. After that, managers must step back, allow the creative process to unfold and then support the results. They cannot assume that people know what is expected or what their role in the overall strategy is. Managers must personally help people make sense of things by communicating what is needed, why and how the individual or group contributes to advancing organizational goals.

Data gleaned from a report is not the same as onsite experience. A leader who really wants to know what is going on at the front line needs to be there, not cloistered away in his home office or hunched over his 'control' desktop. Spreadsheets, dashboards or performance measurement reports cannot replace personal interaction with people actually doing a job. Managers may have all the data at their fingertips but still lack a feel for what is happening or how the environment is changing.

People-centric management demands individualizing leadership, which is different from managing from the corner office. There is no leadership style that fits all situations or people. People-centric leaders interact regularly with those at all levels and attempt to meet the needs of every individual. Employees will appreciate the interaction and the effort, even if the attempt to meet their needs falls short. The relationship between leader and subordinate will strengthen regardless of the result. Hence, effective leadership comes in different styles for different people.

BUILDING DELEGATION CAPABILITIES

Management systems are the tools that allow professional managers to intervene when needed, to keep the organization on track. Systems provide essential information that is necessary to guide strategy, task implementation, shared beliefs and authority boundaries. Integrated systems allow managers to keep an eye on operations from a distance, which permits front-line workers to apply their problem-solving skills and creativity within predetermined boundaries.

INFORMATION

Information systems help managers and the team know what is going on with clarity. Information, sense-making and a shared understanding create responsiveness, which gives the organization the ability to identify valuable business opportunities or threats early (Figure 36). Speed, relevance and sensitivity are essential attributes for management systems to act as an early-warning system, so managers can take swift and effective action to take advantage of opportunities or respond to threats.

Help your team achieve clarity by answering the following questions:
- **Information.** What is going on? Is the team looking at the right (relevant) data?
- **Sense-making.** What does the information mean? Does it provide insight with sensitivity, for early warning?
- **Shared understanding.** What is the team's shared understanding? Do team members know what to do with information when they have it?
- **Responsiveness.** How does the team respond to client needs? Does the information stimulate swift and effective action?

If you are satisfied with the answers, then the information part of your Leadership Scorecard likely reflects responsiveness.

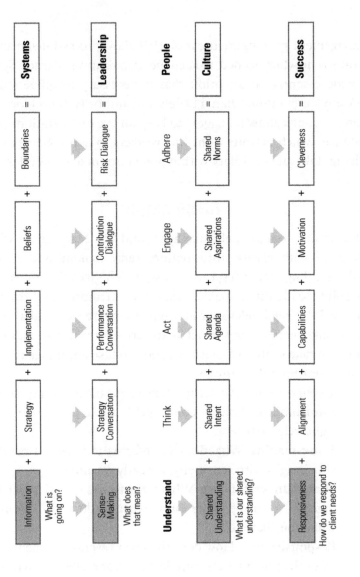

FIGURE 36: INFORMATION SYSTEMS

How do we know with clarity when and how to respond to events or issues? Awareness enables people to *understand*, and then engage with others who share a deep sense of purpose. Awareness becomes an essential key to managing in a complex environment.

Awareness is sensing by translating observed data into relevant information and assessing it objectively so that swift action can be taken. It is about having a clear understanding of the present, which helps guide effective action that shapes a positive future. Non-judgmental awareness is the best way to sense what is really happening. We have seen many experienced managers either fail to act, or take ineffective action, because their interpretation of information was influenced by preconceived notions or bias. It is important to note that more information is not necessarily better information. We have also seen executives become desensitized or overwhelmed, so that they overlook the important messages these signals contain.

Information followed by immediate feedback to people raises awareness of what is important. This feedback helps them understand what matters and focus on the issues at hand. Superior understanding requires that sensors are not muted by too much — or irrelevant — data, and that amplifiers work properly.

Information and feedback mechanisms connect every organizational unit and employee then pulls them under the umbrella of the organization. For example, performance information is reported to the management centre as part of individual accountability procedures, whereas directional feedback information moves to the periphery or front line of an organization. Managers and supervisors at the front line have the duty to inform employees about strategy and what their role is in the grand plan.

Figure 37 summarizes the differences between traditional and people-centric operating systems. Highly responsive systems tend to apply people-centric philosophies that enable people throughout the organization to know what is going on. Effective systems can help them make sense and answer the question 'What does that mean?' by translating data into information then transform that information into knowledge with meaning. Sense-making is the technique that managers use to help people find meaning. The culture of the organization helps to answer the question, 'What is our shared understanding?'

	Traditional	**People-centric**
Context	Knowledge at the top	Distributed knowledge
Information	Executive information, extensive performance measurement	Diagnostic information, few metrics, instant feedback
Sense-making	Rigorous routines to tell people what to do	Interactive sense-making to find purpose
Shared understanding	Individual awareness, executive control	Collective awareness, shared understanding
Responsiveness	Reaction to problems	Fulfil customer expectations

FIGURE 37: THE OPERATING SYSTEM TO UNDERSTAND

As summarized in Figure 37, traditional information systems that emphasize command and control assume that knowledge is at the top of the organizational hierarchy. Executive information systems ensure that decisions are made based on data. Detailed performance information processes provide evaluative data that becomes the basis for essential feedback on necessary corrective action. Rigorous performance routines ensure that people know what they are supposed to do and how well they are doing. The result is a culture based on executive control.

Dynamic information systems support self-responsible people with knowledge that is distributed throughout the organization. Information has a diagnostic quality that highlights critical functions. Few but targeted metrics offer feedback to people working on the front line. In dynamic systems, managers focus on interactions among employees and with the external environment, and help people interpret what is happening to make sense of it. Collective awareness throughout the organization creates a culture with a shared understanding and purpose at its roots.

The application of people-centric management principles, agile qualities and dynamic operating systems helps resolve the tension between complexity and clarity. Resolving this natural tension comes from managers helping people at work understand with clarity and raise awareness of actions that matter. Purpose is the food that helps self-responsible people grow and become personally engaged. With a strong sense of purpose, they search for opportunities to grow and contribute, despite the complexity of work. A strong sense of purpose gives employees meaning and motivation to become highly engaged.

Here is your checklist:

Signs of ineffective information systems. When your organization:

- Ignores or responds slowly to customer needs, overlooks early warning signals, disregards information and feedback, allows bias or preconceived ideas to shape decisions, makes wrong decisions using out-of-date or irrelevant information, acts passively or reactively.

Signs of mastery on how to know with clarity.

When your organization:

- Is readily aware of customer needs, swiftly responds to internal and external challenges, is reliable, creates shared meaning and purpose, enables objectively informed decisions based on timely and relevant information, has an early-warning system to detect changes in the environment, creates broad awareness, learns quickly and converts new lessons to positive action, establishes a shared agenda.

STRATEGY

The strategy component of systems helps all individuals in the organization move in one direction. One of the primary objectives for developing strategic plans is alignment. Everyone in the organization, key players in the supply chain or other external players who are critical for success should have a clear understanding of the strategic objectives, how the strategy is being implemented, and what their role is. Each person should understand how daily decisions impact the strategic plan, so they can evaluate various options and choose the one that best promotes the strategy. Strategic objectives, strategy conversation and shared intent help establish alignment as the capability needed to meet strategic goals that fuel growth. Figure 38 illustrates the relationship between these four components and systems.

Engage your team, which may include supply chain members or others external to the organization, to move in one direction by answering the following questions:

- **Strategy.** What game are we playing? Do all key players have a clear understanding of the strategic goals and objectives?
- **Strategy conversation.** Why are we going there? What have we learned? Do all key players have a clear understanding of their role, and what decisions support the strategic goals?
- **Shared intent.** What is our shared intent? Do all key players support the plan and are they fully engaged in the strategic plan's success?
- **Alignment.** Do the strategy and the organization fit? Does the strategic plan build on existing core capabilities or leverage them to explore new opportunities?

If you are satisfied with the answers, then the strategy part of the Leadership Scorecard suggests that you have alignment from all key participants. Broad alignment means that individuals will make decisions that support the strategy and increase the probability of successfully meeting strategic goals.

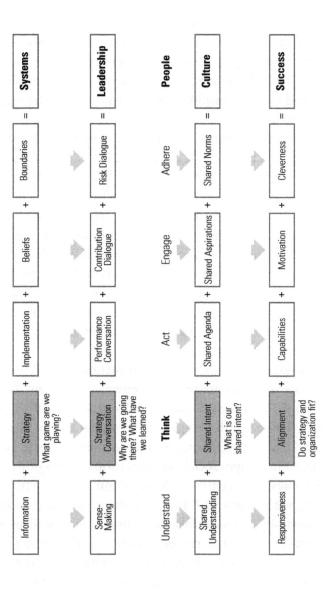

FIGURE 38: STRATEGY SYSTEMS

The question now becomes *how* can leaders get everyone moving in one direction. The answer is freedom of choice. Managers at all levels must engage with key people inside and outside of the organization to develop shared intent. Then, people must make a conscious decision to support the strategic goals and shape their decisions accordingly. They must feely choose to support the plans and modify their *thinking* to assume responsibility. Freedom of choice and self-responsibility are needed to move the organization in one direction.

Choice is the prerequisite for self-responsibility. However, rules and procedures that provide direction and freedom of choice do not naturally correspond. Self-responsibility gives people the choice to take charge and move in the desired direction or not. Choice implies self-determination, where individuals set their own boundaries. Conversely, rules and procedures are set by managers and enforced from the top. In an ambiguous environment, people need freedom of choice to select the action that best serves the customer and reinforces the company's strategic goals. Managers must find a balance between the natural urge to control people through rules and the people-centric approach of giving self-responsible individuals freedom of choice in the VUCA world.

Knowledge workers have a set of mental maps that help them make sense of situations and make effective decisions. The benefits for an organization come not only from individual thinking, but also from collective thinking. The old saying 'two brains are better than one' is very true. Managers should work to create an environment that encourages socialization in formal teams or work groups, or informally, during the workday or after hours. The activity of engaging with others with the same shared intent gives employees an opportunity to create meaning, stimulates new ideas and helps people make a deliberate choice to move together in one direction.

Creating an environment that encourages all the individual brains to focus on the same thing, so that the collective brain thinks of new ideas that have meaning, requires the conventionally trained manager to understand the differences between traditional and people-centric philosophies. Figure 39 summarizes these differences. People-centric environments give employees freedom of choice and direction, which enables moving together in one direction, and aligning, so their work reinforces corporate strategy and supports one another. Executives in a VUCA environment must be agile when developing and implementing strategies. An important part of being able to adjust and quickly move is having an effective feedback mechanism. Conducting frequent and meaningful dialogue with people helps inform key players about the strategy and their role in the game. An agile strategy leads to a shared intent at scale, which becomes particularly important when conditions change unexpectedly.

	Traditional	People-centric
Context	Strategy as power	Strategy as learning
Strategy	Executive retreat, planning as a strategy process, separated from implementation	Strategy as an integrated thought and action model, a creative learning process for every team
Strategy conversation	One-directional messaging	Interactive strategy conversations
Shared intent	Choice restricted to executives, executive decisions, individual intent	Team contributions, shared intent
Alignment	Scattered energy	Aligned energy with an attractive offering

FIGURE 39: THE OPERATING SYSTEM TO THINK

Traditional strategy development processes support executive thinking to provide clarity about the strategy and goals. Executive retreats for strategy and planning are commonly used to facilitate the sharing of ideas and set direction with the leadership team. Leaders then communicate strategic direction throughout the organizationby breaking the strategy down into the unit goals with individual performance measures intended to help everyone achieve those goals. The result is a culture based on executive control and power through hierarchy. These processes work fine when the environment is stable, with little change, but become highly detrimental when the rate of change increases.

Traditional strategy development and implementation requires stability to be effective. The rational process to develop strategy, and then move people in one direction, assumes that the environment remains stable for some time. This is rarely the case in the VUCA 21st century. The result is that strategies and initiatives are abandoned so frequently that they appear to reflect a lack of attention. The opportunities or threats emerge so quickly from different directions that the time- and resource-consuming linear processes cannot keep up. The result is that employees are not able to adapt and align their actions or decisions to advance the company. Confusion, poor morale and loss of engagement are frequently the unintended result, which begins a destructive cycle. It is very difficult for people to know where the organization is heading when things keep changing, so they begin to lose heart and commitment.

Dynamic strategy systems are needed in the VUCA environment, to enable critical thinking and release innovation. Strategy development and implementation are part of a continuous learning process. Leaders must interact on a personal level and offer strategic insights to people throughout the organization. This continuous learning process, driven by leaders who truly engage with people, creates a culture based on a shared intent. When unexpected events occur that disrupt existing strategic initiatives, it is likely that someone senses it and has an answer. Dynamic strategy systems connect people throughout the organization so that creative ideas swiftly reach key decision-makers who can convert the idea into action.

People-centric management principles power dynamic strategy systems that help resolve the tension between ambiguity and need for direction. Resolution of this tension comes from providing freedom of choice to self-responsible people with delegated responsibility. Relationships connect people with knowledge needed to take advantage of valuable opportunities to swiftly respond to threats and then align everyone in an ambiguous environment.

Here is your checklist:

Signs of ineffective strategy systems. When your organization:

- Has missed opportunities, reacts slowly to threats, loses business, has shareholders leave, lacks clarity and direction, has disengaged employees, wastes resources.

Signs that effective strategy systems promote alignment. When your organization:

- Leverages core competencies to explore new opportunities, swiftly responds to threats, wins new clients, attracts the right talent, accumulates capital, has employees who are focused and engaged, aligns resources to maximize returns, releases productive energy, establishes shared intent.

IMPLEMENTATION

Implementation systems help executives mobilize the inherent energy of the team. Effective implementation is driven by frequent and personalized performance conversations with people at all levels. These conversations give people clarity on what their role is and how they are doing to support strategic goals. The result is a shared agenda that maximizes the capabilities of individuals, which drives the organization to deliver on expectations (Figure 40).

Engage your team to mobilize the energy by answering the following questions:

- **Implementation.** How does the team succeed? Is the team focused on the right drivers of success?
- **Performance conversation.** Is the team on track? How is the team doing? What does the teem need to do? What should you do next to help the team continue supporting the strategy?
- **Shared agenda.** Does the team get the right things done? Is everyone on the team focused on the key drivers of the strategy?
- **Capabilities.** Does the team have the right capabilities to support the strategy? Are the team's core capabilities being used effectively?

If you are satisfied with the answers, then the implementation component of systems on your Leadership Scorecard suggests that you are developing the right system capabilities for a VUCA world.

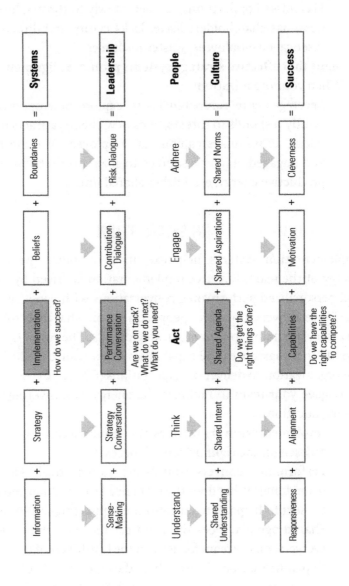

FIGURE 40: IMPLEMENTATION SYSTEMS

Having the right implementation capabilities is good but mobilizing them into focused action requires that one more question be answered. How do we mobilize resources to support implementation? Trust is a prerequisite for self-responsible people in self-organized organizations. Leaders must have trust in teams that organize themselves, and teams must trust their own expertise and instincts in an uncertain environment. Decisions must be made with less-than-perfect information, which introduces risk into every decision and action. Trust in oneself and others becomes the essential quality needed to cope with high uncertainty.

Trust generates speed in the decision-making process and gives organizations agile qualities necessary to react to unexpected events, quickly and effectively. Trust is the most basic management concept ever to exist and is the foundation for every business transaction. As we said earlier, with trust there is no need for renegotiation of contracts when conditions change, and it makes revising prior agreements relatively painless. Managers make a conscious decision to choose between trust and mistrust when dealing with people, both inside and outside of the organization. This is largely shaped by the manager's view of human nature, per McGregor's Theory X and Theory Y. The manager's basic beliefs about humanity determine whether he or she sees people as self-responsible or needing to be tightly control from above. However, trust must be earned. The best way to earn it is by delivering on promises. Again, as we have noted, that means managers must say what they do, do what the say and, ultimately, treat employees fairly and respectfully.

Building trust provides the support that people need to act with focus and energy. As such, we explore some of the options for how managers can help people collaborate by sharing their unique knowledge and skills. Then, we identify and suggest implementation systems that bundle and focus energies at scale, throughout the organization.

Uncertainty makes it difficult to convert opportunities into value-adding propositions. Risks and obstacles are everywhere. People-centric management is based on trust. Trust mobilizes the energy of people who have confidence in their capabilities and the ability of collaborators to overcome uncertainties and obstacles to create value.

Implementation systems facilitate the allocation, coordination and engagement of people to support others and gain support from each other to get work done. Trust becomes the essential ingredient for effective implementation systems.

The task for managers is to mobilize the collective energy of the group to get things done. People put their energy into tasks that are meaningful, and those they care about. Meaningful action requires that people be given the opportunity to apply their special knowledge and expertise with management support that balances freedom with necessary constraints. Dynamic operating systems are powered by people's trust in their own capabilities, and their trust in others.

The operating system needed to enable the organization to act swiftly connects all organizational units through conversations about their performance. A rich communication process promotes constructive dialogue that encourages effective collaboration. These processes make management structures scalable. This means that organizations with rich communication processes can grow without adding more expensive and complex infrastructure. This meaningful communication creates a culture with a shared agenda. Figure 41 summarizes the differences between traditional management practices and people-centric practices.

	Traditional	People-centric
Context	Bureaucracy	Self-organization
Implementation	Plans and budgets, performance reports	Resource allocation on demand, flexible targets, agile implementation, business reviews
Performance conversation	Performance target setting and reviews	Interactive performance conversations
Shared agenda	Trust in processes, individual agenda	Team contributions, shared agenda
Capabilities	Generic capabilities	The right capabilities in place

FIGURE 41: THE OPERATING SYSTEM TO ACT

Traditional implementation systems get things done through bureaucratic processes that work well in highly predictable environments. Plans, budgets and performance management techniques facilitate target setting and business reviews. These are the tools traditional managers use to coordinate work.

Dynamic systems for implementation enable action in self-organized teams when uncertainty is high. Resources are allocated to targeted initiatives on demand, to maximize returns. Plans become flexible and decentralized business reviews track progress to support implementation and make mid-stream adjustments as needed. Leaders interactively challenge teams. Together, these practices lead to a culture with a shared agenda that facilitates the collaboration.

People-centric principles, agile practices and dynamic systems resolve the tension between uncertainty and energy. The key is trusting people and their ability to act on their own. Collaboration in and among self-organized teams gives the organization the ability to act quickly, despite uncertainty.

Here is your checklist:

Signs of ineffective implementation systems. When your organization:

- Is slow to respond, demands constant change initiatives, stalls, or frequently changes direction, has unclear responsibilities and accountability, drives a political agenda, has bureaucracy that dominates.

Signs of mastery on how to mobilize the energy. When your organization:

- Gets things done quickly, leverages core competencies to create competitive advantage, is stable and focused despite uncertainty and external pressure, stays on track, implements strategy quickly and effectively, performs well, uses resources effectively, creates a shared agenda.

BELIEFS AND BOUNDARIES

Beliefs and boundary systems (Figure 42) help you and your team establish and maintain focus. Beliefs combined with contribution dialogue and shared aspirations facilitate motivation to maintain focus on things that matter. Boundaries combined with risk dialogue and shared norms help establish cleverness as an entrepreneurial capability needed for growth.

Engage your team to establish and maintain the focus and develop internal entrepreneurs by answering the following questions:

- **Beliefs and boundaries.** What are our personal and organizational ambitions? Are they widely shared? Where are the limits of authority? Do the limits restrict actions that could improve response time or provide adequate freedom for people to take initiative?
- **Contribution and risk dialogues.** Do people have a firm grasp of their role and how they can contribute to meeting organizational goals? What level of risk can we tolerate? What are the risks? Does management encourage and support reasonable risk taking, or discourage it with penalties or punitive action?
- **Shared aspirations and norms.** Do people share a strong sense of purpose? Is the organizational purpose socially stimulating or a rallying objective that generates emotion? What gets you ahead? Do people understand which actions earn recognition and possible promotion?
- **Motivation and cleverness.** Are people highly motivated to perform at their peak? Do they regularly go above and beyond the call of duty? Do we use the entire playing field to explore new ideas or opportunities? Does the environment encourage or discourage individuality and experimentation?

If you are satisfied with your answers, then the beliefs and boundaries part of your Leadership Scorecard likely are motivating people and establish cleverness.

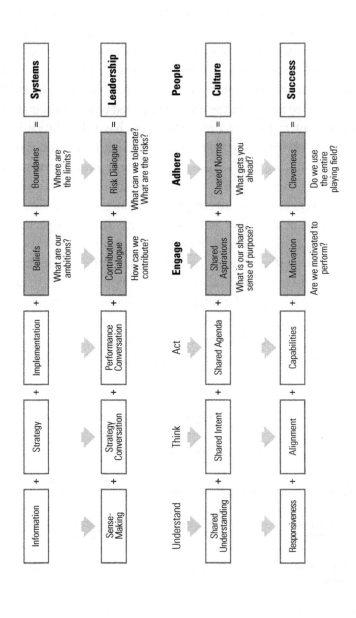

FIGURE 42: BELIEFS AND BOUNDARY SYSTEMS

How do we maintain focus? Being able to focus attention is an essential skill for people to learn, which allows them to perform at their peak. Attentive and focused people are better at dealing with a fast-changing environment. They are more able to sense danger, and then sort through the various options and choose the best one. Focus enables self-initiated attention on what matters most. It is a purposeful act of concentration that requires energy. The challenge for people is to maintain the energy required to focus their attention on important tasks over time. Managers have the choice between creating an environment that promotes self-initiated focus of attention or attempting to drive goal achievement with rewards or force. Additionally, they must be very aware of unintended consequences of interferences from interruptions, changes in orders, unclear instructions, or any other action or inaction that disrupts focus.

The operating system to engage and keep people at work on their tasks (Figure 43) is defined by beliefs and boundaries that enable them to maintain focus on their search for opportunities to excel and be recognized. Figure 43 contrasts the difference between traditional approaches that force people to engage and adhere, using directed targets, and the people-centric approach, based on using intrinsic motivators on the assumption that people are self-responsible.

	Targets	Attention
Context	Performance objectives	Focus of attention
Beliefs and boundaries	Vision, mission, performance objectives	Beliefs and boundaries (values as verbs)
Contribution and risk dialogues	Management by objectives	Interactive contribution dialogue, risk dialogue
Shared aspirations and norms	Individual incentives for goal achievement	Shared aspirations and norms
Motivation and cleverness	Leadership interaction and systems controls	Values and self-responsibility

FIGURE 43: THE OPERATING SYSTEM TO ENGAGE AND ADHERE

Widely shared beliefs link people to organizational vision, values and meaning to help them find a higher purpose in their activities. Accepted norms of behaviour and attire prompt them to accept standards and comply with governance. Beliefs and boundaries set the framework for the actions that are within or outside the limits of the individual's space. The nature of the challenges the organization has decided to tackle determines much of the system design, how it is used and the effectiveness of these controls, whether traditional or people-centric. This is why beliefs and boundary systems must be uniquely designed to fit your specific situation, in support of people-centric management techniques. As with a good car, the brakes and the engine must be suitable for road conditions and the nature of your intended trip. Clearly, the family SUV used by mom and pop to take the kids to football practice is very different from a high-performance Formula One race car. Organizations are no different.

Traditional approaches to defining beliefs and boundaries attempt to focus people's attention through detailed targets that work well when knowledge is assumed to be at the top of the org chart. Vision, mission and goals set by senior executives establish performance targets and offer clarity on what is in and out of scope. Rigorous management by objectives is intended to provide motivation and direction for employees. Incentive plans attempt to encourage people to stick to their targets and respond like rabbits to carrots.

Dynamic beliefs and boundary systems that help people focus their attention promote internally generated engagement and adherence to aspirations and accepted norms. This becomes essential in an environment where knowledge and decision-making authority are distributed throughout the organization. In this distributed environment, managers must continuously interact and engage in dialogue with people on their role and contribution, along with discussing the acceptable risks. Shared aspirations and norms create a strong culture at scale that becomes resilient and flexible. People engaged in direct interaction with stakeholders become able to react to threats quickly and take advantage of opportunities when they arise.

Agile techniques and dynamic systems help resolve the tension between volatility and focus by applying people-centric management principles in a dynamic environment. The resolution of this tension comes from helping people focus their attention on what matters most. Learning is the catalyst for people, and the organization at scale, to stick to chosen opportunities, despite the challenges of higher volatility.

Here is your checklist:

Signs of ineffective beliefs and boundary systems.

When your organization:

- Is inflexible and fights change, blocks ideas from getting to decision-makers, has overloaded leaders who spend their day just putting out fires, lacks guidance so that people are unclear what their role is, has employees who hide and avoid getting involved, waits for the next big thing instead of creating the next big thing.
- Lacks awareness of risks, puts reputation at risk with ventures with low probability of success, stifles knowledge sharing and motivation by creating fear among employees, has a leadership vacuum where managers have a *laisse fare* attitude and avoid confrontation, routinely changes standards and expectations.

Signs of mastery of how to maintain the focus.

When your organization:

- Is agile and quickly responds to unexpected developments, senses, and anticipates change to get ahead of it, continuously develops new ways of operating, encourages employees to self-organize to address issues, is highly motivated, has clear standards and shared aspirations.
- Stretches the boundaries so people have adequate freedom to act, has entrepreneurial spirit, protects, and builds on competitive advantage, takes reasonable risks, behaves entrepreneurially, shares standards and norms.

Here are important questions for you to consider on solving the autonomy crisis:

- How do you solve the crisis of autonomy?
- What is your organization's delegation capacity?
- Are key decisions made at the top or distributed throughout the organization?
- Do you have open channels of communication across the business and are they being used effectively?

- What are your answers on the Leadership Scorecard questions?
- Do people have a clear understanding of their role and how they can contribute to meeting organizational goals?
- Are your people motivated by a higher sense of purpose or are they there just to get a paycheck?
- How does your organization meet the standards of management systems?
- What can you do to succeed with the transition to applying people-centric management techniques?

Next up, Chapter 15 describes how to transition from the delegation stage to the coordination stage, and how to overcome the crisis of control with a dynamic operating system.

PEOPLE-CENTRIC MANAGEMENT

Delegation solves the crisis of autonomy, which emerges during the direction stage of growth. Effective transition from the direction state to the delegation state requires the application of people-centric and engagement-based management principles. Improved management systems solve the tension between people-centric capabilities and the need for control.

KEY CHAPTER IDEAS

- People-centric management principles allow people to take charge.
- The engagement-based mode resolves the crisis of autonomy.
- People-centric management enables delegated decision-making and leadership.

ACTION AGENDA

- Delegate responsibility through the application of people-centric management techniques.
- Review your organization's delegation capabilities.
- Assess the Leadership Scorecard questions with your team.
- Activate an engagement-based management mode.
- Manage decentralized organizations through five management systems.

FURTHER READING

Managerial perspective on people-centric management:
Michel, L (2020). *People-Centric Management: How Managers Use Four Levers to Bring Out the Greatness of Others.* London: LID Publishing.

Expert perspective on management systems:
Michel, L (2021). *Diagnostic Mentoring: How to Transform the Way We Manage.* London: LID Publishing.

Related research on the engagement-based mode:
Michel, L; Anzengruber, J; Wolfe, M; and Hixson, N (2018). Under What Conditions do Rules-Based and Capabilities-based Management Modes Dominate? *Special Issue Risks in Financial and Real Estate Markets Journal,* 6(32).

DYNAMIC OPERATIONS

The third transition is the move from the delegation stage to the coordination stage of growth. The crisis of control emerges at the delegation stage, which inhibits continued growth to the coordination state. The task at this point is to adopt a change-based mode of operation guided by the components of the Leadership Scorecard. Developing dynamic capabilities becomes essential to successfully support managers with delegated responsibility and accountability of segment-type units.

Chapter 15 describes how to transition to the coordination stage by developing diagnostic systems, interactive leadership, shared culture and clearly defined measures of success.

SOLVING THE CRISIS OF CONTROL

Transitioning from a decentralized to a segmented organization requires change-based management supported by a dynamic operating system. Dynamic systems are the most effective choices for an emergent, self-organized and delegated environment. Armed with these tools, managers are able to coordinate activities through interactive leadership and a shared culture that generates intangible value.

DYNAMIC OPERATING SYSTEM

The different management modes (Figure 44) describe bundles of managerial principles and capabilities that characterize operations in stable or dynamic environments. Dynamic operating systems are a feature of better management. Such systems enable the organization to deal with a VUCA environment and limit the risks by preventing people from taking short-cuts, which undermine the operating system and create an infected culture.

To solve the crisis of control of decentralized units, better management principles require a dynamic operating system as the pre-condition for the coordination of segment organizations. Dynamic operating systems differentiate from traditional systems that work in a stable context through a choice of four levers.

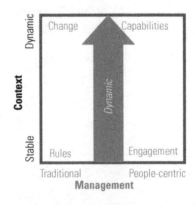

FIGURE 44: DYNAMIC OPERATING SYSTEM

Like the people-centric levers, four context levers add more depth to the analysis and define characteristics that differentiate a stable environment from a dynamic one. Traditional tools, routines, interactions and standards work well in a stable environment. However, they fail to support management in a dynamic context. In a dynamic environment, the entire toolbox requires a design with dynamic features. Figure 45 illustrates the levers that determine the context part of the dominant management mode. Context levers describe characteristics that vary depending on whether the environment is stable or dynamic. There is no absolute value, so the levers exist on a sliding scale that represents the degree to which the organization demonstrates the lever.

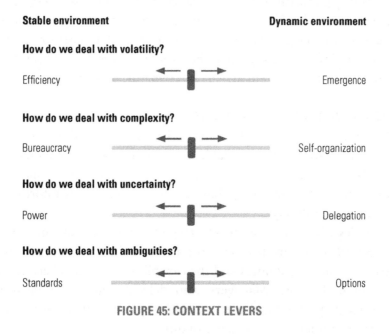

FIGURE 45: CONTEXT LEVERS

HOW DO WE DEAL WITH VOLATILITY?

Efficiency is the hallmark of traditional management. While no business succeeds without it, an exclusive focus on cost, productivity and risk prevention leaves no room for creativity and emergence. Efficiency gained with tight performance objectives and measurement hooks businesses into operating with the use of tools designed for a stable environment.

Emergence means flexibility and anticipation. Management tools focus people's attention on the tasks that matter and generate value. Managers trust self-responsible people who develop individual capabilities that can handle a dynamic context.

HOW DO WE HANDLE COMPLEXITY?

Bureaucracy involves establishing rigorous processes with multiple levels of approval that work well in a stable context. The resulting rigid structure and set of procedures are not flexible enough to deal with complexity. While routines provide a stable platform, they need dynamic design to support complexity.

Self-organization relies on teams of motivated, self-responsible people with flexible routines to deal with increasing complexity. Teams with delegated authority may be formed to meet some situations, and then go away when the situation is resolved. This reliably outperforms layers of managers in a dynamic context.

HOW DO WE HANDLE UNCERTAINTY?

Power and decision-making authority concentrated at the top of the hierarchy works in a stable environment where outcomes are easily determined. Effective use of power assumes that managers know what they are doing, have access to all relevant information and act accordingly.

Delegation and trust in self-responsible people are the keys to effectively managing in an uncertain context. In times of uncertainty, trust in one's capabilities and the capabilities of others becomes an essential dynamic. Managers who delegate important decisions deserve respect because they are giving up personal power by trusting the abilities and good sense of others.

HOW DO WE HANDLE AMBIGUITIES?

Standards, as in 'standard operating procedure' or work instructions, work well in a stable and clear context. When work is repetitive, uniform and measurable, outcomes can be predetermined, and standards work well.

Options are needed in a time of ambiguous contexts. People who form mental models for what can and cannot be done in a situation develop multiple responses that can be unique to each situation. The result is that people are capable of dealing with multiple situations to yield multiple outcomes that create value. This flexibility can help you succeed in a dynamic environment.

The dominant principles that emerge from the levers should align with each other for maximum performance. If the slides are not aligned, a tension is formed that degrades performance. For example, if emergence is strong (slide on the right side of the scale) and centralized power for decisions is strong (slide on the left side of the scale), they contradict each other. The resulting gap creates an atmosphere where managers want to believe they are trusting self-responsible people to make good decisions but haven't actually done so. This discrepancy can lead to poor morale and lost opportunities, as people ask themselves, 'Why bother when the boss is just going to overrule my decision?'

THE CHANGE-BASED MODE

The change-based mode of operating is the best solution in a segmented organization where coordination is essential and the environment is dynamic. Top management must be able to quickly alter structures to serve the needs of a specific segment and stick to the growth plan as opportunities or threats appear and disappear.

For organizations in a dynamic market environment with centralized decision-making, direct intervention by senior executives in the change mode becomes the dominant management style (Figure 46). Dynamic systems (the means) meet traditional ways to lead people (the ends).

Organizations in the change mode operate and adjust to market conditions in response to opportunities or threats. Managers alter the resource base, align interests through incentives and restructure accountabilities in response to market changes to increase responsiveness.

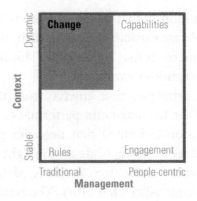

FIGURE 46: CHANGE-BASED MODE

Such organizations apply rigorous targets, tying people and teams to outcomes that align with the firm's overall performance objectives. Such organizations favour disciplined, one-step change programmes to adapt to changes in the environment. This is the traditional way to react to the new context, as taught in most MBA programmes. Managers are taught to delegate the response to change while simultaneously trying to maintain control of it.

Change-based management works with systems that facilitate the scaling of management in an organization. Diagnostic systems, interactive leadership, shared culture and clarity on intangible capabilities allow top management to scale operations as needed.

BUILDING COORDINATION CAPABILITIES

A dynamic operating system serves as the means for top management to control operations through diagnostic systems, interactive leadership and shared culture, with intangible capabilities as keys to success. Once implemented, the dynamic operating system works like a compass for the entire organization.

DIAGNOSTIC SYSTEMS

These five components of diagnostic systems (Figure 47) function as controls to guide people on what needs to get done. Engage your team by answering the following questions:

1. **Information.** What is going on? Are you getting the right information to the team needed to make an informed decision?
2. **Strategy.** What game are you playing? Does everyone on the team know the strategy and have they bought into it?
3. **Implementation.** How do you succeed? Does everyone on the team know what needs to be done to be successful and what their role is?
4. **Beliefs.** What are the shared and individual ambitions of the team and it's members? Do people on the team aspire to reach similar objectives?
5. **Boundaries.** Where are the limits? Do team members recognize the limits of their authority and responsibilities?

If you are satisfied with the answers, you can be sure that the diagnostic system of your Leadership Scorecard supports the coordination of multiple segments in your organization.

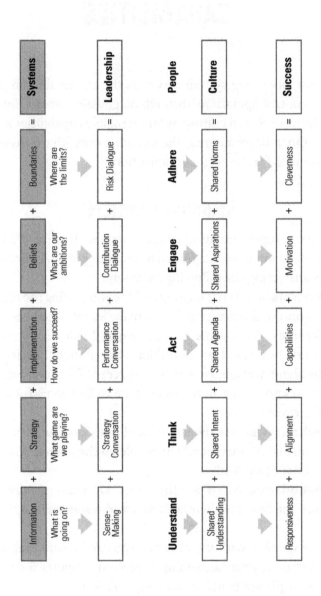

FIGURE 47: FIVE DIAGNOSTIC SYSTEMS

For better coordination, ask yourself these questions as a leader:

- **Information.** Do people at all levels have access to timely and relevant information needed to keep them abreast of what is going on inside and outside the organization to help them make informed decisions?
- **Strategy.** Do they clearly understand the rules of the game and what is needed to align their actions and decisions to move together in one direction?
- **Implementation.** Do all employees clearly understand what is needed to mobilize the energy and implement the strategy? Do they understand their role and responsibilities in implementing the strategy?
- **Beliefs.** Do people across the organization have a shared ambition to focus their energy and abilities on supporting the strategy?
- **Boundaries.** Does everyone have a firm understanding of boundaries or limits to their decisions or authority?

BUREAUCRATIC SYSTEMS FOR A STABLE CONTEXT

In traditional bureaucratic systems, information resides at the top, with extensive metrics serving the control needs of leadership. Executives participate in planning and strategy sessions at closed-door retreats, in isolation from the rest of the organization. The strategy development process is effectively walled off from those who are then charged with implementing strategy. Plans and budgets are used for annual resource allocations. Performance reports from organizational units are used for oversight and to enhance control. Vision, mission and performance objectives guide behaviours of both middle managers and front-line employees.

DIAGNOSTIC SYSTEMS FOR A DYNAMIC CONTEXT

Diagnostic systems generate information that is available where decisions are made. Identifying the few relevant metrics that drive the business provides constant feedback. More is not necessarily better in this regard, so identifying the critical few metrics becomes essential. Strategy development works through an integrated thought process unique to each organization. It is a creative learning process for teams at all levels in the organization. Resources in dynamic systems are allocated on demand, not according to a predetermined plan that may be obsolete in six months. Flexible targets that can change in response to changes in business conditions help with coordination and engagement. Business reviews secure the commitment of all teams and help disseminate knowledge across leadership of the rest of the organization. Values align the behaviours of people to support the strategy and implementation plan.

Here is your checklist on systems:

Signs of ineffective systems. When your organization:

- Works around the systems (people circumvent them), creates bureaucracy, has processes that interfere with focus, mutes awareness, creates mistrust, wastes time and effort, takes too long with approvals or decisions, runs out of energy.

Signs of mastery. When your organization:

- Works in the system (people use the processes), establishes a productive culture, has timely approvals or decisions, exploits potential opportunities, responds quickly to threats, properly does things that add value, applies rigor and discipline.

INTERACTIVE LEADERSHIP

Five conversations that managers should have with subordinates (Figure 48) function as interactive controls that guide people on how to get work done. The conversations should be routine, frequent, and personal, so every individual clearly understands their role. Engage your team by answering the following questions:

1. **Sense-making.** What does it all mean? Why are the company goals important? How do company objectives contribute to broader social good?
2. **Strategy conversation.** Why and how is the team trying to reach the goals? What has the team learned from past mistakes or from new information?
3. **Performance conversation.** Is the team on track? What should the group and group members do next?

4. **Contribution dialogue.** How can each team member contribute? What is each person's role in supporting the company's strategy and goals? How is each team member doing and is their contribution making a difference?
5. **Risk dialogue.** What level of risk can the company tolerate? What are the potential risks? What risks will be supported by management in the event of a poor outcome?

If you are satisfied with the answers, you can be sure that the leadership interactions with your Leadership Scorecard support coordination among various segments of the business.

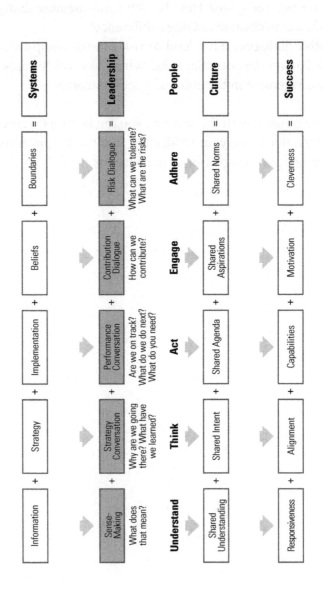

FIGURE 48: FIVE LEADERSHIP INTERACTIONS

For better coordination, ask yourself as a leader:

- **Sense-making.** Do you have the capability to sense changes in internal and external environments and then interpret their meaning?
- **Strategy.** Do you understand why the organization has established strategic goals? Are goals founded on lessons from the past with a clear vision for the future?
- **Performance.** Do you have a clear understanding of whether the organization is on track? What actions should be taken to remain on track and achieve superior performance?
- **Contribution.** Do leaders and employees throughout the organization have a clear understanding of their role and what they can do to move the ball forward? Do leaders and employees have a clear understanding of how they are contributing to meeting goals?
- **Risk.** Do leaders and employees understand the potential risks, and the ultimate level of risk the organization can tolerate? Do front-line people have a clear understanding of their boundaries regarding risk taking? Are you prepared to defence someone who took a reasonable risk that went bad?

People-centric management demands *high-touch* interaction with people. Interactions should be regular and personal. Remember, leadership is a contact sport, so sending out emails in not enough. However, when the boss shows up unannounced, it is often seen as an interference or interruption. Employees naturally ask, 'Why is he here? What have we done?' Front-line employees should be focused on clients, not leaders. Therefore, it is important to show up regularly, to establish relationships and provide encouragement. Regular visits by the boss — so-called 'managing by walking around' — then becomes normal, and people will feel comfortable enough with that to engage in productive, on-the-fly dialogue. Face-to-face encouragement demonstrates management support for the front-line workers. Leadership presence is important to establish trusting relationships that enable constructive dialogue of the five conversations.

COMMAND AND CONTROL FOR A STABLE CONTEXT

Traditional leaders create rigorous routines to tell people what needs to be done, and how to do it, and then create detailed performance metrics to compel compliance and drive performance. Strategy development is what top management does. Senior executives inform lower-level managers and employees about the strategic direction in town hall presentations, published intranet communiqués or emails. Then, people are given targets to pursue, with performance reviews that check on how they are doing. Such performance management techniques assume that people must be directed and driven to perform. Most decisions are made by managers who tell employees what to do and how it should be done. These types of practices work adequately as long as the environment remains stable.

INTERACTIVE LEADERSHIP FOR A DYNAMIC CONTEXT

Effective leaders interact with everyone on a personal level, helping people to make sense of what is going on, find purpose and develop a shared sense of direction. They must make a concerted and purposeful effort to establish trusting relationships with people across the organization. This takes time and effort. Self-determined teams interpret corporate strategy, figure out their contribution and share their performance expectations with management interactively. Such teams, populated by self-responsible individuals, ask management for advice on what needs attention and for critical decisions. In a dynamic environment, it is impossible to anticipate every situation that might come up. Therefore, it is impossible to have predetermined management guidance covering all eventualities. The assumption is that self-responsible people working together for a common good will find the best way to respond to virtually any situation.

Here is your checklist:

Signs of ineffective leadership. When leaders in your organization:

* Make all decisions at the top, focus on meetings, spend an inordinate amount of time with budgets and plans, miss potential opportunities because of slow reaction time, spend more time writing emails than talking to people.

Signs of mastery. When leaders in your organization:

- Delegate decisions throughout the company, give lower-level managers and front-line employees a high degree of freedom to act, maintain rich dialogue through personal interactions, set clear standards and expectations, trust line managers.

SHARED CULTURE

These five culture elements (Figure 49) work as invisible guides to establish a shared mindset on why and how things need to get done. Engage your team by answering the following questions:

1. **Shared understanding.** What is the team's shared understanding? Do people throughout the organization have a firm grasp of corporate strategy and why it is like it is? Is there unified support for the strategy?
2. **Shared intent.** What is your team's shared intent? What is the higher purpose (social value) of the organization and is this purpose widely shared?
3. **Shared agenda.** Does your team get the right things done? Are people focusing their attention and capabilities on tasks that add value and support organizational goals?
4. **Shared aspirations.** What is your team's shared sense of purpose? Do people have common personal goals that reinforce company goals while providing personal growth opportunities?
5. **Shared norms.** What gets the team and team members ahead? Do people understand the expectations or rules for advancement? Do they have a common ethical foundation that guides behaviours?

If you are satisfied with the answers, then you can be sure that the culture of your Leadership Scorecard supports the shared coordination.

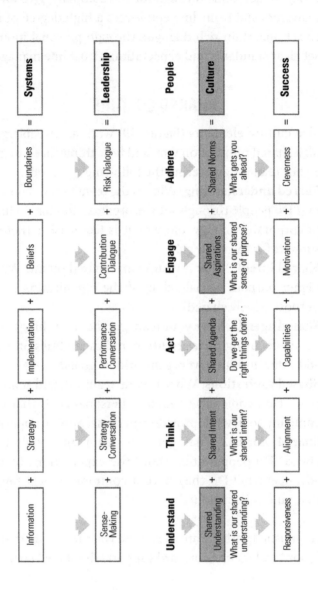

FIGURE 49: FIVE CULTURE ELEMENTS

For better coordination, ask yourself as a leader:

- **Understanding.** Have you created a shared understanding of where the organization is and where it is going (or attempting to go)? Have you brought your people bought into the plan?
- **Intent.** Have you nurtured a shared a common intent for how to move the organization forward to meet goals and objectives?
- **Agenda.** Have you developed and shared a common agenda detailing what needs to be done to move the organization forward?
- **Aspirations.** Have you generated a common sense of energy and allocated resources needed to implement strategy?
- **Norms.** Have you established a common set of norms of behaviour needed to maintain focus?

It is important to note that changing culture is much more than changing individual mindsets. It is represented by the collective behaviours of a group of people that have become automatic and a habit. People adjust to and become part of the organizational culture by having positive reinforcement for exhibiting behaviours that work. Such systems, made up of many people, can only be changed by action, experience and feedback that generate positive experience, rather than the cognitive abstractions of new values. This is why culture is an outcome with systems and leadership as its triggers.

HEROIC LEADERSHIP FOR A STABLE CONTEXT

Executives create their own understanding for what matters most in any environment or industry. However, in many traditionally managed organizations, freedom of choice for key decisions is restricted to top management. Issues are passed along the chain of command to the top managers, who pass judgement and then dictate actions to the lower levels. Executives expect that people trust in their way of doing things, under the assumption that they know more. Incentive programmes rolled out by leaders are meant to promote goal achievement, drive actions and shape behaviours and decisions. This traditional style of management works just fine in a stable environment where change is happening slowly.

SHARED CULTURE FOR A DYNAMIC CONTEXT

In an environment that is dynamic, where change is happening quickly, the traditional approaches to management become burdensome anchors that slow responsiveness and dull senses. In organizations build for a dynamic environment, knowledge and decision-making responsibility is distributed throughout. In such an environment, developing collective awareness for what matters creates a shared understanding so that decisions reinforce the company goals. Self-organized teams create a shared intent, with a shared agenda that determines the group's contribution. Shared aspirations and accepted norms of behaviour create energy.

Here is your checklist:

Signs of an ineffective culture. When people in your organization:

- Act reactively, run after fires to put them out, reinvent work, hoard information as a way to increase personal importance or position, ignore valuable knowledge and input from others, question the credibility of managers, have low levels of trust in leadership.

Signs of mastery. When people in your organization:

- Are well prepared, are proactive in anticipating problems and taking action, promote best practices even if it was not their idea, freely share knowledge across the organization, coordinate work with self-formed teams, align efforts of people and segments to support the strategy.

SUCCESS – THE INTANGIBLE VALUE

We view traditional measures of success, like profits or returns to shareholders, as outcomes resulting from developing key attributes in the organization. We have identified five attributes (Figure 50) that define the primary, intangible organizational value-creating elements that drive success. They are as follows:

1. **Responsiveness.** Identifying valuable opportunities, and then responding quickly and effectively to take advantage of them, or mitigating threats.
2. **Alignment.** Promoting a vision of company goals that encourages people to rally behind the strategy so that everyone is pulling in one direction.

3. **Capabilities.** Delivering the necessary tangible and intangible resources so that individuals, and the organization, have the necessary capabilities to achieve the goals.

4. **Motivation.** Maintaining energy throughout the organization with intrinsic values that engage individuals and encourage them to go above and beyond the minimum expectations.

5. **Cleverness.** Encouraging entrepreneurship and experimentation by recognizing innovation and rewarding experiments that do not work. People will not explore new ideas if they believe they might be punished if they fail.

Our belief is that if your organization has all of these intangible attributes, you are likely to be successful in any endeavour, whether for-profit or not-for-profit. If you are satisfied with the answers in the Leadership Scorecard, then you can be confident that invisible capabilities support effective coordination of multiple segments.

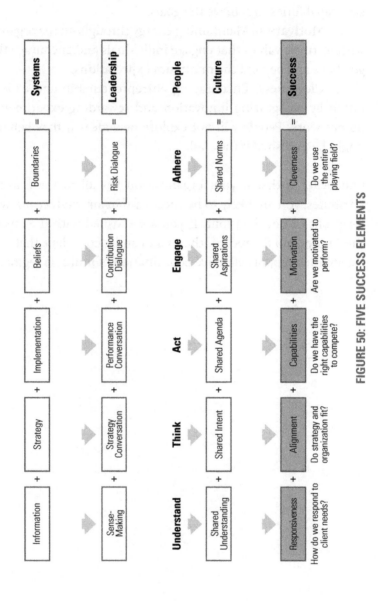

FIGURE 50: FIVE SUCCESS ELEMENTS

For better coordination, ask yourself as a leader:

- **Responsiveness.** Is the organization flexible and able to react to changes in the environment? How does the organization respond to client needs? How does the organization respond to unexpected events?
- **Alignment.** Is the direction of the organization clear? Is it shared broadly and are employees aligned to support the organizational strategies? Do strategy and organizational structure fit?
- **Capabilities.** Does the organization have the right capabilities and skills needed to deliver on promises?
- **Motivation.** Are employees inspired and motivated to perform above and beyond expectations?
- **Cleverness.** Are employees empowered to be creative and to use their creativity to exceed expectations within boundaries that do not stifle creativity?

SUCCESS IN A STABLE CONTEXT

In traditionally structured organizations, managers provide detailed commands on what to do and how to do it and engage in change projects in response to problems. The organizational energy is where the power is (with managers), capabilities are generic rather than specific to a task and people are not aligned. In such an environment, workers may not be equipped with the tools or learning needed to be effective and may be unknowingly working against each other. The same situation applies to various business segments. Leaders proactively try to motivate people with speeches or calls to action, and then create control systems to keep them within rigid, predetermined boundaries.

SUCCESS IN A DYNAMIC CONTEXT

In successful companies in a dynamic environment, self-responsible people with delegated authority and knowledge respond to customer needs or threats. Managers effectively communicate where the company is trying to go, and then trust employees to make the best choice on how to get there. The organizational energy is well aligned, with the right capabilities in place to give individuals and segments the tools to act quickly and effectively. Self-responsibility drives motivation, and shared values and norms keep everyone within the boundaries.

Here are several questions for you to think through on solving the control crisis:

- How do you solve the crisis of control?
- Is your general business environment stable or dynamic?
- Do your management levers tend more toward the traditional style or a people-centric style?
- What is your organization's coordination capacity?
- What are your answers on the Leadership Scorecard questions?
- Are the attributes for success strong or weak in your organization?
- How does your company meet the standards of management systems?
- What can you do to succeed with the transition from traditional management in a stable environment to a people-centric style suitable for a dynamic environment?

Up next, Chapter 16 describes how to overcome the crisis of red tape to transition from the coordination stage to the collaboration phase with an agile organization.

DYNAMIC OPERATIONS

Coordination resolves the crisis of control that inhibits coordination. Efficient transition from the delegation stage to the coordination stage requires dynamic systems with change-based management principles. Better management operating systems resolve the tension between dynamic capabilities and the red-tape crisis.

KEY CHAPTER IDEAS

- Dynamic systems mobilize people to coordinate their activities.
- Change-based techniques address the control crisis.
- The Performance Triangle principles support the coordination of work.

ACTION AGENDA

- Coordinate activities through a dynamic operating system.
- Review your organization's coordination capabilities.
- Answer the Leadership Scorecard questions with your team.
- Activate a change-based management mode.
- Manage powerful segments through diagnostic systems, interactive leadership and a shared culture.
- Pay close attention to the intangibles of culture and success.

FURTHER READING

Managerial perspective on systems, leadership, culture and success:
Michel, L (2013). *The Performance Triangle: Diagnostic Mentoring to Manage Organizations and People for Superior Performance in Turbulent Times.* London: LID Publishing.

Expert perspective on management systems:
Michel, L (2021). *Diagnostic Mentoring: How to Transform the Way We Manage.* London: LID Publishing.

Related research on the change-based mode:
Michel, L; Anzengruber, J; Wolfe, M; and Hixson, N (2018). Under What Conditions do Rules-Based and Capabilities-based Management Modes Dominate? *Special Issue Risks in Financial and Real Estate Markets Journal,* 6(32).

CHAPTER 16

AGILE ORGANIZATION

The fourth transition is the move from the coordination stage to the collaboration stage of growth. The networked organization emerges at this stage. The networked organization connects the various business segments with external business partners in the supply chain, or one of many strategic relationships, like partnerships or joint ventures. The key to making this move is to solve the crisis of red tape. As the organization grows and becomes increasingly complex and segmented, executives implement vast numbers of policies, procedures and processes designed to facilitate control and coordination.

Many of us who have worked in large, complex organizations have experienced the crisis of red tape, where it takes volumes of documentation moving through multiple levels of approvals to get anything done. The red tape is not only frustrating to workers on the front line, but it slows the organization's ability to react or adjust to unusual or changing situations. Solving the crisis of red tape requires the organization to adopt a capabilities-base mode of operating, with an emphasis on a common purpose, effective collaboration, healthy relationships and learning, to support the many actors attempting to navigate procedure-driven, network-type structures.

Chapter 16 describes how to transition to the collaboration stage by building an agile organization founded on people-centric principles with dynamic operating systems.

SOLVING THE CRISIS OF RED TAPE

Moving from a segmented to a networked organization requires capabilities-based management with a focus on purpose, collaboration, relationships, and learning. These four elements require distinct strategies to transition from traditional management structures and techniques to agile management.

AGILE ORGANIZATION

Management modes (Figure 51) group bundles of managerial principles and capabilities into four categories, represented by the four quadrants of the square. Agile management principles enable the organization to sense and anticipate changes in the environment, proactively adapt, and manage changes that yield superior performance in the new environment. Agility helps people perform at their peak and value is created despite ongoing changes.

To solve the red tape crisis, agile management uses four strategies that guide leaders to reach their flow line by creating meaning through purpose, connecting knowledge through relationships, navigating ecosystems through collaboration, and learning through experience. Learning helps people work *on* the system rather than *in* or *against* the system.

Agile management requires the application of people-centric management techniques and the development of dynamic capabilities. The attributes of the Leadership Scorecard in a specific work environment and the dominant operating mode help leaders build agile capabilities to resolve the crisis of red tape that accompanies complexity.

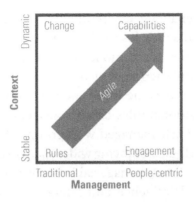

FIGURE 51: AGILE ORGANIZATION

THE CAPABILITIES-BASED MODE

Developing dynamic capabilities is the solution to operating in a network-type organization, where collaboration across national, cultural, legal and other lines becomes essential. The many, varied players need to establish shared meaning that provides a common basis for people to cooperate and generate sustained growth.

In a dynamic environment, with critical knowledge widely distributed throughout the network, the capabilities-based mode (Figure 52) dominates. Dynamic systems provide the means for executives to effectively practise people-centric management (the end) so that people throughout the network operate in a state of flow.

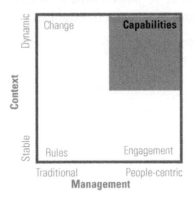

FIGURE 52: CAPABILITIES-BASED MODE

In dynamic and enabling environments, traditional rules-based management approaches lose effectiveness. Under these conditions, the capabilities-based mode supports fast decision-making and proactive, flexible action, which lead to robust outcomes. The essential capabilities become speed and flexibility, neither of which is apparent in traditional rules-based management techniques.

The creation of self-managed workgroups of individuals, with shared purpose and goals, enjoying wider spans of control, decreases the importance of direct managerial influence. The importance of using interpersonal influence and lateral coordination to direct and motivate work broadens and changes the necessary management skills. Peer control, where peers' direct attention serves to motivate and encourage performance, emerges as a primary influence on leaders.

Capabilities-based organizations require people-centric managerial competencies and a talent base that favours creativity and continuous innovation. Learning and access to knowledge through networks becomes as essential to superior performance as continuously reassessing the resource base. In this operating mode, change is ongoing, but not as a disruptive process. Many small adjustments eventually result in changing the entire organization in ways that may be almost imperceptible at any one point in time. It is the development and refinement of dynamic systems capability that makes organizations agile and nimble.

Shared purpose, close collaboration and healthy relationships are prerequisites and the means to establish new connections that grow the network.

BUILDING COLLABORATION CAPABILITIES

Four capabilities — purpose, collaboration, relationships and learning — are the means to operate in a networked organization. Once developed, these capabilities support people as they navigate through networks and ecosystems.

FOUR CAPABILITIES

Solving the red-tape crisis has four parts: shared purpose, healthy relationships, close collaboration and continuous learning (Figure 53). Each element requires the development of a distinct operating environment, with a distinct culture, distinct leadership and distinct systems. All of these emerge and coalesce, triggering four fundamental shifts, if we combine agile, people-centric and dynamic systems principles.

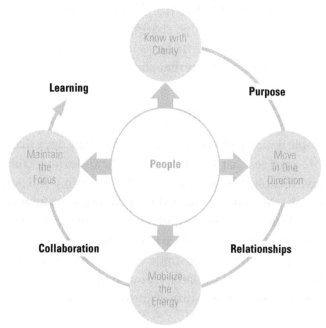

FIGURE 53: FOUR SHFTS

These four capabilities are characterized as follows:

1. **Purpose.** The goal of the organization shifts from making money to delighting the customer or serving some greater social good. The role of the manager at this stage is to help people find purpose and higher meaning in what they do, rather than telling them what to do. Individual motivation becomes intrinsic rather than extrinsic.

2. **Relationship.** The relationship between individuals and their direct manager shifts to teams with delegated responsibility. With is pivot, the role of the manager is to offer direction and create a supportive work environment, not to check on people's work. The manager becomes more of a coach than a commander.

3. **Collaboration.** Instead of work being coordinated by bureaucracy with rules, plans, and reports, work is coordinated by self-organizing teams using agile approaches. Teams of self-responsible individuals reach out to other teams to collectively establish their own rules of engagement and norms.

4. **Learning.** Rather than preoccupation with goals, efficiency and predictability, teams rely on transparency, ongoing learning and knowledge sharing, and strive for continuous improvement. These attributes help teams maintain focus on what matters and tasks that add value.

PURPOSE STRATEGIES

When people understand the meaning of what they do, a shared sense of purpose emerges that binds them together. Meaning comes from systems with explicit beliefs and boundaries (vision, mission, offering and goals). Meaning is enabled by a culture with implicit values and standards that help people find purpose, gain awareness, become intrinsically motivated, get creative and unlock their talents. With purpose, people identify opportunities, stick with them and effectively deal with complexity and volatility. Four purpose modes (Figure 54) can be used to identify the nature of 'meaning' in your organization.

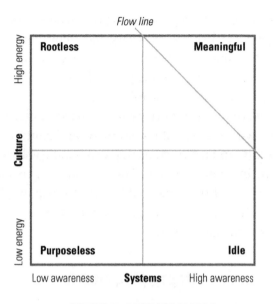

FIGURE 54: PURPOSE MODES

Here is what the purpose modes mean:

Rootless purpose: low awareness, high energy; thoughtless, haphazard change reigns	**Meaningful purpose:** high awareness, high energy; people find purpose in what they do
Productivity and 'being busy' are often mixed up; action dominates	People are motivated, convinced, creative, and they contribute
Intensity of work is often ineffective and needs ongoing justification	Awareness, accountability and self-determination prevail
Themes and initiatives keep changing and ignore reality	Vision, values and direction provide meaning
Purposeless meaning: low awareness, low energy; demotivation saps energy	**Idle purpose:** high awareness, low energy; the lack of energy kills motivation
People are unmotivated, have no choice and are 'busy' all the time	People and teams are exhausted, and constantly sapping energy
Individuals lack resources, routine work dominates and complexity takes over	Defensive reactions prevail and are part of the culture
Initiatives are blocked and direction is confusing	Risk and boundaries dominate decisions and action

The flow line in Figure 54 represents to point where people enter the state of flow, where work becomes easy and enjoyable. Strategies for reaching the flow line with purpose include knowing with clarity, raising awareness, and helping people find purpose. Moving people toward the flow line involves the following:

- **Build awareness and nurture a productive culture.** Use agile systems with vision, values, strategy, and routines to reduce complexity, and utilize tools that can handle volatility.
- **Remove interference.** Fix flawed systems generating irrelevant data, and then marshal leaders to help employees find purpose through personal interaction. The fix is developing systems with agile features.

CREATE MEANING

The first step is to help people know what is going on with clarity and find purpose in what they do. This leads to a shift from traditional command and control to engaging self-responsible individuals and teams, with the goal of delighting the customer and being flexible.

Traditional command-style management assumes that people need detailed, constant guidance to get things done. Guidance may range from giving precise orders, to control of actions or behaviours, to gentle observation. All these approaches are ingrained in the traditional control mindset. Thy come with conventional 'plan, do, check and act' management techniques that are driven by extensive performance measurement and information tools.

In contrast, self-responsibility builds on intrinsic motivation and trust that people will make sensible decisions on their own. By definition, self-responsible people are motivated by the ability to say no to things. They are driven by a sense of purpose that powers their engagement. Individuals willingly apply their creativity and special knowledge to deal with complex issues when allowed to use their own free will.

The first step is to give people meaning that enables them to find higher purpose in their jobs. This requires a different managerial mindset, and a new set of skills and enabling tools that build on distributed knowledge for a dynamic era. Figure 55 summarizes the difference between traditional and agile management philosophies.

Management	From Traditional	To Agile
Principle	Command	Self-responsibility
Shared understanding	Hierarchy	Shared understanding, awareness
Sense-making	Control	Interactive sense-making for feedback and clarity
Information: Measurement	Budget review	Self-control
Information and feedback	Restricted, limited to the top	Accessibility and transparency
Performance indicators	Many detailed metrics	Few relevant outcome metrics

FIGURE 55: PURPOSE – FOR A DEEP UNDERSTANDING

The mindset shift to self-responsibility. Self-responsibility is the prerequisite for intrinsic motivation. Supervising self-responsible individuals requires that leaders let go of traditional command and control modes of operating. In an environment where knowledge is widely distributed, agile principles assume that people want to contribute and perform. They do not need to be told or forced to perform.

The shift to skills for feedback and sense-making. Internally motivated people require a higher purpose to power their actions. They need continuous feedback, with information that helps them make sense of what is going on. Agile management demands active sense-making that is provided by the systems and a manager who helps interpret the information.

The shift of tools that deepen understanding. Agile management techniques work with a toolbox that raises awareness of what matters most and creates a shared understanding.

Mastery of agile management builds on a strong, stable foundation of basic human nature. A successful shift to self-responsibility always builds on solid belief in the underlying goodness in people, along with fundamental capabilities that enable people to know with clarity. Organizational stability comes from personal skills and systemic tools that assess market moves and performance indicators, which offer reliable, relevant feedback. Without high-quality diagnostic information, movement to agile management becomes a risky shift.

RELATIONSHIP STRATEGIES

Connectivity facilitates healthy relationships. It comes from leadership through personal interactions and a culture that supports people with clear direction, offers choice, delegates authority and uses knowledge to stimulate continuous learning. Remember, knowledge is the only resource that grows with use. Connectivity helps people select the right opportunities and effectively deal with ambiguity. Four relationship modes (Figure 56) can be used to identify the nature of connectivity in your organization and help chart a course toward the flow line.

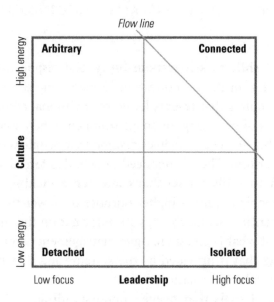

FIGURE 56: RELATIONSHIPS MODES

Here is what the relationship modes mean:

Arbitrary relationships: low focus, high energy; people are busy with scattered initiatives People are always busy and need ongoing motivation from management Teams miss opportunities, or the right timing Leaders are blind to inefficiencies	**Connected relationships:** high focus, high energy; creative people with choice build knowledge Employees have choice in how to do things They get the right things done Leaders interact, offer clarity and support learning
Detached relationships: low focus, low energy; people are isolated and mediocrity prevails People stand in each other's way for no apparent reason Teams resist change and are mobilized by others It becomes hard to escape the negative spiral	**Isolated relationships:** high focus, low energy; leaders keep people busy Employees use up resources with long hours There is no capacity for anything else Teams work on projects in the dark, with little impact

Strategies for reaching the flow line and building reliable relationships include moving together in one direction, enabling choice, and building relationships between people to enhance knowledge sharing. Getting to the flow line involves:

- **Strengthening the focus and energizing the culture.** Use agile systems (built for creativity and innovation) and rethink the culture (desired behaviours, decisions, and actions).
- **Removing interference.** Fix flawed or irrelevant systems, identify and eliminate viruses from the culture (see Tool #1 for more on viruses), and then vaccinate the culture against new infection.

CONNECTING KNOWLEDGE

The second shift is for people to move in one direction and build relationships to enhance knowledge sharing. This represents a pivot from managerial power and control to delegated responsibility in teams.

Traditional power and control practices originate from a mindset with an industrial background of low-skilled work, where people need to be told what to do, how do to it, and are then forced to comply. Industrial thinking fundamentally implies hierarchy with knowledge concentrated at the top. Relationships are established through pre-set structures and formal authority based on titles. Power is exercised in many ways, and it is important to note that power and authority are neither inherently bad nor good. It depends on how power is exercised and the effect it has on subordinates. There are times, such as in a crisis, when exercising unilateral power and authority is the only way to get things done quickly.

Delegation of authority and accountability assumes that knowledge is widely distributed throughout the organization, and those who assume responsibility have special knowledge that equips them to do what they are doing. People who assume delegated responsibility enjoy freedom of choice to make effective and timely decisions. The organizational challenge comes from the need to align widely dispersed people and parts of the organization, so they move in one direction that supports organizational goals. Alignment with strategy must come from intense personal conversations and sharing the rationale for the strategy, which establishes productive relationships.

The relationship shift from traditional to agile mindset (Figure 57) enables people to build healthy and productive relationships. Agile approaches require a new set of conversational and interaction skills that help embed the shared intent throughout the organization.

Management	From Traditional	To Agile
Principle	Power	Decentralization, delegation, teams
Shared intent	Personal agenda	Choice
Strategy conversation	Top-down messaging	Interactive, encouragement to take risks
Strategy: Strategic management	Analysis	Modelling, testing
Strategy development	Competitive advantage	Search for opportunities
Strategy	A three- to five-year plan	Thinking, value proposition

FIGURE 57: RELATIONSHIP – TO ENABLE THE THINKING

The shift of mindset to delegation. Delegating responsibility requires managers to establish relationships with workers possessing distributed power, who are accountable for their actions. This requires a concerted effort by managers to take the time to build individual relationships to communicate goals, purpose and expectations, in order to align actions. Agile capabilities ensure that people synch up their actions and move in one direction. As such, distributed delegation offers a new and superior kind of control.

The shift to skills for strategy conversations. Delegation requires connectivity with people throughout the organization, knowledge sharing and personal interaction. Developing agile capabilities relies on engaging people with conversations and deep dialogue about strategy that enhances the employer brand, and eventually employee loyalty.

The shift to tools that support critical thinking. While traditional strategy tools rely on detailed analysis and rational process, agile tools encourage delegated critical thinking throughout the organization. People are encouraged to ask *how* or *why*, and offer new insights drawn from their unique knowledge and experience. Agile principles promote freedom of choice, and simultaneously enhance the bonding of employees with each other and with organizational goals, through a shared intent.

The shift from a traditional power approach to delegation does not mean that leaders lose control. Conventional power structures are the stable platform or starting point from which the shift to delegation can be successfully made. Delegation demands a higher level of personal interaction between leaders and employees on strategy and the way to get there. Consequently, transitioning from traditional to agile management requires managers to rethink how they interact with people and take time to build trust in delegated decisions.

COLLABORATION STRATEGIES

Cooperation enhances collaboration. Cooperation is facilitated by systems (rules, routines and tools) and leaders who connect people and encourage trusting interaction. Trust in oneself and others is essential to mobilize resources and turn opportunities into value, despite uncertainty. Four collaboration modes (Figure 58) can be helpful to identify the nature of cooperation in organizations.

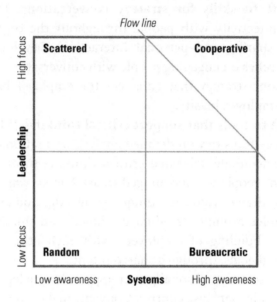

FIGURE 58: COLLABORATION MODES

Here are the characteristics of the four collaboration modes:

Scattered collaboration: low awareness, high focus; private agendas determine work priority People move in different directions and miss opportunities Teams miss out on synergies and only follow orders Leaders follow their own agendas	**Cooperative collaboration:** high awareness, high focus; trust mobilizes people and resources People connect to share and collaborate with others Teams address important themes quickly and effectively Leaders provide resources and trust decisions made by teams
Random collaboration: low awareness, low focus; people cooperate where there is trust, but trust is low People don't know what is important and who to go to for information Teams work in isolation without getting things done; may be counterproductive Leaders are uncertain and out of their depth, and tend to keep their heads down	**Bureaucratic collaboration:** high awareness, low focus; systems are in control People and teams must navigate bureaucracy to get things done Routines and rules govern actions and decisions Leaders are torn between many priorities

Strategies for reaching the flow line of superior collaboration include mobilizing energy, building trust, and facilitating collaboration. The path to get to flow involves the following:

- **Build awareness and focus attention on collaboration.** Use agile systems (with 'management by objectives' that focuses action on value-adding outcomes, rules and routines that allow freedom to act, and collaboration tools) and marshal leaders to work *in* the system (see Chapter 1).
- **Remove interference.** Fix flawed systems that are not timely and do not generate irrelevant information, remove faulty leadership entrenched in traditional management styles and train leaders the agile way.

NAVIGATING ECOSYSTEMS

The third shift focuses on people who mobilize energy and collaborate across organizational boundaries. This shift describes transitions from bureaucracy to coordination, followed by collaboration in self-organized teams.

Bureaucracy builds organizational structures to maximize efficiency with leaders, rules and routines to coordinate work. Bureaucratic structures work well with repetitive tasks in a stable environment, and where little collaboration across departments or segments is required. The perceived need for bureaucracy is founded in fundamental beliefs about human nature, where mistrust prevails. This worldview holds that employees cannot be trusted to make sound decisions on their own, so they must be ruled over, and told what to do and how to do it. However, there are alternatives to traditional bureaucracies, based on the countervailing conviction that people are fundamentally self-responsible, want to do the right thing and have the necessary knowledge to make informed decisions.

Self-organization builds on natural trust and assumes that people at the front line are better equipped to coordinate where the work is done. The belief is that front-line individuals have the necessary knowledge and will to make solid decisions. Self-responsible people are capable of self-organizing to find solutions to issues quickly and efficiently. However, self-organization does not just happen. It requires energy from the outside in the form of leadership. Such direction differs from traditional control techniques because leaders develop tools that enable teams to function effectively in an uncertain environment, while simultaneously keeping the leader informed. The leader or manager may only become personally involved if asked for help or if the team begins to veer too far off course.

The collaboration shift (Figure 59) summarizes the differences between traditional management and agile management. Agile techniques enable people to collaborate with a new set of skills and tools that create trust and a shared agenda throughout the organization.

Management	From Traditional	To Agile
Principle	Bureaucracy	Self-organization
Shared agenda	Plan-fulfilment, goal achievement	Resource flexibility, trust, shared agenda, value creation
Performance conversation	Planning	Interactive and dynamic coordination
Implementation: Performance management	Budgeting and resource allocation	Planning as a continuous and engaging process
Performance planning	Annual top-down budgeting	Just-in-time resource availability, rigorous peer business reviews
Performance plans and reports	Fixed budgets, often linked to incentives	Relative goals

FIGURE 59: COLLABORATION – TO FOCUS ON DELIVERY

The shift of mindset to self-organization. Managers must shift their thinking away from fixed bureaucratic procedures to explore flexibility with resource allocation. This mindset change is not easy for educated managers, who have been indoctrinated in MBA programmes on the need for control and likely inherit sophisticated structures in existing companies. Moving toward self-organization requires creativity to develop better business capabilities. These include making resources available on demand where most needed, not according to some annual budget that may be an obsolete result of political infighting.

The shift to skills for performance conversations. Personal interactions across organizational boundaries enhance collaboration. People-centric, peer review-based conversations should focus on value creation rather than goal achievement. Personal dialogue among peers and supervisors should emphasize and evaluate activities that create value rather than just meeting numerical goals handed down through the bureaucratic chain of command.

The shift to tools that focus on delivery. Traditional management-by-objectives systems should be replaced by business plans and reviews owned by self-organized teams. Planning and reviews facilitate collaboration with a shared agenda, based on trust, which replaces top-down bureaucracy.

The shift from bureaucracy to self-organization enables collaboration across the company. Bureaucracy provides a stable platform, with rigorous routines on which to build a self-organizing enterprise that provides the flexibility of combining resources.

LEARNING

The fourth shift from traditional to agile management is to build an environment that promotes continuous learning and helps people focus their efforts on tasks that add value. It is the shift from managers' preoccupation with narrow individual targets, which theoretically motivates by enabling teams to maintain focus through ongoing learning, knowledge sharing and continuous improvement.

Narrow targets typically limit the scope of action beyond team assignment or job descriptions. They become time-limited goals set by managers to drive performance. The use of narrow targets assumes that managers understand the drivers of the business and what motivates people. However, Drucker observed that most of the time managers do not have a firm understanding of either. Goal setting may range from fixed targets established by managers to an agreement with employees. Yet, hard annual goals become a tool that cannot cope with higher volatility, prompting employees to 'game the system' with actions that might meet goals but can be counterproductive to growth. The negative effects of gaming the target-setting process are widely discussed in the professional literature. While working with many companies, we have observed people meeting annual goals in October, and then taking November and December off for vacation. Their rational is that if they continue beyond an assigned quota, the goal will be increased the following year. In this example, the company met annual goals, but the unintended consequence was to stunt growth.

In contrast, promoting focus of attention by providing broad direction offers freedom of action and encourages people to focus on actions that yield value-adding results. At the same time, focus is a tool that helps people continuously learn and improve upon what they are doing.

Figure 60 summarizes the difference in mindset between traditional approaches with agile management. Managers must develop new tools that work well in a volatile environment, where knowledge is critical.

Management	From Traditional	To Agile
Principle	Narrow targets	Broad direction
Shared beliefs and boundaries	Risk prevention	Energy, entrepreneurship, accumulating knowledge
Contribution and risk dialogues	Control	Interactive interventions, performance, learning and joy, entrepreneurial decisions
Beliefs and boundaries: Engagement and governance	Performance targets, rules and incentives	Shared value, social control, entrepreneurship
Objectives alignment, risk management	Incentive plans	Trust in teams and self-control
Vision, values, contributions, mission, risks, structures	Narrow objectives with wordy directives	Focus of attention, basing accountability on holistic factors and broad direction

FIGURE 60: LEARNING – TO FRAME ENGAGEMENT AND ADHERENCE

The shift of mindset to focus of attention. The primary managerial focus of attention becomes seeing the whole business rather than digging into all the detail. This is a shift away from goal setting with detailed, fixed targets. The aim is to create an environment that enables people to focus on value-adding actions within the framework that provides broad direction.

The shift of skills to contribution and risk dialogues. These conversations zero in on how to maintain focus on value-adding activities rather than how to meet hard goals. Managers must personally engage with individuals to refocus those who might get off track, recognize outstanding performance, and applaud learning and new ideas. Helping people focus their efforts directly impacts performance, whereas mere goals are an intellectual construct created by managers that do not necessarily provide direction for individual action.

The shift of tools to engage and adhere. Focus of attention promotes continuous learning. Agile techniques establish broad boundaries of the playing field, with beliefs and norms that frame entrepreneurial behaviours and actions. Broad direction and shared beliefs stretch the boundaries, whereas common norms of behaviour ensure that no one steps over existing boundaries.

The learning shift changes the task of leadership from applying detailed targets to communicating broad direction in support of entrepreneurial behaviours and actions. However, it assumes that leaders have given some thought to the direction they want to take and a course of action. A successful shift to a people-centric approach builds on the stable systems platform that helps people maintain their focus and continuously learn.

Here is a set of questions for you to answer on solving the red tape crisis:

- Does it take too long to make decisions?
- Have you missed opportunities or reacted poorly to threats because of procedures, processes or debate?
- How do you solve the crisis of red tape?
- What is your organization's collaboration capacity?
- Do you allow self-organized teams to make decisions?
- How does your company meet the standards of the three capabilities?
- How pervasive are goals and hard targets?
- Do managers personally engage with employees or are they anchored at their desk?
- What can you do to succeed with the transition to agile management?

Coming up, Part V introduces the management process for transitions from stage to stage, starting with Chapter 17: Work *on* the System.

AGILE ORGANIZATION

Collaboration resolves the crisis of red tape. The transition from coordination to collaboration demands the development of three capabilities and capabilities-based management. Management techniques that emphasize purpose, collaboration and relationships help solve the tension between traditional and agile management and the next crisis.

KEY CHAPTER IDEAS

- Purpose and relationships enable people to collaborate.
- The capabilities-based management techniques address the crisis of red tape.

ACTION AGENDA

- Collaborate through purpose and relationship.
- Review your organization's collaboration capabilities.
- Activate a capabilities-based management mode.
- Navigate through networks and ecosystem with the right work environment.

FURTHER READING

Managerial perspective on purpose, collaboration and relationships:
Michel, L (2013). *The Performance Triangle: Diagnostic Mentoring to Manage Organizations and People for Superior Performance in Turbulent Times.* London: LID Publishing.

Expert perspective on the work environment:
Michel, L (2021). *Diagnostic Mentoring: How to Transform the Way We Manage.* London: LID Publishing.

Related research on the capabilities-based mode:
Michel, L; Anzengruber, J; Wolfe, M; and Hixson, N (2018). Under What Conditions do Rules-Based and Capabilities-based Management Modes Dominate? *Special Issue Risks in Financial and Real Estate Markets Journal,* 6(32).

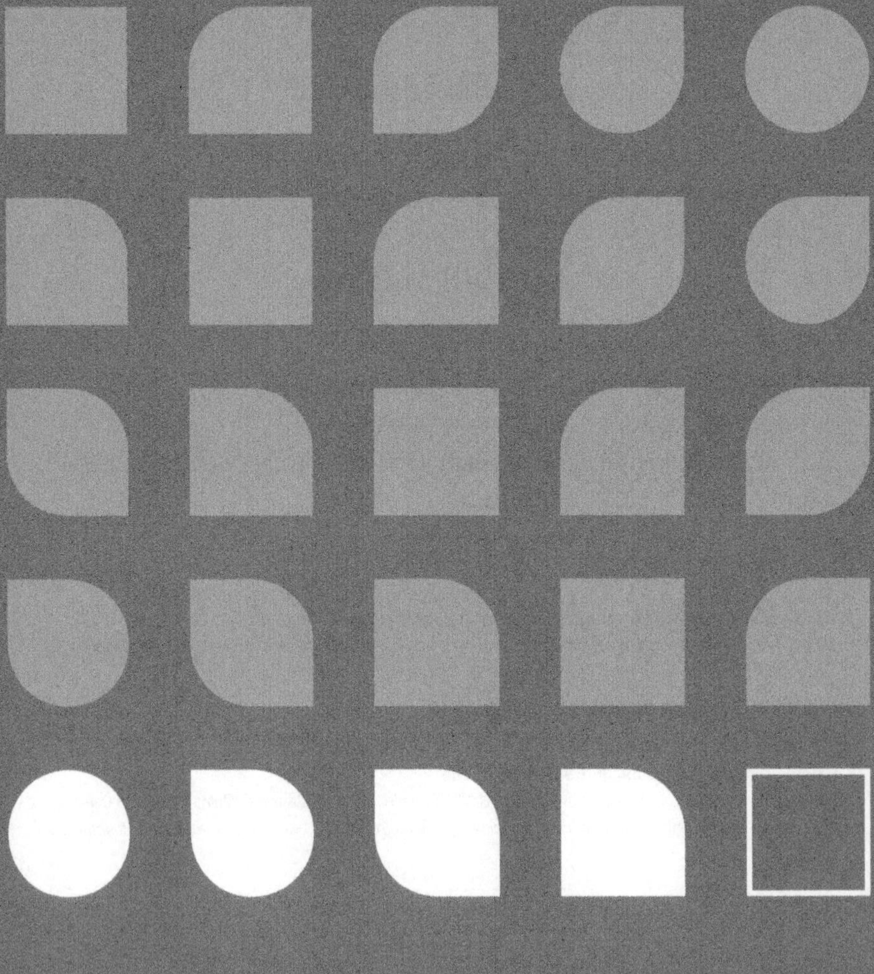

PART V

MANAGING TRANSITIONS

Organizational growth, as outlined by Greiner, follows five stages. Four transitions, from one stage to the next, build the structures, capabilities and systems needed to navigate through the life cycle. Managing these transitions becomes every manager's job, with mastery of better management principles as the target. By managing these transitions effectively, organizations can convert their management from a necessary burden into a competitive advantage.

Part V introduces management techniques to assist in these transitions, starting with Chapter 17, which introduces the concept of working *on* the system.

CHAPTER 17

WORK *ON* THE SYSTEM

There are two intervention paths to select in preparing to navigate the transitions. One represents an evolution while the other a disruption. Although every phase features some attributes of both an evolution and a revolution, the concept of working *on* the system helps balance the tension between the two approaches. Diagnostic mentoring is the methodology that assists executives in balancing evolution and disruption by working *on* the system to make the transitions.

Chapter 17 explains the process of working *on* the system to help take you there.

TWO INTERVENTION PATHS

There are two alternate paths that set different priorities for the intervention: evolution and disruption.

Figure 61 illustrates the divergent paths these intervention approaches take. Disruption as an intervention first alters systems to scale agility, and then develops leadership to individualize people-centric management. Managers adapt their leadership style to fit the new systems. Conversely, evolution first trains leaders on people-centric management techniques, before scaling people-centric principles throughout the organizations as systems are changed to meet the new approach.

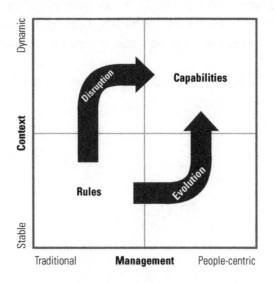

FIGURE 61: TWO INTERVENTION PATHS

Executives therefore have a choice of approaches, with different assumptions. The disruptive approach assumes that individual behaviours change through altering the rules, routines and tools for people to get work done. This approach assumes that it is time to introduce and train managers on people-centric management *after* the systems designed for a dynamic environment are in place. On the other hand, the evolution approach assumes that leaders with the right attitude, training and mindset engage in people-centric management and *then* change systems to fit the new style in a dynamic environment.

Philosopher and organizational behaviour author Charles Handy (2015), in his seminal book, *The Second Curve*, introduced an S-shaped curve to project the future. The lower point on the S-shape denotes an initial period of investment when input exceeds the output. As you begin to show results and progress is made, the business moves up the curve. Inevitably, the curve peaks and begins its descent down the far end of the 'S,' as productivity falls. The good news is that there is always a second curve. Disruptive innovations create that second curve (Christensen, 2015).

Traditional management practices (Figure 62) followed the first curve pattern over the past 100 years. This described a success story during a period of relative stability. Application of better manage-ment principles produces the second curve as traditional manage-ment is disrupted and the company continues to evolve and grow. When speed is important, but systems and processes slow you down, you know that the need for induced disruption has arrived. The organization and leadership teams are at an inflection point and must choose between continuing to apply traditional approaches or searching for better approaches to managing knowledge, using people-centric principles.

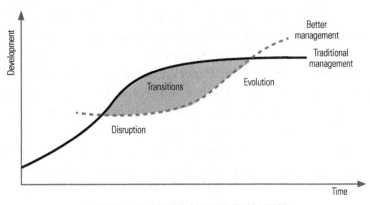

FIGURE 62: DISRUPTION AND EVOLUTION

Adoption of better management principles disrupts traditional management structures, but legacy traditional structures and thinking will continue for a while. In fact, efficiency and reliability attributes resulting from traditional management will be needed more than ever to satisfy customers. Traditional structures and thinking will not go away altogether. The transformation means that both traditional processes and better management techniques will coexist and perform as intended: traditional for exploitation and better management for exploration. This coexistence will require ambidextrous managers who can visualize both the past and the future state simultaneously to navigate the transitions.

Over time, evolution replaces disruption. The transformational shift will take the organization from adopting the operating system to training leaders and employees how to be effective in the new operating mode. Extensive training and education of open-minded managers is essential. Harvard Business School's Amy Edmondson (2018) suggested that organizations need 'fertile soil' in place before 'seeds' of training for interventions can grow. She noted that people need a sense of 'psychological safety' at work for transformations to succeed.

Can you first evolve and then disrupt? While companies spend billions annually on training and education (Beer, Finnström and Schrader, 2016), the evidence of success is slim. Why do executives continue what clearly does not work, consistently failing to deliver a good return on investment?

First, we have observed that organizations are viewed as aggregations of individuals. By that logic, people must be selected, then then trained on the right skills, knowledge and attitudes. The conventional expectation is that this process translates into changed organizational capabilities. However, organizations and systems consist of interconnected sub-systems and processes that drive behaviour and performance. If systems do not change, they will not provide incentive to promote changes in individual behaviour. Second, it is hard to confront senior executives with the uncomfortable truth that failure to change or implement new systems is not rooted in individuals' deficiencies but in the policies and practices created by top management. It is difficult for leaders to admit that they are in fact the cause of many of the problems, rather than failure of employees to do what they are told.

The work on better management principles (evolution) always resolves the crisis (disruption) that makes transitions and change painful and inefficient.

Here are some questions for you to consider on the matter of intervention paths:

- How do you manage the tension between disruption and evolution?
- Do you have leaders who can think ambidextrously?
- Has your leadership team made an honest and objective assessment of the processes and procedures that they implement?
- How do you substitute traditional practices for better management techniques?

TAPPING INTO EXPERIENCE

Diagnostic mentoring is a methodology for working *on* the system based on experiential learning and the inner-game principles. Work *on* the system involves five activities (Figure 63): understanding context, applying inner-game principles, following people-centric techniques, designing the toolbox and making the shift to work *in* the system to yield positive outcomes.

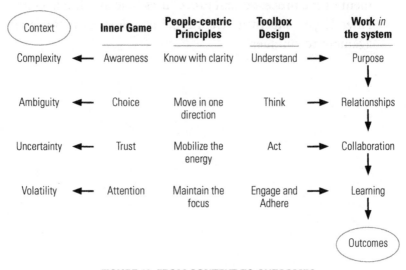

FIGURE 63: FROM CONTEXT TO OUTCOMES

Every part requires your work *on* the system.

Understand context. With increasing challenges from the VUCA environment, utilizing agile principles, people-centric management and dynamic capabilities will help your organization quickly adapt to the new environment. These techniques help resolve the tensions between the challenges of the new context and the need for clarity, direction, energy and focus.

Play the inner game. People are best equipped to resolve the tensions the new context poses. Individuals apply four inner-game principles — awareness, choice, trust and attention — to address the challenges of the outer game in the new context. Developing inner-game attributes is a mindset question for managers that has implications for the design of the operating system. Managers must change their thinking from 'How can I control people?' to 'How can I develop awareness, choice, trust, and attention?'

Design a dynamic toolbox. Following the principles of management design enables you to determine the optimal operating system. Managers will have to think about the right design to fit the current context and promote the inner game.

Work *in* the system. With the right design of your toolbox, leaders can establish a higher sense of purpose as the source of intrinsic motivation, connect people to nurture healthy relationships, facilitate collaboration to coordinate work and expedite learning as the means to perform, innovate and grow.

Use diagnostic mentoring methodologies to help your team design a dynamic toolbox that fits the people-centric approach. Applying diagnostic mentoring techniques helps you deal with a dynamic environment and deliver superior business outcomes.

With your personal shift to capabilities-based management, you are ready to engage your team in the same way that you made your journey through experiential learning. Getting the most from experiential learning assumes that your talents are adequate, you are motivated and you want to learn to gain that experience fast. This learning requires an investment in the skills required to play the inner game, use resources the agile way and make more effective decisions.

Experiential learning is the process that develops leadership skills everywhere. The most effective leaders in history learned valuable lessons from mistakes, and then adjusted their leadership style to fit the situation. Working *on* the system requires leaders to develop agile skills, refine customer focus on results that add value and create an environment that promotes superior performance. Working *on* the system requires creating an atmosphere to promote the inner game (awareness, choice, trust and focus) to build experience among your team. All members of the team must have positive inner-game experiences to adopt behaviours, purpose, and norms that are shared by the group. At the same time, working *on* the system uses the inner game to lead the agile way. Understanding the principles of the inner game is easy. Applying them requires skill and dedication.

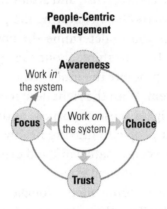

FIGURE 64: WORK *ON* THE SYSTEM

Experiential learning (Figure 64) simultaneously involves work *on* the system and work *in* the system. Start in one place in your organization and then expand the idea across all other units. Do not experiment — one does not experiment with people. Introduce the concept of experiential learning to improve work, organization and management.

The goal is to navigate and accelerate the transition from traditional management to master better management techniques. Awareness of what is happening around you initiates the learning process and gets you started. The people-centric approach must become your chosen leadership style. People-centric practices replace traditional change initiatives, which never worked anyway. Trust your team to care about clients and do the right thing for the right reason. Focus your attention on creating an environment that stimulates superior performance, innovation and growth.

Experience is the opposite of education. Experience combines work *on* the system with work *in* the system. Do not try to educate your leaders by force-feeding them through yet another executive development programme. Engage managers and future leaders in creating systems that support the transformation journey. Remember that learning by experience also involves the occasional failure, so patience becomes essential. To support your engagement, *Agile by Choice*, a previous book we have cited here, offers 14 nudges to guide your team, and the wider organization, to make the shift to better management.

Here are several questions for you to consider on tapping into experience:

- How do you develop better management?
- Have you created an environment that allows people to develop their inner game?
- Are you practising people-centric management techniques?
- Does the toolbox provide the right tools to help people think and act effectively?
- Are people working *in* the system rather than *on* the system to produce valuable outcomes?
- Are you satisfied with the outcomes?
- If you are not, what actions can you take to facilitate the transition to better management?

Next, in Chapter 18, we introduce the methodology of diagnostic mentoring, consisting of three steps that help the organizations successfully navigate transitions from one stage to another.

WORK *ON* THE SYSTEM

Work *on* the system is needed for the transition across the growth life cycle. This helps resolve the tensions between evolution and disruption. Diagnostic mentoring is the methodology to manage the transitions. Experiential learning is a key process to help people learn to work *on* the system and play their inner game.

KEY CHAPTER IDEAS

- Work *on* the system follows similar principles as work *in* the system.
- Diagnostic mentoring is about understanding current context, playing the inner game and designing the toolbox to return to work in the system.
- Experiential learning is a key process to help make transitions.

ACTION AGENDA

- What action can you take to meet your transition challenges?
- What action can you take to resolve the crisis holding you back from advancing to the next growth stage?
- What actions can you take to help people develop their inner game, apply people-centric techniques and build a better toolbox?

FURTHER READING

Managerial perspective about work on the system:
Michel, L (2021). *Management Design: Managing People and Organizations in Turbulent times (Third ed.)*. London: LID Publishing.

Individual executive perspective on transitions:
Michel, L (2021). *Agile by Choice: How You Can Make the Shift to Establish Leadership Everywhere*. London: LID Publishing.

Expert perspective on the work environment:
Michel, L (2021). *Diagnostic Mentoring: How to Transform the Way We Manage*. London: LID Publishing.

Related research on the capabilities-based mode:
Nold, H; and Michel, L (2016). The Performance Triangle: A Model for Corporate Agility. *Leadership & Organizational Development Journal*, 37(3).

THREE
STEPS

CHAPTER 18

THREE STEPS

Transitioning from one life cycle stage to another need not be lengthy, painful or disorganized. Diagnostic mentoring methodology can help executives plot a course to making the transition quickly and in an orderly fashion. The diagnostic mentoring methodology consists of three steps that facilitate change. The survey instrument developed by the authors helps executives identify and then decode key elements needed for successful transition. Taking targeted action is the primary responsibility of top management. In the VUCA environment, leaders do not have the luxury of taking time to try multiple approaches to navigate the transition. The diagnostic mentoring methodology provides a tool for them to target the key areas that need strengthening to move to the next growth stage.

Chapter 18 introduces diagnostic mentoring methodology that consists of three steps to help executives prepare for and manage a successful transition.

WHY GUESS?

Does the analysis of the current Leadership Scorecard indicate the presence of people-centric management, agile capabilities and dynamic operating systems? Diagnostic mentoring methodologies review current operations and environment then offer insight into critical areas needed to become people-centric, agile and dynamic.

Monitoring is the discipline needed to observe then take proactive action to alter capabilities. By observing (scanning) critical capabilities, potential faults and malfunctions can be spotted at an early stage. In becoming aware of critical signals, potential design requirements can be surfaced and acted on. With this, leaders can decide whether to address certain issues or ignore them. As such, monitoring helps initiate changes in capabilities.

Gaining new perspectives — constructive, multi-voice input — is an integral part of the monitoring. Taking a step back, objectively observing and challenging the use and effectiveness of current capabilities helps avoid the risk of getting locked into 'We have always done it that way' or 'It worked just fine in the past' ways of thinking. Organizations should regularly review their tools, routines and behaviours in view of the current environment because the landscape has likely changed since the last review. What worked five years ago may not necessarily be effective in today's environment.

Monitoring the effectiveness of tools, routines and behaviours is a risk management activity. The use of managerial tools and processes is selective and can be changed to adapt to new conditions. For all environments, leaders select specific systems and processes that support them in managing their organization in that specific situation. When conditions change, the toolbox also should change, and be adapted to fit the new environment. Diagnosing systems, leadership and culture helps prevent organizations from misapplying tools, ignoring critical events or being threatened by changes in their operating environment.

Taking an objective arms-length stance, careful observation and critique of organizational design and capabilities helps identify and mitigate risks. These might include thoughtless reproduction of organizational designs and capabilities through path dependency, structural inertia and lock-in. Early-warning systems, including monitoring and reflection, can help reduce these risks. This first step, raising awareness, is such an early-warning system.

People-centric principles, agile capabilities and dynamic systems are not directly observable. They require indirect measurement. Monitoring such things as institutionalized, rules-based reflection is not a routine practice. Therefore, few relevant tools exist. If such monitoring is to be worthwhile, it must be transparent and routine. Only then is it possible to detect extraordinary signals that call the validity of current organizational design and capabilities into question.

Monitoring must include the internal and external environment. While internal factors can be identified, external factors are wide open and largely without boundaries. Crises, both internal and external, are regularly preceded by weak signals that, if detected early enough, could prompt leaders to take pre-emptive action and prevent potential problems from becoming a full-blown crisis. The interpretation of weak signals requires unique skills (Ansoff, 1980), as well as systems capable of sensing the early warning signs and bringing them to management's attention.

Routine scanning and observation of the environment should be followed by action, with systematic methods for generating, modifying and improving capabilities. The monitoring routines themselves need to be evaluated and updated regularly to prevent traps and path-effects as the environment changes. Using the professional Executive Survey to ensure effective monitoring, along with continuous investments in the tool, helps prevent falling into these traps.

It is important to encourage all units, sub-units and individual members of an organization to actively participate in capability monitoring. Providing a supportive environment and social climate is key for effective monitoring. Leadership briefings establish the environment and set the rules and tone for a non-political, objective approach to organizational design monitoring.

Capability monitoring is a relatively new concept so people with the necessary tools and expertise are rare. This makes the process too costly to own and perform in-house for most organizations.

It makes sense to use an outside supplier with proven tools and expertise, experience and investment in professional surveys. We have observed hundreds of organizations and executives who sense that something is not right, or could be better, but without clear direction must guess about the problem and how to fix it. The result is that most leaders end up initiating a series of change initiatives or hiring various consultants with little effect, or they chose to do nothing at all.

Here are several questions for you to consider regarding capabilities monitoring:

- Do you sense that something is not quite right or could be better?
- Do you have clear indications as to the root cause of issues that you might sense?
- Do you continue to guess at the root of a problem rather than seeking clear insight?
- If you have insight into unseen root issues, could you take targeted action?
- Who can support you in your search for unseen issues that hinder your transition to the next growth stage?

DIAGNOSTIC MENTORING

Diagnostic mentoring creates the learning experience needed to successfully create your new scorecard and transform the organization using better management practices. Awareness, insights and learning guide your journey, with proven tools to engage your team (Figure 65).

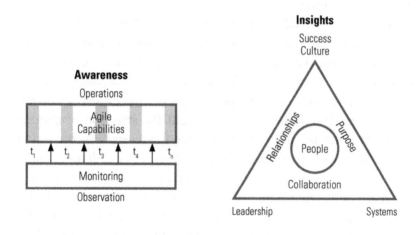

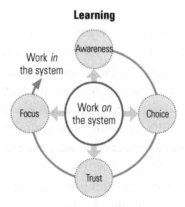

FIGURE 65: DIAGNOSTIC MENTORING TOOLS

Raise awareness for the transition. Diagnostics using proven tools establishes quantifiable observation points. Monitoring is a discipline that can be used to observe the current state and alter design for an improved future state. By observing (scanning) capabilities, potential faults and malfunctions that are typically overlooked can be spotted at an early stage. By becoming aware of critical but unseen signals, potentially beneficial design requirements can be identified. In this way, leaders can decide whether to address issues by taking targeted action. As such, monitoring initiates design changes to improve capabilities.

Act on your insights on your transition. The Performance Triangle model distils the elements of better management into practical components. The application of agile principles, people-centric management, dynamic capabilities and organizational design is selective. The decision to employ a specific design excludes other alternatives. The design process is about the selection of managerial tools, routines and rules that make for mastery in the unique context of the organization. Effective organizational design requires objective reflection and personal interactions. It is not free from internal politics, but enlightened leaders will make every effort to remain objective and minimize political infighting for the good of the organization. The setting and tone of these conversations determines much about the design's quality.

Expedite the learning about your transition. The inner game describes the techniques for continuous learning. Monitoring assumes that the design can be changed and not frozen in place. While deeply embedded in organizational practices and rooted in the past, managerial design and capabilities can be changed through interventions. The shift to better management demands specific capability development projects that advance the decisions on what needs to be changed. In this way, the idea of permanent change is replaced by the notion of combining learning and doing into an iterative process of continuous improvement.

The transformation to adopt agile, people-centric and dynamic capabilities begins with a personal mindset shift away from traditional thinking that every leader needs to make. Reliance on self-responsibility, delegation, self-organization and focus of attention are not typically principles that are part of the education or experience of most leaders. It takes experience to recognize the need for change then navigate the shift. This is why we suggest that leaders first work through *Agile by Choice*, the book that offers gentle nudges for the transition.

The traditional negative assumptions about people, and the dominant Cartesian mindset — where everything is *either/or*, rather than fluidly integrated — are the main obstacles to any transformation. Success depends on applying the same people-centric, agile and dynamic principles to the transformation that are necessary for better management. These attributes build on the humanistic tradition in Europe. Readers can find the details in *People-Centric Management*, the book that serves as a model for mastery.

Here are the questions a few for you to consider on diagnostic mentoring:

- What is your approach to succeed with the transition?
- Can you identify specific conditions, beliefs, values or shared assumptions within your workforce that interfere with success or change?
- How can you minimize the risk of your transition?
- Can you take targeted action to resolve unseen conditions that add risk to the transition?
- How can you quickly get back on your growth path?
- Are there any tools available to help you chart the quickest and most efficient path to guide the transition?

THE EXECUTIVE SURVEY

Capability monitoring with a professional, research-based survey tool creates awareness and the necessary insights for managers to develop people-centric, agile and dynamic capabilities.

The responses to questions in the survey tool force participants to step back, observe from a distance and challenge the current management and organization in a non-threatening environment. Non-routine monitoring, using a proven diagnostic instrument, detects weak signals and serves as an early-warning system that promotes institutionalized reflection.

The Executive Survey is an online questionnaire for managers and employees that takes less than a half-hour to complete and is available with 33, 47 and 59 questions. The selected size depends on the type and scope of issues to be explored. Unlike traditional employee surveys, the diagnostic yields significant results with as few as seven participants. It is therefore not necessary to involve an entire organization, which may only create false expectations. However, the instrument can be designed to capture and evaluate data from multiple segments, departments or cover the organization from top to bottom. The choice rests with executive leadership and the type of issues to be explored.

The Executive Survey is extensively documented in *The Performance Triangle* book, with definitions of all factors, visual presentation, a foundation in research, examples, business cases and tips for crafting the right design. The survey has been extensively tested in practice and validated through independent research (Nold et al., 2018).

Seven dimensions combine to assess current agile characteristics, people-centric management, dynamic capabilities and outcomes of the organization:

- **Agile organization.** Agile maturity with 11 Performance Triangle elements
- **People-centric management.** 10 people-centric levers plus the 20 elements of the Leadership Scorecard.
- **Dynamic capabilities.** Four dynamic levers, speed, agility and resilience, plus elements of the Leadership Toolbox.

- **Outcomes.** Performance, innovation and growth.

Depending on the survey chosen and the issues to be explored, as many as 30 'result reports' can be available to support every part of the process. A wide range of feedback, in the form of executive summaries, workbooks for workshops, technical reports for the design, and guides for agile and people-centric development are available and customized to fit the needs of every organization.

The Executive Survey differs from traditional cultural assessments and employee surveys in various ways:

- **The Executive Survey** offers the non-routine assessment of dynamic capabilities.
- **Culture Assessments** evaluate gaps with predetermined culture attributes.
- **Employee Surveys** identify faulty behaviours and flawed leadership.

Conducting the assessment creates awareness and establishes a shared understanding of the context and the issues that require attention. Participating in the survey is a first intervention. Objective reflection and dialogue about the results among executives triggers the thinking about *how we do things here* and *what mastery in management looks like*. Therefore, engaging people in the survey, and the following steps, means using the knowledge and brainpower throughout the organization to work *on* the system.

Here are a few questions about the assessment for you to consider:

- How do you assess the state of your organization?
- Do you sense that 'Something else is going here' or ask, 'Why is this happening?'
- Do you wish you could look under the hood to discover what people are *really* thinking?
- What are the capabilities, systems, and structure that require your attention?
- How close is your next crisis?
- What can you do to resolve your crisis fast or prevent it in the first place?

HOLISTIC AND COMPLEMENTARY

As we have seen, systems, leadership and culture frame the operating system of an organization. These elements complement and depend on each other, forming a dynamic system. Diagnostic mentoring is a holistic approach that addresses all elements of this dynamic system. Quick fixes targeting one component, like Six Sigma or leadership training seminars, miss the point. Systems and leadership are natural constraints on culture, while the culture helps shape systems design and leadership style (Figure 66).

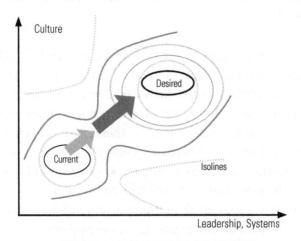

FIGURE 66: CONSTRAINTS ON CULTURE

We often hear executives say, 'We need to change the culture to improve results.' However, culture is an outcome of systems and leadership interventions. People typically adapt their beliefs and behaviours to be successful in the system and under the leadership of the organization when they join the team. One infamous example of this was how good, upstanding people were corrupted by the leadership and systems at Enron — the energy giant that flamed out in a massive criminal fraud scandal — into taking actions that were clearly unethical. Effective intervention can only be achieved by altering the managerial system or updating the skills of leaders. Changing the culture requires significant, simultaneous, changes to systems and leadership. Addressing one component without the others will yield less than desirable results that will not be permanent and likely be very expensive.

The transition from current capabilities to the desired ones requires getting rid of the old and developing the new system or interrelationships. Think of it as a mountaineering tour, where you visualize climbing the next peak as you stand on your current peak. You first must walk down your current mountain to then climb to the desired summit. If your current peak represents your current capabilities, and the next mountain your wished-for future capabilities, it becomes clear that the descent requires getting rid of some of the weight of your current capabilities to build the desired new ones.

In organizational theory, the descent is called 'unlearning.' It is often a necessary step to enable new systems, leadership, behaviours and culture.

It is often the case that optimizing current capabilities is insufficient for success in a dynamic environment. As we have noted previously, the business graveyard is littered with iconic names like Sears, Kodak, DEC and Polaroid because leaders focused on exploiting current capabilities rather than exploring new opportunities. Rather than asking, 'Can't we do better?' a true transformational leader asks, 'Can we not do it *differently* much better?' This mindset opens the unique and undiscovered potential in organizations. Most transitions demand that leaders overcome the current structures, system and capabilities that are holding them back. They start by asking questions, sharing points of view and challenging the present, beyond the comfort zone.

Here are questions for you to consider about holistic and complementary approaches:

- What are the elements that simultaneously require your attention?
- Have you gotten satisfactory returns from prior initiatives that focus on one of the three major components? If not, why not?
- What has changed in your internal and external environment in recent years?
- When was the last time you had an objective assessment of current leadership styles, systems, and cultural characteristics?
- What are your transition issues to overcome to advance to the next growth stage?

WHO IS RESPONSIBLE?

Attaining mastery in better management, whether it is a disruption or an evolution, is about learning. The question becomes who is responsible for facilitating organizational learning that is key to effectively navigating the shift in the operating system.

Learning has three components: readiness, capabilities and opportunity. Readiness rests with the individual. Learning is an individual accountability, so people must be in the proper frame of mind and open to new ideas. Learning requires awareness, focus, trust and choice. Capability is a shared responsibility between people and the institution. People must have essential skills and the organization must provide the necessary tools and environment that supports the individuals. Leaders need to provide opportunities for people to learn, and then support the effort. At that point it is up to the individual to take advantage of the opportunity. Providing opportunity resides with the institution. As such, institutions and individuals have different roles and accountabilities in navigating the shift to better management.

Without exception, any decision to pursue a transformation lies with top management. The organizational system, comprising a web of dependent relationships among management systems, leadership and culture, is at stake. Such transformations fundamentally alter the DNA of the organization. Transforming it using people-centric approaches assumes individual self-responsibility, which is an altogether different image of mankind than he traditional way of thinking. Many relevant decisions are delegated to front-line people or groups. Networks of teams with a wide range of authority organize themselves to achieve common purpose. Broad objectives, rather than individual performance measures, inspire people and help them maintain focus on actions that add value.

At the same time, this dramatic change alters the role of leaders. It becomes their task to establish a work environment where people can unlock their full potential. Leaders establish and maintain control through personal interaction, rather than by command, with feedback loops for control. Such leadership requires an onsite presence and engaging in meaningful dialogue to help people understand goals, expectations and roles, and provide support for people to get work done.

The transition through life cycle stages alters the fundamental functioning of an entire organization. Team or department-level change projects, without considering the effects on complex dependencies that link systems, leadership and culture, are doomed to fail.

Here are some questions for you to consider regarding your responsibility:

- Who, if not you, is responsible for charting and driving the transition of your organization?
- What are the key performance drivers and core competencies of your organization?
- Who can you rely on to get complex projects done?

Next, Chapter 19 provides a roadmap and developmental activities to assist you in transitioning from one stage to the next.

THREE STEPS

Diagnostic mentoring is the three-step process to help organizations succeed with the life cycle transition. It provides deep insight into unseen and rarely discussed elements of systems, leadership and culture. Major organizational transformations require leaders at the top to adopt a new mindset that views people as self-r esponsible. Top executives must recognize that all components of the organization are closely interconnected, in a complex web of dependent relationships. It is the manager's responsibility to drive the transformation.

KEY CHAPTER IDEAS

- Rather than guessing, organizations are better off diagnosing their crisis resilience and transition readiness.
- Transformation leaders must adapt their thinking to view people as self-responsible and the organization as a complex web of mutually dependent functions.
- Diagnostic mentoring raises awareness, acts on insights and expedites the learning process, which increases the transformation's speed and probability of success.
- The transition is holistic and complementary.

ACTION AGENDA

- Diagnose your organization's capabilities, structures and systems.
- Be objective and keep an open mind to new ideas. Fight bias.
- Plan your transition with the help of a diagnostic mentoring expert.

FURTHER READING

Managerial perspective on better management:
Michel, L (2022). *Better Management: Six Principles for Leaders to Make Management their Competitive Advantage.* London: LID Publishing.

Get personally ready for the transition:
Michel, L (2021). *Agile by Choice: How You Can Make the Shift to Establish Leadership Everywhere.* London: LID Publishing.

Expert perspective on the three steps:
Michel, L (2021). *Diagnostic Mentoring: How to Transform the Way We Manage.* London: LID Publishing.

Related research on the capabilities-based mode:
Nold, H; Anzengruber, J; Michel, L; and Wolfle, M (2018). Organizational Agility: Testing Validity and Reliability of a Diagnostic Instrument. *Journal of Organizational Psychology*, 18(3).

THE TRANSITION ROADMAP

There are three telltale triggers that indicate the need for a transition and act as roadblocks for a growth life cycle transition. The roadmap presented in this chapter describes the capabilities needed for a successful transition. Working *in* the system charts a path to follow on the roadmap. Regular fitness checks help managers evaluate the progress of the transition and make course corrections when needed.

Chapter 19 describes the activities and roadmap for the transition.

THREE TRIGGERS

Three triggers indicate when transformation is needed and act as roadblocks to be overcome for a successful transition to the next growth stage. We often hear from executive teams that they need to be more people-centric, agile and dynamic. Unless you have already made that decision, here are three triggers to be aware of, that signal when you need to get going. These triggers indicate when a change in the design of leadership and systems is needed:

- **Interference and unused potential.** When your organization lacks performance, innovation, and growth.
- **Faulty operating mode.** When your leadership and systems are stuck in old (traditional) modes of thinking and operating.
- **Change in context.** When your business environment has changed.

INTERFERENCE AND UNUSED POTENTIAL

When interference and unused potential limit performance (Figure 67), it is time to consider the people-centric shift. Over time, unseen and typically unrecognized interferences creep into an organization. Like a virus infecting a living organism, the interference is not readily apparent, but it will degrade performance. Interferences must be diagnosed and eliminated to improve performance. You notice interferences when your leadership requires lots of time to fix what should be normal. When fluctuation in performance increases, it is time to look at unused potential.

Interferences stem from faulty systems, flawed leadership, or a virus-infected culture. All three require a fix. Since these are interdependent, you must consider how the entire organizational system functions. Actions to address one element without considering the other parts rarely yield satisfactory results, because of unintended consequences in other parts. The fix may indicate a need to adopt people-centric approaches. For example, tools in the toolbox that do not fit the current situation may create undesired and unintended behaviours. Or you may discover that attempting to emphasize self-responsibility while retaining detailed performance targets creates a mismatch or interference. These consequences cause loss of control and stifle employee motivation and engagement, resulting in poor performance and lack of innovation.

Unused potential is a major cost driver and stunts growth. It does not make sense to hire the best talent and then limit their ability to apply their skills and expertise. Systems and leadership are a frequent cause of such inefficiencies. For example, control-oriented leadership may drive efficiency, but it limits creativity. As we noted earlier, when people take orders, they will typically follow these directives but do no more. As a result, organizations miss out on the creative potential and, eventually, the innovation capacity.

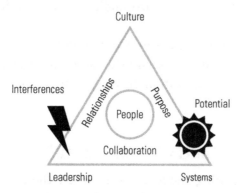

FIGURE 67: INTERFERENCE AND POTENTIAL

What do you fix first: leaders, culture or systems? Imagine that you have decided to make the transformation to people-centric management, agile techniques and dynamic operating systems. Where do you start your intervention?

Culture? That is an outcome that requires interventions in leadership and systems. Over time, transforming leadership style and systems will result in an effective culture.

Leadership? This is where most companies begin. But why would you train leaders with new techniques on Friday, only for them to come back to the office on Monday morning and find themselves in the same mess?

Here is what works best. First, fix systems, and then retrain leaders to use them interactively with people-centric principles. Over time, the resulting success will establish a strong shared culture as people adopt new beliefs and values, compelled by positive reinforcement. The starting place is to remove interferences caused by legacy systems before attempting to develop new leadership styles.

In their *Harvard Business Review* article, 'Why Leadership Training Fails, and What to Do About It,' management consultants Michael Beer, Magnus Finnström and Derek Schrader (2016) made the following point: "The problem was that even well-trained and motivated employees could not apply their new knowledge and skills when they returned to their units, which were entrenched in established ways of doing things. In short, the individuals had less power to change the system surrounding them than the system had to shape them."

Systems, structures, and processes that define roles, routines and rules have a strong impact on individuals' mindsets, behaviours and the culture of the organization. If the system does not change, people will be set up to fail.

FAULTY OPERATING MODE

The wrong operating mode emerges when there is a mismatch between the dominant operating mode and the environment. We have observed countless companies try to compete in a VUCA environment while shackled with rigid bureaucratic structures. They are constrained by processes and procedures that emphasize command and control, using techniques developed in last century. Such a mismatch allows interferences to become entrenched, the organization is unable to react quickly to threats and opportunities are lost.

The degree of external challenges and the rate of change, along with the distribution of knowledge throughout the organization, are the two triggers that determine the choice of your operating mode. Rules-based and engagement-based modes work in a stable environment that characterized the 20th century. However, a dynamic environment typical of the 21st century needs dynamic capabilities. Effective knowledge-based management is rooted in the engagement mode, with people-centric capabilities. Context and operations need to match to generate superior performance. Executives should routinely step back and objectively assess what might have changed then ask whether the current operating mode is aligned with the context.

CHANGE IN CONTEXT

When VUCA conditions change, it is time to adjust your operating mode. For example, fixed performance targets and volatility do not go together. In a rapidly changing environment, annual goals prevent people from adapting to the change. Remember that targets are agreed upon, so they represent a contract between the employee and the organization. Targets that make sense in January may be inappropriate by July, so you end up reinforcing less than desirable behaviours for half the year. In addition, it is unfair to ask an employee to bend a contract and accept a disadvantage to follow the change. A system that works well in a stable environment may hurt employees, and the wider organization, when the context changes.

How do we know? Over the last 20 years, we have learned that it makes sense to routinely diagnose your context and the operating system for viruses and unused potential. This is not easy because executives who have spent long careers advancing up the management ladder become desensitized and fail to recognize that the operating system is out of sync, as everything looks familiar and normal. Overcoming this condition, along with bias and political infighting, makes it hard for executives to be objective and critical. An objective diagnosis of the operating system typically requires a neutral outside perspective to provide clarity on what requires change and how to initiate that development.

We also understand why it is hard to abandon or change traditional approaches that may have worked fine for decades. Many executives may have been instrumental in instituting the existing process, so there is pride of ownership. Few leaders are willing to admit that the processes they spent their careers developing should change and that they must abandon their comfort zone for the chaos of uncharted territory. It is a risk that many are unwilling to take. Additionally, a cognitive bias known as the Dunning-Kruger effect

(Dunning, 2011) suggests that many leaders overestimate their own capabilities and those of their organization while underestimating the abilities of others. As a leader, self-confidence is essential and is part of their DNA. However, overconfidence and risk-aversion are like boomerangs. They can circle back and hit you in the head. The resulting demotivation throughout the ranks, and the feeling that change is impossible, spreads like a virus. Consequently, the over-confident leader gets very lonely, giving rise to the conviction that he or she must do all the work. And so, there we are, stuck in a vicious cycle, getting nowhere fast.

The enabling operating mode is better management, and better management is every manager's primary job. Diagnostic Mentoring is the guide for managers and their teams to work *on* the system and develop the enabling mode. Clarity on the specific trigger initiates the transformation.

Here are questions for you to consider on the triggers for your transition roadmap:

- What causes you to initiate a life cycle transition?
- Is your organization performing poorly, does it lack innovation, and is growth slow?
- When was the last time you stepped back and took a good look to see if your operating mode is aligned with the environment?
- Has the environment changed? If so, how, and how quickly?
- What do the triggers tell you about your crisis?
- If you have identified triggers that stunt growth, what actions can you take today to begin the process of transforming the organization?

BUILDING TRANSITION CAPABILITIES

Better management combines people-centric practices, agile principles and dynamic capabilities, which are key to successfully transitioning to the next growth stage. Diagnostic mentoring includes a variety of learning opportunities that help leaders develop these capabilities throughout their organization.

PEOPLE-CENTRIC

Four principles and the dominant leadership style define people-centric management. Figure 68 offers materials for learning and development opportunities to help managers understand people-centric management principles.

Elements	Learning Opportunities
People-centric principles	Practise the exercises with Nudges 1-6 from *Agile by Choice*
	Define and implement transition initiatives in line with four shifts based on *People-Centric* Management

FIGURE 68: PEOPLE-CENTRIC CAPABILITIES

Altering basic managerial principles is a deep intervention. As such, it requires a carefully selected, comprehensive set of development and education initiatives. Moreover, better management is not a quick fix that adds to your existing way of running a business. It is a fundamental change in every mindset, principle, process and practice. While early successes will quickly materialize, it takes years of hard work, combined with a large dose of patience, to complete the transformation.

AGILE

The Performance Triangle frames the capabilities of an agile organization. Figure 69 identifies essential materials that provide instruction on the capabilities of the Leadership Scorecard. The scorecard summarizes the people, organization and work learning opportunities.

Elements	Learning Opportunities
People: The inner game with focus, awareness, choice and trust	Practise the exercises with Nudges 3-6 from *Agile by Choice*
Organization: Systems, leadership and culture	Practise the exercises with Nudge 2 from *Agile by Choice* Use the definitions, practices, insights and literature cited in *The Performance Triangle*
Work: Purpose, relationships and collaboration	Practise the exercises with Nudge 2 from *Agile by Choice* Use the definitions, practices, insights and literature cited in *The Performance Triangle*

FIGURE 69: AGILE CAPABILITIES

The inner-game technique come naturally to some people. However, few are aware of their innate capabilities because they lost the natural proficiency to learn that they had as a child. Moreover, executives who have been indoctrinated with conventional management thinking and are accustomed to the command-and-control style cannot imagine what the inner game can do for them and their teams. That is why we created exercises in *Agile by Choice* to help leaders gain that personal experience and learn to appreciate the value of the inner game.

Return on management is a conceptual formula to measure how effectively companies use resources. Like the inner game, practising of time, attention, energy and space requires experience and grows with use. To get started, *Agile by Choice* offers another set of exercises.

In *The Performance Triangle*, we extensively documented the purpose, definitions, practices, insights and literature on the agile features of systems, leadership, culture, purpose, relationships and collaboration. With this introduction, executives become familiar with the survey instrument, which is followed by a team workshop that provides the best opportunity for development. Applying the participants' own insights on the unique conditions of the company to the results from the survey becomes the best motivation for successful change.

DYNAMIC

The Leadership Scorecard and its related Leadership Toolbox reveal the dynamic features of the operating system, or lack thereof. Figure 70 introduces learning and development materials for executives to become familiar with the Leadership Scorecard.

Elements	Learning Opportunities
The Leadership Scorecard	Use the definitions, practices, insights and literature cited in *The Performance Triangle*
	Educate leaders on the people-centric scorecard
The operating system	Learn about diagnostic mentoring to decide on your dominant management context, the operating model and the principles to determine the design of your Leadership Toolbox. Use the definitions, practices, insights and literature from *The Performance Triangle*
	Purpose: Identify the toolbox that fits the operating model
	Features: Close the gaps in your existing toolbox
	Choice: Select the elements that meet the needs of your organization's demographics
	Develop and implement systems through specific transformation initiatives
	Train and counsel leaders in the use of systems through dedicated leadership development programmes

FIGURE 70: DYNAMIC CAPABILITIES

The Leadership Scorecard identifies the key capabilities needed for transformation to better management. The Performance Triangle describes the details of these capabilities in 20 elements. Embedding these capabilities into the organization takes education, time and patience. Changing behaviour and the decision-making approach is hard, as old patterns dominate everything we do. It takes training and persistence for a new leadership style to evolve.

The Leadership Toolbox is the most effective resource to help identify important capabilities necessary for success in a dynamic environment. The design of a toolbox with dynamic features is the most important intervention in any organization. This is why the development and implementation of a new toolbox requires special care.

A large part of *Diagnostic Mentoring* is dedicated to the design of the toolbox with dynamic features. While design is an expert task, leaders need to understand how to use the toolbox to their own benefit. Its design, development and implementation follow specific transformation initiatives. While change in the toolbox is a comparably easy intervention, it does not just happen by itself.

The Leadership Scorecard is the tool to help executives scale leadership across an entire organization. A poorly stocked scorecard has long legs; it infiltrates all parts of an organization. This is why the design of the scorecard is expert work and requires the CEO's attention. With a dynamic scorecard, businesses have the capabilities to enable effective leadership everywhere.

Here are a couple of questions for you to ask about your transition roadmap:

- What are the capabilities that require your attention?
- How do you develop these capabilities?

MEASURING TRANSITION SUCCESS

In a previous chapter we introduced the concept of management as a competitive advantage. This now serves as the foundation to evaluate the progress and fitness for your transition. Fitness is handy, as it allows managers to compare the capabilities of their organization with others in the same category. The fitness check example in Figure 71 helps managers review the impact of their roadmap programme.

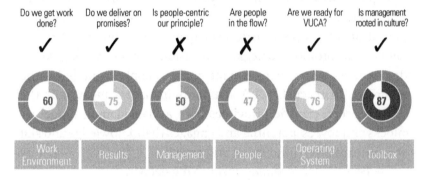

FIGURE 71: SIX LEVELS OF FITNESS

Assessing six levels of fitness provides an actionable overview with the option to dig deeper. Every level comes with a specific standard, based on a scale from 0 to 100, that we established based on analysing survey results from hundreds of organizations in many industries. A check mark means that the organization fulfils the criteria. An X indicates that there remains work to be done.

Level 1: Work Environment reviews the capabilities that make up an engaging workplace. Meeting the threshold indicates that the organization has established 'solid organizational practices 101' related to culture, purpose, relationships and collaboration. Can employees fully engage and perform? To reach Level 1 standards executives must remove the interferences that keep people from engaging with each other in the digital economy.

Use *The Performance Triangle* to dig deeper.

Level 2: Results assesses the elements that represent outcomes. The threshold is an average organization that delivers in the green zone on people performance, innovation, growth and success factors. Does the company deliver results? To reach Level 2 standards executives must determine the elements that drive results, identify the levers and then take targeted action that will help build the desired capabilities.

Use *Agile by Choice* to dig deeper.

Level 3: Management assesses the basic principles of management that dominate the leadership style. Level 3 looks at traditional or people-centric management styles, and then tells you which style dominates. The threshold is a score of 75, which indicates strong application of people-centric principles. These build self-responsibility and promote delegated decision-making among knowledge workers. Does management enable people to mobilize their resources? To reach Level 3 standards managers must shift their focus to people-centric principles with a management model that unlocks employees' potential and engages their knowledge and skills for more creativity, innovation and growth.

Use *People-Centric Management* to dig deeper.

Level 4: People assesses employees' ability to perform and learn based on inner-game principles. The standard is set by top-tier organizations with a score of 75. High scores indicate that the environment helps people experience flow more often. Can employees unlock their potential and perform at the peak? To reach Level 4 standards managers must apply the principles of the inner game to focus their attention and release more energy in times of stress. People at all levels learn how to deal with adversity and master unexpected challenges.

Use *Agile by Choice* to dig deeper.

Level 5: Operating System assesses the range of capabilities enabled by the operating system. Level 5 tells you whether you have a traditional and dynamic system, along a scale from 0 to 100. The standard is set at 75 for dynamic capabilities. These enable organizations to better deal with internal and external challenges. Can operations deal with disruptions, volatility, and complexity? To reach Level 5 standards executives must align the systems principles with the unique challenges in the current environment, and then equip the operating system with dynamic features.

Use *Management Design* to dig deeper.

Level 6: Toolbox assesses the fit of the management systems with people. The standard is set by organizations in the top tier and a score of 75. High scores indicate a management toolbox that enables people to deliver peak performance and take on greater challenges. Does the toolbox support people in tackling tougher new challenges? To reach Level 6 standards executives must design the toolbox to have interactive and diagnostic features that perfectly fit management principles for handling people. This includes the challenges presented by the employee demographics of your organization.

Use *Diagnostic Mentoring* to dig deeper.

In the example in Figure 70, management passes the first two levels: work environment and results. However, it misses the mark for management and people. Both levels are related, as they deal with the people side in organizations. The example company met the standard for systems levels, the operating system and the toolbox. What this says is that it is doing ok, and has the structural foundation to achieve superior performance, but is not maximizing the talents and capabilities of its people. Leadership could do better by rethinking fundamental beliefs about people and retraining managers to get them to apply people-centric principles and create flow.

The six levels of fitness offer a high-level review of capabilities. They show increasing sophistication, with Level 1 being the easiest and Level 6 the most difficult to achieve. As with the example in Figure 31, it is possible to reach higher levels without passing lower levels because they are all independent. Fixing weak levels starts with going after low-hanging fruit, to align with the more challenging levels. In the example, the first target would be to improve fundamental management principles, and then help people achieve flow.

Here are questions for you to ponder regarding your organization's state at this point:

- What is your organization's post-transition fitness?
- What are the areas that require further attention to continue developing and growing?

WORK *IN* THE SYSTEM

Mastering the transition to generate continued growth is to work *in* the system. With the people in mind, managers now can apply the four principles of working *in* the system as a roadmap to continue making transitions to higher levels with their team. Managing continuing transitions follows principles of work *in* the system (Figure 72).

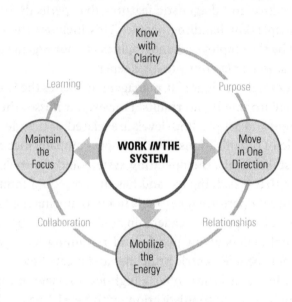

FIGURE 72: WORK *IN* THE SYSTEM

1. **Know with clarity: raise awareness. Help people find purpose.** They know that motivation stems from self-responsibility. Shared sense of purpose replaces material incentives. All leaders need to do for people is help them make sense of what truly matters. That is the best way to identify opportunities and deal with the complexity in your business.
2. **Move in one direction: enable choice. Relate with people to enhance knowledge.** People-centric leaders delegate decisions and relate with people on individual levels to enhance their

skills and knowledge. Providing choice and direction become means to bundle the energy and help employees select the right opportunities and move in one direction as their way of dealing with ambiguity.

3. **Mobilize the energy: build trust. Facilitate collaboration.** People-centric leaders facilitate self-organization based on trust as the means to deal with uncertainty. They mobilize resources in ways that enable collaboration across organizational boundaries, which turns opportunities into value.

4. **Maintain the focus: focus attention. Enable learning.** People-centric leaders use beliefs and boundaries to keep attention centred on what truly matters. They know that focus enables learning as the means to unlock creativity and stick with chosen opportunities, despite the turbulence of higher volatility.

Applying better management techniques is working *in* the system. You should expect all your managers to follow these four principles and develop their enabling approach to management, which caters to the people as individuals.

Here are questions for you to consider on your work in the system:

- How do you get your managers to work *in* your system?
- What can you do to embed your management deeply into the culture?

REIGNITING GROWTH

Here are a few closing thoughts to consider and reflect on:
- The digital economy and technology expedite and accelerate life cycles and growth.
- Greiner identified six known life cycle patterns, but they are not the end. There are more to come, and growth should be continuous.
- Mastery of better management techniques is needed to convert management from a necessary evil to a competitive advantage.
- Applying better management techniques helps an organization successfully transition from one growth stage to another.
- Every stage and transition is different.
- Success at each growth stage requires different capabilities.
- Organizational leaders should be developing essential capabilities at their current stage, while simultaneously looking toward the future and laying the groundwork to transition to the next stage.
- Mastering transitions from one stage to the next follows three steps.
- The goal is to generate continuous growth in the digital economy.
- Developing dynamic systems and an environment that allow people to use all their innate talents releases energy to respond to threats or generate innovative ideas.

In *The Transition of Organizations*, we explored various common patterns of management styles to offer transition strategies that help managers succeed in the digital economy.

THE TRANSITION ROADMAP

Work *in* the system implements the transition roadmap. With the fitness check, managers can review the current state of their transition. They can take targeted action to fix weak areas that hinder the transition. The overall goal is to generate continuous growth.

KEY CHAPTER IDEAS

- Three triggers indicate the need for a transition roadmap.
- The roadmap is the plan to build the transition capabilities.
- Managers implement the transitions as the work *in* the system.
- The fitness check reviews the progress of the transition.

ACTION AGENDA

- Watch out for the triggers.
- Create the transition roadmap.
- Review fitness from time to time.
- Ensure that everyone works *in* the system.

FURTHER READING

Managerial perspective on the transition:
Michel, L (2022). *Better Management: Six Principles for Leaders to Make Management their Competitive Advantage*. London: LID Publishing.

Get personally ready for the transition:
Michel, L (2021). *Agile by Choice: How You Can Make the Shift to Establish Leadership Everywhere*. London: LID Publishing.

Expert perspective on the transition:
Michel, L (2021). *Diagnostic Mentoring: How to Transform the Way We Manage*. London: LID Publishing.

Related research on the fitness check:
Nold, H; Anzengruber, J; Michel, L; and Wolfle, M (2018). Organizational Agility: Testing Validity and Reliability of a Diagnostic Instrument. *Journal of Organizational Psychology*, 18(3).

APPENDIX
LIFE CYCLE TRANSITIONS

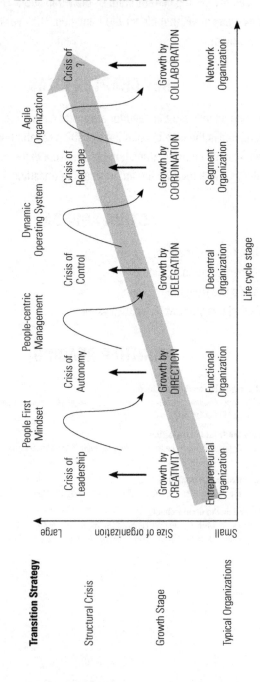

Management Index	70	65	68	70	72
Capabilities	75	61	75	64	67
Outcomes	65	66	58	75	79
Management Context	Enagement	Rules	Enagement	Change	Capabilities
Competitive Advantage	✓	✗	✗	✗	✗
Work Environment	✗	✗	✗	✓	✓
Results	✓	✗	✓	✗	✓
Management	✓	✗	✓	✗	✗
People	✗	✗	✗	✓	✓
Operating System	✗	✗	✗	✗	✗
Toolbox	Outbound	Outbound	Cultivating	Cultivating	Cultivating
Leadership Style					

BIBLIOGRAPHY

Ansoff, H (1980). Strategic issue management. *Strategic Management Journal*, 1, 131-148.

Barney, JB (1991). Firm Resources and Sustained Competitive Advantage. *Journal of Management*, 17(1): 99-120.

Beer, M; Finnström, M; and Schrader, D (2016). Why Leadership Training Fails – And What to Do About It. *Harvard Business Review*. June.

Christensen, Clayton M (2015). *The Innovator's Dilemma: When New Technologies Cause Great Firms to Fail.* Boston: Harvard Business Review Press.

Csikszentmihalyi, M (1990). *The Psychology of the Optimal Experience.* New York: Harper & Row.

Dunning, D (2011). The Dunning–Kruger Effect: On Being Ignorant of One's Own Ignorance. *Advances in Experimental Social Psychology*, 44: 247-296.

Drucker, PF (2006). *The Effective Executive: The Definitive Guide to Getting the Right Things Done.* New York: Harper Business Essentials.

Edmondson, A (2018). *The Fearless Organization: Creating Psychological Safety in the workplace for Learning, Innovation, and Growth.* Hoboken, New Jersey: Wiley.

Gallwey, WT (2000). *The Inner Game of Work.* New York: Random House.

Greiner, L. E. (1998). Evolution and Revolution as Organizations Grow. *Harvard Business Review:* Mai-June.

Habermas, J (1988). *Moralbewusstsein und kommunikatives Handeln.* 3. Aufl. Frankfurt a M.

Handy, C (2015). *The Second Curve: Thoughts on Reinventing Society.* London: Random House.

Michel, L; and Anzengruber, J (2023). *The New Leadership Scorecard: Perspectives, Dimensions and Patterns for Mastery in the Digital Economy.* London: LID Publishing.

Michel, L (2022). *Better Management: Six Principles for Leaders to Make Management their Competitive Advantage.* London: LID Publishing.

Michel, L (2021). *Diagnostic Mentoring: How to Transform the Way We Manage.* London: LID Publishing.

Michel, L (2021). *Management Design: Managing People and Organizations in Turbulent Times* (Third ed.). London: LID Publishing.

Michel, L (2021). *Agile by Choice: How You Can Make the Shift to Establish Leadership Everywhere.* London: LID Publishing.

Michel, L (2020). *People-Centric Management: How Managers Use Four Levers to Bring Out the Greatness of Others.* London: LID Publishing.

Michel, L; Anzengruber, J; Wolfe, M; and Hixson, N (2018). Under What Conditions do Rules-Based and Capabilities-based Management Modes Dominate? *Special Issue Risks in Financial and Real Estate Markets Journal,* 6(32).

Michel, L (2013). *The Performance Triangle: Diagnostic Mentoring to Manage Organizations and People for Superior Performance in Turbulent Times.* London: LID Publishing.

Mintzberg, H; Ahlstrand B; and Lampel J (1998). *Strategy Safari: A Guide through the Wilds of Strategic Management.* Prentice Hall Europe.

Nold, H; Anzengruber, J; Michel, L; and Wolfle, M (2018). Organizational Agility: Testing Validity and Reliability of a Diagnostic Instrument. *Journal of Organizational Psychology,* 18(3).

Nold, H; and Michel, L (2016). The Performance Triangle: A Model for Corporate Agility. *Leadership & Organizational Development Journal,* 37(3).

Nold, H (2012). Linking Knowledge Processes with Firm Performance: Organizational Culture. *Journal of Intellectual Capital,* vol. 13, no. 1, 16-38.

O'Reilly, Charles A., III, and Michael L. Tushman. "The Ambidextrous Organization." *Harvard Business Review* 82, no. 4 (April 2004): 74–81.

O'Reilly III, C. & Tushman, M (2016). *Lead and Disrupt: How to Solve the Innovator's Dilemma,* Stanford, CA: Stanford University Press.

Porter, M (1985). *Competitive Advantage: Creating and Sustaining Superior Performance.* New York: Free Press.

Simons, Robert (1995). *Levers of Control: How Managers Use Innovative Control Systems to Drive Strategic Renewal.* Boston: Harvard Business School Press.

LIST OF FIGURES

FIGURE 1: GREINER'S FIVE LIFE CYCLE STAGES   27

FIGURE 2: LEVERS OF CONTROL   32

FIGURE 3: CONTROL SYSTEMS   36

FIGURE 4: FOUR OPERATING MODES   41

FIGURE 5: THREE MANAGERIAL ECOSYSTEMS   45

FIGURE 6: PEOPLE-CENTRIC LEVERS   60

FIGURE 7: THE PERFORMANCE TRIANGLE   68

FIGURE 8: THE INDIVIDUAL ENVIRONMENT   74

FIGURE 9: CONTRASTING KNOWLEDGE WORK   76

FIGURE 10: ASSUMPTIONS ABOUT WORK   77

FIGURE 11: THE OPERATING ENVIRONMENT   79

FIGURE 12: THE WORK ENVIRONMENT   87

FIGURE 13: DYNAMIC CAPABILITIES AND OUTCOMES   92

FIGURE 14: RETURN ON MANAGEMENT   104

FIGURE 15: FOUR OPERATING SYSTEMS   105

FIGURE 16: FEATURES OF OPERATING SYSTEMS   106

FIGURE 17: THE LEADERSHIP SCORECARD   119

FIGURE 18: MANAGEMENT AS A COMPETITIVE ADVANTAGE   127

FIGURE 19: SIX MATURITY LEVELS   130

FIGURE 20: CREATIVITY AS A COMPETITIVE ADVANTAGE   141

FIGURE 21: THE LEADERSHIP SCORECARD FOR CREATIVITY   143

FIGURE 22: DIRECTION AS A COMPETITIVE ADVANTAGE   151

FIGURE 23: THE LEADERSHIP SCORECARD FOR DIRECTION   153

FIGURE 24: DELEGATION AS A COMPETITIVE ADVANTAGE   161

FIGURE 25: THE LEADERSHIP SCORECARD FOR DELEGATION   163

FIGURE 26: COORDINATION AS A COMPETITIVE ADVANTAGE   171

FIGURE 27: THE LEADERSHIP SCORECARD FOR COORDINATION   173

FIGURE 28: COLLABORATION AS A COMPETITIVE ADVANTAGE   181

FIGURE 29: THE LEADERSHIP SCORECARD FOR COLLABORATION   183

FIGURE 30: PEOPLE FIRST   193

FIGURE 31: RULES-BASED MODE   195

FIGURE 32: FLOW   199

FIGURE 33: PEOPLE-CENTRIC MANAGEMENT   207

FIGURE 34: FOUR MANAGEMENT LEVERS   208

FIGURE 35: ENGAGEMENT-BASED MODE   211

FIGURE 36: INFORMATION SYSTEMS   214

FIGURE 37: THE OPERATING SYSTEM TO UNDERSTAND   216

FIGURE 38: STRATEGY SYSTEMS   219

FIGURE 39: THE OPERATING SYSTEM TO THINK   221

FIGURE 40: IMPLEMENTATION SYSTEMS   224

FIGURE 41: THE OPERATING SYSTEM TO ACT   226

FIGURE 42: BELIEFS AND BOUNDARY SYSTEMS   229

FIGURE 43: THE OPERATING SYSTEM TO ENGAGE AND ADHERE   230

FIGURE 44: DYNAMIC OPERATING SYSTEM   238

FIGURE 45: CONTEXT LEVERS   239

FIGURE 46: CHANGE-BASED MODE   242

FIGURE 47: FIVE DIAGNOSTIC SYSTEMS   244

FIGURE 48: FIVE LEADERSHIP INTERACTIONS   248

FIGURE 49: FIVE CULTURE ELEMENTS   252

FIGURE 50: FIVE SUCCESS ELEMENTS   256

FIGURE 51: AGILE ORGANIZATION   263

FIGURE 52: CAPABILITIES-BASED MODE   263

FIGURE 53: FOUR SHFTS   265

FIGURE 54: PURPOSE MODES   267

FIGURE 55: PURPOSE – FOR A DEEP UNDERSTANDING   269

FIGURE 56: RELATIONSHIPS MODES   270

FIGURE 57: RELATIONSHIP – TO ENABLE THE THINKING   272

FIGURE 58: COLLABORATION MODES   274

FIGURE 59: COLLABORATION – TO FOCUS ON DELIVERY   277

FIGURE 60: LEARNING – TO FRAME ENGAGEMENT AND ADHERENCE   279

FIGURE 61: TWO INTERVENTION PATHS   286

FIGURE 62: DISRUPTION AND EVOLUTION   287

FIGURE 63: FROM CONTEXT TO OUTCOMES   290

FIGURE 64: WORK *ON* THE SYSTEM   292

FIGURE 65: DIAGNOSTIC MENTORING TOOLS   301

FIGURE 66: CONSTRAINTS ON CULTURE   306

FIGURE 67: INTERFERENCE AND POTENTIAL   315

FIGURE 68: PEOPLE-CENTRIC CAPABILITIES   319

FIGURE 69: AGILE CAPABILITIES   320

FIGURE 70: DYNAMIC CAPABILITIES   321

FIGURE 71: SIX LEVELS OF FITNESS   323

FIGURE 72: WORK *IN* THE SYSTEM   326

ACKNOWLEDGEMENTS

The Transition of Organizations is the result of 20 years of work with clients around the globe and the related research that enabled us to conclude that there are patterns of deliberate strategies companies can follow to overcome their inherent structural crises.

Our thanks go to all our clients, the members of our professional community, and the many participants in the annual Global Drucker Forum management conference in Vienna. First, we appreciated the many conversations we had with clients on their challenges over the past few years. When we analysed the insights they'd gained, compelling transition strategies fell into place. Second, many of our accredited partners have augmented their clients' work with 'management twins' — virtual mirror representations of the organization that can help predict how transition strategies and processes might perform. Taken together, we were able to distil these learnings into a consistent concept. Third, conversations with colleagues around the world convinced us to put it all into writing.

Thank you to everyone who contributed to our research, and the writing of this book on patterns of mastery.

ABOUT THE AUTHORS

Lukas Michel is the owner of Management Insights, which is based in Switzerland and encompasses a global network of experienced management mentors.

In addition to lecturing at universities, licensing his own diagnostic mentoring methodology, writing on management issues and building his consulting network, Lukas is a business leader with a track record of balance sheet accountability in his work for global corporations in Europe and Asia.

Over the course of his 40-year career, he has worked with executive teams around the world, focusing on management in a diverse range of local, national and global organizations.

For the last 20 years Lukas has been developing the methodology, framework and language for scaling agile, people-centric and dynamic capabilities across all organizational levels.

He holds an MS in Management from North Carolina State University, and bachelor's degrees in textile management and teaching.

Lukas is the author of six previous books: *The Performance Triangle, Management Design, People-Centric Management, Agile by Choice, Diagnostic Mentoring* and *Better Management.*

Dr Herb Nold is a Professor of Business Administration at Polk State College in Winter Haven/ Lakeland, Florida. Herb earned a Doctor of Management in Organizational Leadership from the University of Phoenix, College of Doctoral Studies, holds master's and bachelor's degrees in education from Northern Illinois University, and is a Certified Public Accountant. Prior to entering academia, Dr Nold had a 30-year business career with private and public companies. Publications include *Agile Strategies for the 21st Century: The Need for Speed*, and numerous journal articles.

Herb's expertise and research interests are in the areas of organizational culture, organizational change and performance optimization. Since earning his doctorate in 2011, his research has been published in numerous academic journals and cited nearly 700 times as of March 2023. Herb received a 2013 Outstanding Paper Award from the *Journal of Intellectual Capital,* and the 2012 International Award for Excellence for the top-ranked paper, published by the *International Journal of Knowledge, Culture and Change.* In 2021, *Agile Strategies for the 21st Century: The Need for Speed,* from Cambridge Scholars Publishing, translated his research into language understandable by undergraduate students and business executives alike.